Modern Literary Criticism and Theory

D0059071

To my children, Hishaam and Hasan

Modern Literary Criticism and Theory

A History

M. A. R. Habib

Blackwell
Publishing

BLACKWELL PUBLISHING
350 Main Street, Malden, MA 02148–5020, USA
9600 Garsington Road, Oxford OX4 2DQ, UK
550 Swanston Street, Carlton, Victoria 3053, Australia

First published 2008 by Blackwell Publishing Ltd
1   2008

Library of Congress Cataloging-in-Publication Data

Habib, Rafey.
   Modern literary criticism and theory : a history / M. A. R. Habib.
      p. cm.
   Includes bibliographical references and index.
   ISBN-13: 978-1-4051-7667-5 (hardcover : alk. paper)
   ISBN-13: 978-1-4051-7666-8 (pbk. : alk. paper)   1. Criticism—History—20th
century. I. Title.
   PN94.H23 2008
   801′.950905—dc22
                              2007036297

A catalogue record for this title is available from the British Library.

Set in 10.5 on 12.5 pt Minion
by SNP Best-set Typesetter Ltd., Hong Kong
Printed and bound in Singapore
by Markono Print Media Pte Ltd

The publisher's policy is to use permanent paper from mills that operate a sustainable forestry policy, and which has been manufactured from pulp processed using acid-free and elementary chlorine-free practices. Furthermore, the publisher ensures that the text paper and cover board used have met acceptable environmental accreditation standards.

For further information on
Blackwell Publishing, visit our website at
www.blackwellpublishing.com

Contents

Acknowledgments

I would like to offer my deepest gratitude to the following people for their guidance, inspiration and support or endorsement: Chris Fitter, Terry Eagleton, Michael Payne, Mughni Tabassum, Joe Barbarese, Robert Grant, Ron Bush, Peter Widdowson, Laurie Garrison, Emma Bennett, Karen Wilson, David Rogers, Danielle Magnusson, Timothy Martin, Stacy Zicarelli, Keith Hall, Mariam Patel, my dear mentor Siddiqua Shabnam, and my Yasmeen.

Introduction

These are turbulent and exciting times for criticism and theory: partly because, nowadays, so much more is at stake than just the reading of a literary text, or talking about the way class or gender is portrayed in literature. The very institutions in which academic and intellectual and free thought flourish are perceived by many as being under threat: the university, the school, the very space of the public sphere in the television media, newspapers, magazines, radio, film, church, synagogue, and masjid. What is at stake – not in some ultimate and underlying way, but now, in the starkest immediacy – is the democratic process itself and the values purportedly enshrined in democracy. There is a new urgency in some circles of academia – not restricted to any given political allegiance – to re-engage and reclaim this public sphere (or counter-public sphere) as an arena of genuine debate, to infuse this sphere with the learning, knowledge, humanity, and high linguistic ability embodied in the best institutions of learning; to extend the province and reach of academic disciplines into the discussion of democracy, war, terror, tolerance, and freedom.

Why this urgency to renew literature's connections with the larger world? The last ten years or so have seen a series of unprecedented political and cultural phenomena. Many of these have a global scope: transnational movements of finance and capital; globalization of media and technological resources; ecological and epidemic risks; the widespread impact of the collapse of Communism; the threat of various forms of authoritarianism; the danger of erosion of democracy; the formation of transnational identities and various kinds of cultural and sexual hybridity; and unprecedented mobility of populations. The sociologist Anthony Giddens sees social interaction as operating across time and space with a rapidity that problematizes the usual understanding of society as a territorially bounded space.[1] What has given these general tendencies a unique character has been a series of world-transforming political events: the First Gulf War, September 11, and the Iraq War, as well as the forms of economic and cultural globalization mentioned above. These vast transformations and events have, in turn, generated an unprecedented series of literary critical responses: a group of literary critics has compiled a book with the singular task of criticizing the Bush administration;[2] a renowned Marxist critic has devoted a book to the subject of terror; an eminent Oxford professor writes in a popular vein, asking *What Good are the Arts?*; a recent critic regards the character of contemporary criticism as specifically a response to terror; a new University in London has set up a Centre of Suburban Studies under the aegis of its English Department; a very large group of academics has engaged in a concerted endeavor to destabilize what they see as *Theory's Empire* and to initiate a rewriting of the recent history of literary criticism.[3]

The aftermath of the attacks of September 11, 2001 demonstrated graphically that what we call culture, and what we think of as the liberal arts, are not somehow peripheral but central to our world civilization. And that what we teach in the literature classroom – whether it is a poem by Emily Dickinson, a Shakespeare play, or verses by contemporary Arab or Israeli poets – can no longer be marooned – either by its content or by its obscure style – from the public sphere in which our lives and values are played out. What used to be thought of as Departments of English have long exploded beyond their conventional boundaries into the areas of cultural studies, film theory, and media. Most recently, they have reached explicitly into the world of politics. Now, there is a new urgency, fueled largely by fears that our own democracy and our own political and cultural values are imperilled, largely from within, from the very administrations purporting to defend them. The values which we academics cherish and are so fond of promoting – the pursuit of knowledge, tolerance, freedom of thought, the understanding of cultural, racial, and sexual difference – are no longer felt to be constrainable within the study of literature. Indeed, the very techniques and methodologies we employ in literary analysis are now often seen as even *more* urgently needed in the public sphere. This is the motivation behind the recent incursion of many academics into the public sphere, into an explicitly political mode, into the discussion of democracy, human freedom, war, imperialism, justice, religious fundamentalism, power, mass media, economic and gender equality, and the public role of the arts. The continuity between literary analysis and broader analyses of culture is re-emerging into a visibility that has been obscured for a number of generations – partly by the very esoteric language in which those connections have hitherto been formulated.

This book aims to offer a concise overview of the major tendencies and figures of modern literary and cultural criticism from the early twentieth century to the present. An endeavor of such broad scope is bound to be incomplete: there is not enough room to include, or even to do justice to, all of the important figures. I do hope, however, that the following account will have the virtues of clarity, close reading, and appropriate contextualization, in making accessible to a general reader these sometimes difficult modern theories, their philosophical premises and their historical contexts. What follows is an outline of the some of the formative moments of literary criticism, then a sketch of the historical background and scope of modern criticism and theory.

Formative Moments in the History of Literary Criticism

Many of the parameters of literary critical study (and philosophy generally) were laid down by Plato and Aristotle. Plato banned poetry from his ideal republic on the grounds that it was three times removed from truth, being merely an imitation of an imitation: it imitated the world of physical appearances, which was itself an imperfect copy of the eternal world of Forms or essences. He also saw poetry as appealing to our lower nature, exciting the mob of passions to rebel against the rule of reason. Aristotle saw poetry as a productive art, and assigned it essentially a moral purpose. He laid down the formulation of tragedy as an action which was complete (and linear, with beginning, middle, and end) and serious, involving significant moral choice. Its language was elevated, and it produced the emotions of pity and terror in an audience through their sympathy and identification with the fall of the hero into misfortune, not through some evil nature but through an overarching human fault or mistake. Classical literary criticism also includes the Roman poet Horace, who urged that poetry must be both pleasing and (morally and intellectually) useful. This insight, regulated into the formula that literature must "teach and delight," dominated much literary criticism until the eighteenth century.

Neoplatonic literary criticism, such as that of Plotinus, saw literature as a direct expression of eternal essences; as such it provided access to the higher spiritual realms and to the divine. The Neoplatonists elaborated notions of allegory which enabled a harmony between the Old and New Testaments, the new being allegorically prefigured in the old. Augustine attempted to trace the appropriate connections between literal and figurative language in the reading of scripture. Medieval criticism, such as that of Aquinas and Dante, refined these notions of allegory: the meanings of language encompassed not just the literal level, but the allegorical (hidden), moral, and anagogical or mystical levels. In general, medieval aesthetics emphasized the beauty, order, and harmony of God's creation. It saw literature as one part of an ordered hierarchy of knowledge leading to the divine, whose apex was theology. Renaissance criticism, such as that of Sir Philip Sidney, became more humanistic and secular, reviving classical learning: Italian writers such as Giraldi and Castelvetro reassessed the classical heritage; the French writers Du Bellay and Ronsard defended the vernacular as a medium of poetic expression; Sidney found it necessary to defend poetry from the many attacks being leveled against it. In general, Renaissance writers re-examined the notions of imitation, the didactic role of literature, and the classification of genres. The neoclassicists of the eighteenth century, such as Pope, Dryden, and Johnson, were even more stringent in observing classical virtues such as rationality, moderation, balance, and decorum (the harmony of form and content), and the dramatic unities of time, place, and action. The use of "wit," a broad term referring to intellectual virtuosity and ability, was much advocated and its meaning disputed. At the same time, Enlightenment thinkers such as John Locke – whose philosophy is one of the foundations of modern bourgeois liberalism – opposed the use of wit, which was metaphorical and ambiguous, and urged instead a language that was clear, distinct, and unambiguous (we have inherited these ideals of writing in our composition courses, designed for success in a world ruled by corporate ethics).

Romantic literary criticism reacted against these strict tendencies; influenced by Kant, it valued Imagination as a higher and more comprehensive faculty than reason, one which united what is given to our senses with the categorizing capacity of our intellect. In his *Critique of Judgment* Kant articulated for the first time a systematic formulation of the autonomy of art and literature, as a domain free of the constraints of morality or utility. Throughout the nineteenth century, this notion of autonomy developed, in the Romantics, the theories of Poe, Baudelaire, and the French symbolists, the aestheticians such as Pater and Wilde, and in writers such as Henry James.

A number of other critical currents arose in the mid- to late nineteenth century: realism (which included requirements of probability and lifelike detail); naturalism, which attempted to model itself on scientific observation of both the internal (psychological) and external worlds; and Marxism, which placed literature in an economic and broad cultural setting; and a number of historical theories, influenced by Hegel, of the evolution of literature and its internal shaping by its unique historical circumstances. The history of literary criticism has yielded a number of enduring concerns, which have persisted into the twenty-first century: the notion of mimesis, the truth value of literature, its connections with tradition, the issue of literature as the production of art or genius, the connection between literal and figurative language, the moral, social, and ideological function of literature, the definition of beauty, literature as a form of knowledge, and its connections with philosophy and rhetoric. The twentieth century added its own concerns, such as the problematic status of language in general, the questioning of identity, the issues of race and gender, and the world of mass media, technology, globalism, and the semiotic codes underlying the functioning of power.

Historical Backgrounds of Modern
Criticism and Theory

Modern history since the early twentieth century is marked by certain colossal events and phenomena which profoundly shaped the worlds of literature, criticism, and theory. These events included the Bolshevik Revolution of 1917 in Russia, the First World War (1914–1918), the great economic depression of the 1930s, the Second World War (1939–1945), the Cold War and the arms race, the predominance of America as a world power, the emergence of the so-called "third world," the social and political unrest of the 1960s, and a general swing in the West toward right-wing politics in the 1980s. Many of these developments culminated in the collapse of much of the Communist bloc by 1989 and of the Soviet Union by 1991. The 1990s witnessed a concerted awareness of the AIDS epidemic and environmental destruction, while the beginning of the new century has overseen the emerging narratives of a new world order and the war on terror, as capitalism emerges, on many levels, into a global phenomenon.

The devastating impact of the First World War, fought between the major powers Germany and Austria on the one side (joined by Turkey and Bulgaria), and France, Russia, and Britain on the other (allied with Japan, Italy, and America), was unprecedented in history. The historian Eric Hobsbawm states that this war "marked the breakdown of the (western) civilization of the nineteenth century."[4] The ideals of the Enlightenment, embodied in the various institutions of the capitalist world, and its ideologies of rational, scientific advance, material and moral progress, individualism, and the economic and cultural centrality of Europe, had culminated in a catastrophe on many levels, economic, political, and moral. The consequent psychological and material devastation and carnage led thinkers in all domains to question not only the heritage of the Enlightenment but also the very foundations of Western civilization. Long-held assumptions – the power of reason, the progress of history, providence, the moral autonomy of human beings, the ability of people and nations to live in harmony, as well as our capacity to know ourselves and the world – were plunged into a mode of moral, spiritual, and intellectual crisis.

Subsequently, the Great Depression of the 1930s represented "a world economic crisis of unprecedented depth," bringing "even the strongest capitalist economies to their knees." Hobsbawm remarks that liberal democratic institutions declined between 1917 and 1942, as fascism and various authoritarian regimes rose to power. The Second World War, waged by the Allies (Britain, America, and France) to contain the expansionist ambitions of Nazi Germany (aided by the totalitarian regimes of Italy and Japan), wrought not only a second wave of wide-scale destruction but also, in its aftermath, the disintegration of the huge colonial empires of Britain, France, Belgium, and the Netherlands, which had subjugated one-third of the world's population. It was the "bizarre" alliance of capitalism and Communism which, ironically, saved the former, with the Red Army playing an essential role in the defeat of Nazi Germany. This alliance, says Hobsbawm, "forms the hinge of twentieth-century history and its decisive moment" (*AE*, 7). Notwithstanding such measures as the formation of the United Nations in 1945, and NATO in 1949, the twentieth century, as Hobsbawm states, "was without doubt the most murderous century of which we have record" (*AE*, 11). All of these phenomena – the two world wars, the rise of fascism, the depression, and decolonization – had a profound impact on literature and criticism.

Then followed a long period, from 1947 to 1973, of considerable growth and prosperity, which harbored, according to Hobsbawm, the greatest and most rapid economic and cultural transformations in recorded history (*AE*, 11). Apart from the unprecedented technological advances, whereby most of the world's population ceased to live in agricultural economies, this era witnessed numerous political and social revolutions, whose principles were variously expressed by Che Guevara in Latin America, Frantz Fanon in Algeria, and the philosopher Herbert Marcuse who inspired radical intellectuals in America and Europe. Political revolutions and movements against colonialism erupted in many parts of Africa; the earlier Black militancy in America, inspired by figures such as Marcus Garvey and later Malcolm X, broadened into the Civil Rights Movement of the 1950s and 1960s, whose leaders included Martin Luther King, assassinated in 1968. Many of the sentiments behind these movements were powerfully expressed in African American literature. The African American heritage has been increasingly explored and theorized in recent decades by critics such as Henry Louis Gates, Jr. In the Middle East, things were no less turbulent. The termination of the British mandate in Palestine and the creation of the state of Israel in 1948 led to persistent conflict between Israel and the Arab nations, fought out in bitter wars in 1948, 1956, 1967, and 1973. This conflict has profoundly shaped the literature and the literary critical principles of the entire region; it was analyzed in the work of the Palestinian American scholar Edward Said, as well as of recent thinkers such as Slavoj Žižek.

Throughout this period, Western capitalism pursued the path of increasing monopoly and consolidation, often employing the principles advocated by economists such as John Maynard Keynes who thought that the inequities of capitalism could be remedied, and prosperity brought to all, using monetary control rather than the nineteenth-century principles of *laissez-faire*. A generation of students in America and Europe, however, reacted against what they saw as the repressive, unjust, sexist, racist, and imperialist nature of the late capitalist world, epitomized for many by American involvement in the Vietnam War. In May 1968, left-wing uprisings of students and workers shook the University of Paris, as well as Berkeley, San Francisco State, Kent State, and elsewhere. Much literary theory in France and America, including feminism, took its impetus from this atmosphere of unrest and agitation. The later twentieth century brought a new awareness of ecology and the extent to which modern industrial life and production had damaged the environment.

As we enter a new century, it is clear that the Cold War has been replaced by a new dynamic, which itself has served as the foundation for much recent criticism and theory. The relatively stable international system of Communism was succeeded by local ethnic, tribal, and religious conflicts in Yugoslavia and areas of the former Soviet Union. Since the early 1990s, the core of this new dynamic has been underlain by America's unopposed predominance as *the* major world power, fueled by formulations of a "New World Order." The relative impotence of the political left has left its mark on the nature of theory, and on what is viewed as radical or conservative. What has occupied center stage since the attacks of September 11 on the World Trade Center has been the "war on terror." Hobsbawm states three ways in which the world has changed from the beginning to the end of the twentieth century: it is no longer Eurocentric, though America, Europe, and Japan are still the most prosperous; the world has in certain important ways become a "single operational unit," primarily in economic terms, but also increasingly in terms of mass culture; and, finally, there has been a massive disintegration of previous patterns of human relationships, with an unprecedented rupture between past and present. Capitalism has become a permanent and continuous revolutionary force that perpetuates itself in time and extends its empire increasingly in space. Modern criticism and theory have broadened to encompass all of these developments.

The Scope of Modern Literary and Cultural Criticism

Since the early twentieth century, literary, criticism and theory have comprised a broad range of tendencies and movements: a humanistic tradition, descended from nineteenth-century writers such as Matthew Arnold and continued into the twentieth century through figures such as Irving Babbitt and F. R. Leavis, surviving in our own day in scholars such as Frank Kermode and John Carey; a neo-Romantic tendency, expressed in the work of D. H. Lawrence, G. Wilson Knight, and others; the New Criticism, arising initially in the 1920s and subsequently formalized and popularized in the 1940s; the tradition of Marxist criticism, traceable to the writings of Marx and Engels themselves, being revived first during the depression of the 1930s through figures such as Christopher Caudwell and then again with the political unrest of the 1960s, in the works of Terry Eagleton and Fredric Jameson; psychoanalytic criticism, whose foundations were laid by Freud and Jung; Russian Formalism, arising in the aftermath of the Russian Revolution; the first wave of feminism, articulated by thinkers such as

Simone de Beauvoir and Virginia Woolf; structuralism, which emerged fully in the 1950s, building on the foundations established in the early twentieth century by Saussure and Lévi-Strauss; and the various forms of criticism which are sometimes subsumed under the label of "poststructuralism": Lacanian psychoanalytic theory, which rewrote Freudian concepts in terms of linguistic categories; deconstruction, as initiated by Jacques Derrida, which emerged in the 1960s, as did the later waves of feminism in writers such as Elaine Showalter, Julia Kristeva, and Hélène Cixous; reader-response theory, whose roots went back to Husserl and Heidegger; and the New Historicism, which arose in the 1980s through Stephen Greenblatt, again tracing its roots to Michel Foucault. This decade gave birth to another pervasive mode of criticism, postcolonialism, which traced its roots through Edward Said back to colonial struggles earlier in the century and their theorists such as Frantz Fanon. The 1990s saw the concerted emergence of gender studies along with gay and lesbian criticism, in figures such as Judith Butler and Eve Kosofsky Sedgwick.

The attacks of September 11, 2001 on the World Trade Center somewhat shifted the gears and parameters of literary and cultural thinking: some critics, both liberal and radical, moved explicitly into the political domain, while more conservative critics – and some liberal critics – reaffirmed a commitment to the aesthetic. Among the most prominent left-wing critics are Slavoj Žižek, who has reformulated, in Lacanian categories, some Marxist imperatives in the light of present political exigencies, such as the Palestinian–Israeli conflict; Antonio Negri and Michael Hardt, who have formulated a new conception of "Empire"; both Marxists such as Terry Eagleton and writers affiliated with poststructuralism such as Jean Baudrillard, who have analyzed the meanings of "terror"; the new liberal humanists including Elaine Scarry, Martha Nussbaum, and John Carey, who have analyzed the public status of the arts, the notions of beauty, justice, and the meanings of democracy and good citizenship; and the new formalistic critics, including figures such as Michael Berube, who wish to reserve a space for the aesthetic, for the study of literature *as* literature.

The foregoing movements represent the scope of this book. They also indicate the ways in which the study of "English" has been transformed over the last few decades, shifting focus from the texts of literature to a dazzling array of cultural and ideological contexts. In general, the present critical scene presents two sharply opposed currents, the one taking literary analysis into the discourses of politics – under the banner of a revived liberal humanism or a reconfigured leftism – and the other almost wishing to repress the memory of theory in its reaffirmation of the project of withdrawal from the world of politics and the world of interdisciplinarity, in an attempt to redraw and reinstall the institutional, disciplinary, and intellectual boundaries of literature. This battle is about to be fought.

Notes

1   A discussion of this and some of the other themes mentioned here can be found in the excellent introduction, *Key Contemporary Social Theorists*, ed. Anthony Elliott and Larry Ray (Oxford: Blackwell, 2003), pp. xi–xviii.
2   *Dissent from the Homeland: Essays After September 11*, ed. Stanley Hauerwas and Frank Lentricchia (Durham, NC, and London: Duke University Press, 2003).
3   *Theory's Empire: An Anthology of Dissent*, ed. Daphne Patai and Will H. Corral (New York: Columbia University Press, 2005).
4   Eric Hobsbawm, *The Age of Extremes: A History of the World, 1914–1991* (New York: Pantheon, 1994), p. 6. Hereafter cited as *AE*.

Chapter 1

The First Decades:
From Liberal Humanism
to Formalism

At the end of the nineteenth century, criticism in Europe and America had been predominantly biographical, historical, psychological, impressionistic, and empirical. With the establishment of English as a separate discipline in England, many influential critics, such as George Saintsbury, A. C. Bradley, and Arthur Quiller-Couch, assumed academic posts. By far the most influential of this early generation of academic critics was A. C. Bradley. In *Shakespearean Tragedy* (1904), Bradley's central thesis, influenced by Hegel and the Hegelians T. H. Greene and F. H. Bradley (his brother), saw Shakespearean tragedy as a dialectic whereby the moral order and harmony of the world were threatened (by the tragic hero) and then re-established.

In America, influential theories of realism and naturalism had been propounded by William Dean Howells, Hamlin Garland, and Frank Norris. An important concern of American critics such as John Macy, Randolph Bourne, and Van Wyck Brooks was to establish a sense of national identity through tracing a specifically American literary tradition. In France, the most pervasive critical mode was the *explication de texte*, based on close readings which drew upon biographical sources and historical context. In the humanist tradition of Matthew Arnold, much of this *fin-de-siècle* criticism saw in literature a refuge from, or remedy for, the ills of modern civilization. In both America and Europe, the defenders and proponents of literature sought to preserve the humanities in the educational curriculum against the onslaughts of reformists such as Harvard University President Charles Eliot and John Dewey, who urged that the College education system be brought into line with prevailing bourgeois scientific and economic interests.

The New Humanists, Neo-Romantics, and Precursors of Formalism

The humanist tradition of the late nineteenth century, as expressed by figures such as Matthew Arnold, vociferously reacted against the commercialism and philistinism of bourgeois society. This tradition was continued and intensified in the polemic of the "New Humanists," as well as by certain neo-Romantic and formalistic critics. Led by Harvard professor Irving Babbitt and including figures such as Paul Elmer More, Norman Foerster, and Stuart Sherman, the New Humanists were conservative in their cultural and political outlook, reacting against what they saw as a relativistic disorder of styles and approaches characterizing early twentieth-century America. They rejected the predominant tendencies stemming from the liberal-bourgeois tradition: a narrow focus on the present at the expense of the past and of tradition; unrestrained freedom in political, moral, and aesthetic domains; a riot of pluralism, a mechanical exaltation of facts and an uninformed worship of science.

Irving Babbitt's humanism posits a unity which might contextualize historically the reductive multiplicity and isolated present of the bourgeois world. Babbitt describes the dilemma of relating the One and the Many, of perceiving unity in the diversity of our experience, as "the ultimate problem of thought."[1] Babbitt sees the Protestant Reformation and the French Revolution as the crucial historical impulses toward modernity. At the heart of these eras of expansive individualism he locates Bacon and Rousseau who respectively embody "scientific" and "sentimental" naturalism, which attempt to explain man's nature and the world on "natural" rather than transcendent foundations. As a result of this misguided veneration of the sciences, affirms Babbitt, "Man has gained immensely in his grasp on facts, but . . . has become so immersed in their multiplicity as to lose that vision of the One by which his lower self was once overawed and restrained."[2]

In *Rousseau and Romanticism* (1919) and *Democracy and Leadership* (1924), Babbitt sees Rousseau as both the father of "radical democracy" and the fullest representative of Romanticism (*RR*, ix, 379). Babbitt here articulates the opposition between Classicism and Romanticism. Classicism expresses what is "normal" and "central" in human experience; it is not local and national but universal and "human"; it thus offers a model of representative human nature (*RR*, xxii, 14–17). Hence it seeks a "true centre," an abiding permanent human element through change. Classicism employs an "ethical" imagination which insists on restraint and proportion. In contrast, Romanticism's pursuit of the strange, extreme, and unique is premised on a conception of imagination, derived from Kant and Schiller, which is utterly free from all constraint. Babbitt's main objection to Romanticism is its fostering of "anarchic individualism" and evasion of

11

moral responsibility. In avoiding a center of human experience, it condemns itself to both intellectual and moral relativism, a blind immersion in the "Many" with no recourse to the stabilizing authority of the "One" (*RR*, 391). Babbitt's humanism, concerned with perfecting the individual, urges a return to the Renaissance ideal of the "complete" man who achieves a Socratic harmony between thought and feeling (*LAC*, 75, 80, 82, 166). Babbitt insists that both life and man constitute a oneness that is always changing, and that experience contains both unity and multiplicity (*RR*, xii). At the foundation of Babbitt's humanism, then, is a view of human nature as essentially fixed through all its surface changes and a view of reality as ultimately a unity.

Literary criticism, according to Babbitt, is infected with the pervasive disease of impressionism.[3] To reaffirm the role of "objective" judgment Babbitt calls for comparative and historical methods which treat the classics "as links in that unbroken chain of literary and intellectual tradition which extends from the ancient to the modern world" (*LAC*, 159–160). The modern obsession with originality, says Babbitt, betrays "the profound doctrine of Aristotle that the final test of art is not its originality, but its truth to the universal . . . Now . . . there is a riot of so-called originality" (*LAC*, 186, 188). These statements will be echoed almost verbatim by writers such as T. S. Eliot and Ezra Pound. Genuine originality, Babbitt suggests, "imposes the task of achieving work that is of general human truth and at the same time intensely individual" (*LAC*, 194–195). What is needed, says Babbitt, is a critic who will use the "historical method" while guarding against its dangers of relativism by seeing "an element in man that is set above the local and the relative . . . in Platonic language, he will perceive the One in the Many" (*RR*, xii). This was a call to which Eliot, Pound, and others enthusiastically responded.

Also reacting against the industrialism and rationalism of the bourgeois world were the neo-Romantic critics in England, including D. H. Lawrence, G. Wilson Knight, John Middleton Murry, Herbert Read, and C. S. Lewis. Lawrence (1885–1930) was an avowed irrationalist, who saw the modern industrial world as sexually repressive and as having stunted human potential. His literary criticism was expressed in several reviews and in his *Studies in Classic American Literature* (1923), as well as in essays on sexuality and the unconscious. In both these works and his fiction, Lawrence advocated a vitalism and individualism which often had parallels in the views of Nietzsche and Freud. He attempted to revaluate various writers in the light of his libidinal and primitivist ideology, urging that their art achieved something contrary to their conscious and morally repressive intentions. His disposition is anti-democratic and even fascistic, reacting, like Nietzsche, against mass mediocrity and moral conventionalism, and urging hope for a new man. In his own highly idiosyncratic way, Lawrence anticipates the stress on the unconscious, the body, and irrational motives in various areas of contemporary criticism.

Of the other neo-Romantic critics mentioned above, Middleton Murry (1889–1957) attempted to reinstate a Romantic belief in pantheism and the organic unity of the world. He saw as a central criterion of genuine poetry that it was not amenable to paraphrase and that it expressed truths inaccessible to reason or concepts. Herbert Read (1893–1968) began as an advocate of imagism and classicism and eventually expressed an allegiance to Romanticism and articulated an organicist aesthetic, viewing poetry as transcending reason. G. Wilson Knight (1897–1985), a Shakespeare scholar, is best known for his *The Wheel of Fire* (1930). Drawing on the findings of anthropologists such as Sir James Frazer concerning myths, rituals, and symbols, Wilson Knight interprets Shakespeare's plays in terms of certain recurring symbols and motifs. As a critic, he distinguished interpretation, which aims empathetically to reconstruct an author's vision, from criticism, which he sees as evaluative. Somewhat like the New Critics, Wilson Knight wished to subordinate considerations drawn from intention or biography or morality to artistic concerns. Another significant critic in this broad Romantic-religious tradition was C. S. Lewis (1898–1963), whose major critical work was *The Allegory of Love* (1936), which, along with his other works, contributed to his mission of promoting understanding of the formality and didacticism of the literature of the Middle Ages and the Renaissance. Finally, mention should be made of the scholar of Milton and Shakespeare, E. M. Tillyard (1889–1962), who engaged in a debate with C. S. Lewis in *The Personal Heresy* (1939) and whose most influential work was *The Elizabethan World Picture* (1943). New Critical trends were also anticipated in America where W. C. Brownell attempted to establish literary criticism as a serious and independent activity, and where James Gibbons Huneker and H. L. Mencken insisted on addressing the aesthetic elements in art as divorced from moral considerations.

Hence, the critical movements of the early twentieth century were already moving in certain directions: the isolation of the aesthetic from moral, religious concerns, and indeed an exaltation of the aesthetic (as transcending reason and the paradigms of bourgeois thought such as utility and pragmatic value) as a last line of defense against a commercialized and dehumanizing world; and a correlative attempt to establish criticism as a serious and "scientific" activity. This broadly humanist trend is far from dead; it has not only persisted through figures such as F. R. Leavis but has also often structured the very forms of critical endeavors which reject it.

The Background of Modernism

Modernism comprised a broad series of movements in Europe and America that came to fruition roughly between 1910 and 1930. Its major exponents and practitioners included Marcel Proust, James Joyce, Ezra Pound, T. S.

Eliot, William Faulkner, Virginia Woolf, Luigi Pirandello, and Franz Kafka. These various modernisms were the results of many complex economic, political, scientific, and religious developments over the nineteenth century, which culminated in the First World War (1914–1918). The vast devastation, psychological demoralization, and economic depression left by the war intensified the already existing reactions against bourgeois modes of thought and economic practice. Rationalism underwent renewed assaults from many directions: from philosophers such as Bergson, from the sphere of psychoanalysis, from neoclassicists such as T. E. Hulme, the New Humanists in America, and neo-Thomists such as Jacques Maritain. These reactions were often underlain by a new understanding of language, as a conventional and historical construct. The modernist writer occupied a world that was often perceived as fragmented, where the old bourgeois ideologies of rationality, science, progress, civilization, and imperialism had been somewhat discredited; where the artist was alienated from the social and political world, and where art and literature were marginalized; where populations had been subjected to processes of mass standardization; where philosophy could no longer offer visions of unity, and where language itself was perceived to be an inadequate instrument for expression and understanding.

A distinct group of artist-critics associated with modernism was the highly iconoclastic Bloomsbury Group. This circle included Virginia Woolf and her sister Vanessa, daughters of the critic and agnostic philosopher Leslie Stephen, the art critics Roger Fry and Clive Bell, the economist John Maynard Keynes, the biographer Lytton Strachey, and the novelist E. M. Forster. Most members of the group fell under the influence of the Cambridge philosopher G. E. Moore's *Principia Ethica*. They saw this text as affirming an "aesthetic" approach to life inasmuch as it stressed the value of allegedly timeless states of consciousness which facilitated the enjoyment of beauty. The Group inevitably fell under many of the influences that had shaped modernism, such as the notion of time advanced in the philosophy of Bergson. It was during this period also that the foundations of the New Criticism were laid by figures such as William Empson and I. A. Richards; the latter's *Principles of Literary Criticism* (1924) and *Practical Criticism* (1929) were widely and enduringly influential. Here, too, the literary artefact was treated as an autonomous and self-contained verbal structure, insulated from the world of prose, as in Richards' distinction between emotive and referential language. In France also, the somewhat positivistic earlier mode of criticism, the *explication de texte*, was opposed by influential figures such as Bergson, whose novel conceptions of time and memory, and whose view of art as uniquely transcending the mechanistic concepts of bourgeois society, profoundly influenced Proust and other modernists. Paul Valéry (1871–1945) formulated a criticism drawing on the earlier French symbolists, one which prioritized the aesthetic verbal structure over historical and contextual elements.

The Poetics of Modernism: W. B. Yeats, Ezra Pound, T. S. Eliot

Over the last fifty years or so, we have come to appreciate more fully the complexity and heterogeneity of literary modernism, in its nature and genesis. It is no longer regarded as simply a symbolist and imagistic reaction against nineteenth-century realism or naturalism or later versions of Romanticism. It is not so much that modernism, notwithstanding the political conservatism of many of its practitioners, turns away from the project of depicting reality; what more profoundly underlies modernistic literary forms is an awareness that the definitions of reality become increasingly complex and problematic. Modernists came to this common awareness by different paths: Yeats drew on the occult, on Irish myth and legend, as well as the Romantics and French symbolists. Proust drew on the insights of Bergson; Virginia Woolf, on Bergson, G. E. Moore, and others; Pound drew on various non-European literatures as well as French writers; T. S. Eliot, whose poetic vision was profoundly eclectic, drew on Dante, the Metaphysical poets, Laforgue, Baudelaire, and a number of philosophers.

In general, literary modernism was marked by a number of features: (1) the affirmation of a continuity, rather than a separation, between the worlds of subject and object, the self and the world. The human self is not viewed as a stable entity which simply engages with an already present external world of objects and other selves; (2) a perception of the complex roles of time, memory, and history in the mutual construction of self and world. Time is not conceived in a static model which separates past, present, and future as discrete elements in linear relation; rather, it is viewed as dynamic, with these elements influencing and changing one another. Human history is thus not already written; even the past can be altered in accordance with present human interests, motives, and viewpoints; (3) a breakdown of any linear narrative structure following the conventional Aristotelian model which prescribes beginning, middle, and end. Modernist poetry tends to be fragmented, creating its own internal 'logic' of emotion, image, sound, symbol, and mood; (4) an acknowledgment of the complexity of experience: any given experience is vastly more complex than can be rendered in literal language. For example, the experience of 'love' could be quite different from one person to another, yet language coercively subsumes these differing experiences under the same word and concept. Modernist poetry tends to veer away from any purported literal use of language which might presume a one-to-one correspondence between words and things; it relies far more on suggestion and allusion rather than overt statement; (5) a self-consciousness regarding the process of literary composition. This embraces both an awareness of how one's own work relates to the literary tradition as a whole, and an ironic stance toward the content of one's own work; (6) finally, and most importantly, an awareness of the problematic nature of language. This indeed underlies the other elements cited above. If there is no simple correspondence between language and reality, and if these realms are mutually constituted through patterns of coherence, then a large part of the poet's task lies in a more precise use of language which offers alternative definitions of reality. Eliot once said that the poet must "distort" language in order to create his meaning.

Twentieth-century modernism, as manifested in the work of the Irish poet and critic W. B. Yeats (1865–1939), the American poet Ezra Pound, and the Anglo-American poet and critic T. S. Eliot, was deeply influenced by symbolism, whether that of the English Romantics such as Blake, Coleridge, Wordsworth, and Shelley, or French symbolism as developed in the work of Baudelaire, Mallarmé, Verlaine, and Rimbaud. French symbolism was introduced to English and American audiences largely through Arthur Symons' book *The Symbolist Movement in Literature* (1899). In this book, Symons explained the history and rationale of French symbolism, which he saw as a reaction against nineteenth-century scientism and materialism. French symbolism saw literature as affirming the reality of a higher, spiritual realm which could be divined not by rational thought but only in glimpses through a pure poetic language divested of any representational pretension. Symbolism is an attempt to reinvest both the world and language – stripped by much bourgeois thought and science to a utilitarian literalness – with metaphor, ambivalence, and mystery. In symbolist poetry, concrete images are used to evoke emotions, moods, and atmospheres otherwise ineffable.

Yeats' own theory and practice of symbolism drew from William Blake, Shelley, Irish mythology, and magic. Yeats affirmed that external objects and scenes could express the profoundest internal states, and that the poet's task is to imbue such scenes and images with a symbolic significance transcending the time and place of their immediate origin. Symbols, for Yeats, evoke what he calls the "Great Mind" and "Great Memory." Yeats' own poetry uses numerous symbols with both private and public associations, such as the rose, the cross, the stairway, and the tower. Yeats worked out his own highly intricate cosmological symbolism in *A Vision* (1925–1937). His assessments of most poets were motivated by a search for symbolic predecessors and an attempt to explain their techniques.

The other major critic of the early twentieth century influenced by French symbolism was the modernist poet T. S. Eliot (1888–1965). Some of the assumptions underlying his renowned critical notions, such as "tradition" (expressed in his seminal essay of 1919, "Tradition and the Individual Talent"), "dissociation of sensibility," and "objective correlative," were derived in part from French writers. Eliot's concept of "dissociation of sensibility," for example, according to which a dissociation of thought from feeling had arisen subsequent to the Metaphysical poets, was informed by his perception of some of the nineteenth-century French poets as "Metaphysical" in their attempt to harmonize these polarized faculties. Both Eliot's "dissociation of sensibility" and "objective correlative" may have had roots in the thought of French symbolists and especially Remy de Gourmont. Other major influences on Eliot's criticism were Ezra Pound's imagism and T. E. Hulme's classicism. Eliot's main critical contributions were (1) to combat provincialism by broadening the notion of "tradition" to include Europe; (2) to advocate, as against the prevailing critical impressionism, a closely analytical and even objective criticism which situated literary works alongside one another in the larger context of tradition. In this, he contributed to the development of notions of artistic autonomy which were taken up by some of the New Critics; and (3) to foster, by his own revaluation of the literary tradition (reacting against the Romantics, for example, and highlighting the virtues of the Metaphysical poets), a dynamic notion of tradition as always in the process of change. Eliot also brought to literary criticism a sophistication drawn from his philosophical studies, which helped to display the intricate connections between literary study and other fields such as religion, philosophy, and psychology. Eliot's criticism, as he acknowledged, was motivated by a desire to explain and propagate the kind of poetry he was writing, as well as to draw attention to the various elements of literary tradition which had proved serviceable to his verse. Hence, his criticism was in part a manifesto of literary modernism, characteristically infused with political conservatism.

Eliot's aesthetics and his notion of tradition were also indebted to Ezra Pound (1885–1972) and the imagist movement. Pound assumed a broad range of critical roles: as poet-critic, he promoted his own work and the works of figures such as Frost, Joyce, and Eliot; he translated numerous texts from Anglo-Saxon, Latin, Greek, and Chinese; and, associating with various schools such as imagism and vorticism, he advocated a poetry which was concise, concrete, precise in expression of emotion, and appropriately informed by a sense of tradition. As a result of his suggestions, Eliot's major poem *The Waste Land* was radically condensed and transformed. The ideas of Pound and Eliot have had a lasting influence but their most forceful impact occurred between the 1920s and the 1940s.

Formalism

The various modernistic groups tended to be formalistic in tendency, focusing in considerable detail on the formal structure of a work of art. Indeed, literary critics and thinkers of various historical periods have placed emphasis on the formal aspects of art and literature. Aristotle, ancient and medieval rhetoricians, Kant, many of the Romantics, and writers in the nineteenth-century movements of symbolism and aestheticism all placed a high priority on literary form. This emphasis reached a new intensity and self-consciousness in the literatures and critical theories of the early twentieth century, beginning with the Formalist movement in Russia and with European modernism, extending subsequently to the New Criticism in England and America and later schools such as the neo-Aristotelians. In general, an emphasis on form parenthesizes concern for the representational, imitative, and cognitive aspects of literature. Literature is no longer viewed as aiming to represent reality or character or to impart moral or intellectual lessons, but is considered to be an object in its own right, autonomous (possessing its own laws) and autotelic (having its aims internal to itself). Moreover, in this formalist view, literature does not convey any clear or paraphrasable message; rather, it communicates what is otherwise ineffable. Literature is regarded as a unique mode of expression, not an extension of rhetoric or philosophy or history or social or psychological documentary. Critics have variously theorized that preoccupation with form betokens social alienation, a withdrawal from the world, an acknowledgment of political helplessness, and a retreat into the aesthetic as a refuge of sensibility and humanistic values. Such an insular disposition also betokens a retreat from history and biography, effectively isolating the literary artefact from both broad social forces and the more localized and personal circumstances of its author.

In both academia and popular culture, we are still today very familiar with terms such as "art for art's sake" and we still hear poetry or music or art spoken of as "ends in themselves," to be enjoyed for their own sake. Most thinkers from Plato to the eighteenth century would not have understood this idea or indeed the desire to read literature *as* literature: while they might admit that one function of literature is to "delight" us via its formal qualities, they would insist that literature has an important moral, religious, or social dimension.

Strange as it may seem, the idea of literature as autonomous, as having no purpose beyond itself, received its first articulate expression not by a poet or a literary critic but by a philosopher: Immanuel Kant. It was Kant's *Critique of Judgment*, first published in 1790, which synthesized previous haphazard attempts toward expressing literary autonomy. This book proved to have a vast influence on subsequent aesthetics and poetry, an influence still alive today in our own reverence for the literary artefact as something which stands above and beyond the demands of morality, education, and politics. Throughout the nineteenth and into the twenty-first century, the notion of literary autonomy – an index of a broader mutual separation and specialization of disciplines in bourgeois society – was developed by many literary figures and movements, ranging from the Romantics, Poe, and the French symbolists through the aestheticism of Pater and Wilde into modernism and current reactions against what are seen as ideological or political readings of literature.

Russian Formalism

Along with movements in futurism and symbolism, the Russian Formalists were a group of writers who flourished during the period of the Russian Revolution of 1917. The Formalists and the futurists were active in the fierce debates of this era concerning art and its connections with ideology. The Formalists and futurists found a common platform in the journal *LEF* (Left Front of Art). The Formalists, focusing on artistic forms and techniques on the basis of linguistic studies, had arisen in pre-revolutionary Russia but now saw their opposition to traditional art as a political gesture, allying them somewhat with the revolution. However, all of these groups were attacked by the most prominent Soviet theoreticians, such as Trotsky, Nikolai Bukharin (1888–1937), Anatoly Lunacharsky (1875–1933), and Voronsky, who decried the attempt to break completely with the past and what they saw as a reductive denial of the social and cognitive aspects of art. V. N. Volosinov and Bakhtin later attempted to harmonize the two sides of the debate, viz., formal linguistic analysis and sociological emphasis by treating language itself as the supreme ideological phenomenon, as the very site of ideological struggle. Other groups, called "Bakhtin Circles," formed around this enterprise.

There were two schools of Russian Formalism. The Moscow Linguistic Circle, led by Roman Jakobson, was formed in 1915; this group also included Osip Brik and Boris Tomashevsky. The second group, the Society for the Study of Poetic Language (*Opoyaz*), was founded in 1916, and its leading figures included Victor Shklovsky, Boris Eichenbaum, and Yuri Tynyanov. Other important critics associated with these movements included Leo Jakubinsky and the folklorist Vladimir Propp.

It should be said that the Russian Formalists' emphasis on form and technique was different in nature from that of the later New Critics. The Formalists' analyses were far more theoretical, seeking to understand the general nature of literature and literary devices, as well as the historical evolution of literary techniques; the New Critics were more concerned with the practice (rather than the theory) of close reading of individual texts. Though Russian Formalism as a school was eclipsed with the rise of Stalin and the official Soviet aesthetic of Socialist Realism, its influence was transmitted through the structuralist analyses of figures such as Jakobson and Tzvetan Todorov to writers such as Roland Barthes and Gerard Genette. Even reception theorists such as Hans Robert Jauss have drawn upon Victor Shklovsky's notion of defamiliarization.

Victor Shklovsky (1893–1984) became a founding member of one of the two schools of Russian Formalism, the Society for the Study of Poetic Language, formed in 1916. His essay "Art as Technique" (1917)[4] was one of the central statements of formalist theory. It is in this paper that Shklovsky introduces defamiliarization, one of the central concepts of Russian

Formalism: as our normal perceptions become habitual, they become automatic and unconscious: in everyday speech, for example, we leave phrases unfinished and words half-expressed. Shklovsky sees this as symptomatic of a process of "algebraization" which infects our ordinary perceptions: "things are replaced by symbols"; we fail to apprehend the object, which "fades and does not leave even a first impression; ultimately even the essence of what it was is forgotten" (AT, 11).

Shklovsky quotes Tolstoy as saying that "the whole complex of lives of many people go on unconsciously . . . such lives are as if they had never been." Hence habituation can devour work, clothes, furniture, one's wife, and the fear of war. It is against this background of ordinary perception in general that art assumes its significance: "art exists that one may recover the sensation of life; it exists to make one feel things, to make the stone *stony* . . . The technique of art is to make objects 'unfamiliar,' to make forms difficult, to increase the difficulty and length of perception because the process of perception is an aesthetic end in itself and must be prolonged. *Art is a way of experiencing the artfulness of an object; the object is not important*" (AT, 12).

Boris Eichenbaum (1886–1959)

Like Shklovsky, Eichenbaum was one of the leaders of the Russian Formalist group known as the Society for the Study of Poetic Language, founded in 1916. Like others of his school, Eichenbaum was denounced by Trotsky. He wrote an important essay, "The Theory of the 'Formal Method'" (1926, 1927), expounding the evolution of the central principles of the formalist method. Eichenbaum begins by stating that formalism is "characterized only by the attempt to create an independent science of literature which studies specifically literary material."[5]

According to Eichenbaum, the Formalists were aware that "history demanded . . . a really revolutionary attitude . . . Hence our Formalist movement was characterized by a new passion for scientific positivism – a rejection of philosophical assumptions, of psychological and aesthetic interpretations . . . Art . . . dictated its own position on things. We had to turn to facts and, abandoning general systems and problems, to begin 'in the middle,' with the facts which art forced upon us" (TFM, 106). It is clear from these lines that the ideology behind Formalism was positivism, an attempt to emulate the models and methods of what is perceived as "science," an attempt to focus on immediately given empirical data rather than on general schemes or theories for uniting and understanding such isolated information. It is hardly surprising that the spokesmen of the official Russian aesthetic saw such a posture as reductive, tearing art from its historical and political contexts, denying its ideological function, and attempting to view it as an independent, autonomous domain. In the context of early twentieth-century Russia, Eichenbaum evidently sees this strategy as revolutionary, as attempting to free art from serving ideological and political ends.

Eichenbaum also argued that poetry uses words differently from their function in ordinary speech, disrupting "ordinary verbal associations" (TFM, 129). The suggestion here is that poetry, or more specifically poetic form, comprises a kind of speech of its own, which is cumulatively developed by a tradition of poets. Rhythms are developed that are peculiar to poetry, and so are shades of meaning and syntactical structures. In this view of poetic form, the notion of content or material, as explained in Yuri Tynyanov's *The Problem of Poetic Language* (1924), does not lie opposed to or outside of or beyond form; rather, content is itself a formal element (TFM, 130). Also, the Formalists adopted a new understanding of literary history which rejected the idea of some linear, unified tradition. Rather, literary tradition involved struggle, a destruction of old values, competition between various schools in a given epoch, and persistence of vanquished movements alongside the newly dominant groups (TFM, 134–135). The Formalists insisted that literary evolution had a distinctive character and that it "stood alone, quite independent of other aspects of culture." Clearly, such a model of literary history anticipates later theories such as those of Pound and T. S. Eliot; the latter saw works of literature as forming an "ideal order" among themselves. For the Formalists, moreover, this evolution was independent of biography and psychology: "For us, the central problem of the history of literature is the problem of evolution without personality – the study of literature as a *self-formed social phenomenon*" (TFM, 136). Such methods clearly anticipate certain tenets of structuralism, such as the location of an author's subjectivity within linguistic and social structures.

Mikhail M. Bakhtin (1895–1975)

Bakhtin is perhaps best known for his radical philosophy of language, as well as his theory of the novel, underpinned by concepts such as "dialogism," "polyphony," and "carnival," themselves resting on the more fundamental concept of "heteroglossia." Bakhtin's writings were produced at a time of momentous upheavals in Russia: the Revolution of 1917 was followed by a civil war (1918–1921), famine, and the dark years of repressive dictatorship under Joseph Stalin. While Bakhtin himself was not a member of the Communist Party, his work has been regarded by some as Marxist in orientation, seeking to provide a corrective to the abstractness of extreme formalism. Despite his critique of formalism, he has also been claimed as a member of the Jakobsonian formalist school, as a poststructuralist, and even as a religious thinker.

Bakhtin's major works as translated into English include *Art and Answerability: Early Philosophical Essays* (1990), *Rabelais and his World* (1965; trans. 1968), *Problems of Dostoevsky's Poetics* (1929; trans. 1973), *The Dialogic Imagination: Four Essays* (1930s; trans. 1981), and *Speech Genres and*

Other Late Essays (1986). His important early essay "Towards a Philosophy of the Act" (1919) was not published until 1986. Bakhtin's interest in the nature of language was formed in part by members of the various "circles" that formed around him during his career. The authorship of some further publications, such as *Marxism and the Philosophy of Language* (1929, 1930), which was published under the name of V. N. Volosinov, is still in dispute.[6]

Bakhtin's major achievements include the formulation of an innovative and radical philosophy of language as well as a comprehensive "theory" of the novel. His essay "Discourse in the Novel" furnishes an integrated statement of both endeavors. Indeed, what purports to be a theory of the novel entails not only a radical account of the nature of language but also a radical critique of the history of philosophy and an innovative explanation of the nature of subjectivity, objectivity, and the very process of understanding. In this essay, Bakhtin defines the novel as a "diversity of social speech types (sometimes even diversity of languages) and a diversity of individual voices, artistically organized" (*DI*, 262). It quickly becomes apparent that Bakhtin's view of the novel is dependent upon his broader view of the nature of language as "dialogic" and as comprised of "heteroglossia." In order to explain the concept of dialogism, we first need to understand the latter term: "heteroglossia" refers to the circumstance that what we usually think of as a single, unitary language is actually comprised of a multiplicity of languages interacting with, and often ideologically competing with, one another. In Bakhtin's terms, any given "language" is actually stratified into several "other languages" ("heteroglossia" might be translated as "other-languageness"). For example, we can break down "any single national language into social dialects, characteristic group behavior, professional jargons, generic languages, languages of generations and age groups, . . . languages of the authorities, of various circles and of passing fashions . . . each day has its own slogan, its own vocabulary, its own emphases." It is this heteroglossia, says Bakhtin, which is "the indispensable prerequisite for the novel as a genre" (*DI*, 263).

"Dialogism" is a little more difficult to explain. On the most basic level, it refers to the fact that the various languages that stratify any "single" language are in dialogue with one another; Bakhtin calls this "the primordial dialogism of discourse," whereby all discourse has a dialogic orientation (*DI*, 275). We might illustrate this using the following example: the language of religious discourse does not exist in a state of ideological and linguistic "neutrality." On the contrary, such discourse might act as a "rejoinder" or "reply" to elements of political discourse. The political discourse might encourage loyalty to the state and adherence to material ambitions, whereas the religious discourse might attempt to displace those loyalties with the pursuit of spiritual goals. Even a work of art does not come, Minerva-like, fully formed from the brain of its author, speaking a single monologic language: it is a response, a rejoinder, to other works, to

certain traditions, and it situates itself within a current of intersecting dialogues (*DI*, 274). Its relation to other works of art and to other languages
(literary and non-literary) is dialogic.

Bakhtin has a further, profounder, explanation of the concept of dialogism. He explains that there is no direct, unmediated relation between a
word and its object: "no living word relates to its object in a *singular* way."
In its path toward the object, the word encounters "the fundamental and
richly varied opposition of . . . other, alien words about the same object."
Any concrete discourse, says Bakhtin, "finds the object at which it was
directed already as it were overlain with qualifications, open to dispute,
charged with value, already enveloped in an obscuring mist – or, on the
contrary, by the 'light' of alien words that have already been spoken about
it. It is entangled, shot through with shared thoughts, points of view, alien
value judgments and accents. The word, directed toward its object, enters
a dialogically agitated and tension-filled environment" (*DI*, 276–277). The
underlying premise here is that language is not somehow a neutral medium,
transparently related to the world of objects. Any utterance, whereby we
assign a given meaning to a word, or use a word in a given way, is composed
not in a vacuum in which the word as we initially encounter it is empty of
significance. Rather, even before we utter the word in our own manner and
with our own signification, it is already invested with many layers of
meaning, and our use of the word must accommodate those other meanings and in some cases compete with them. Our utterance will in its very
nature be dialogic: it is born as one voice in a dialogue that is already constituted; it cannot speak monologically, as the only voice, in some register
isolated from all social, historical, and ideological contexts. We might
illustrate this notion of dialogism with an example taken from the stage of
modern international politics. Those of us living in Europe or America
tend to think of the word (and concept of) "democracy" as invested with
a broad range of positive associations: we might relate it generally with
the idea of political progress, with a history of emancipation from feudal
economic and political constraints, with what we think of as "civilization,"
with a secular and scientific world view, and perhaps above all with the
notion of individual freedom. But when we attempt to export this word,
this concept, to another culture such as that of Iraq, we find that *our*
use of this word encounters a great deal of resistance in the linguistic and
ideological registers of that nation. For one thing, the word "democracy"
may be overlain in that culture with associations of a foreign power, and
with some of the ills attendant upon democracy (as noted by thinkers
from Plato to Alexis de Tocqueville): high crime rates, unrestrained individualism, the breakdown of family structure, a lack of reverence for the
past, a disrespect for authority and a threat to religious doctrine and values.
What occurs here, then, is precisely what Bakhtin speaks of: an ideological
battle *within* the word itself, a battle for meaning, for the signification of
the word, an endeavor to make one's own use of the word predominate.

Similar struggles occur over words such as "terrorism," welded by the Western media to a certain image of Islam, and qualified in the Arab media with prefixes such as "state-sponsored." In such struggles, the word itself becomes the site of intense ideological conflict. Hence, language is not somehow neutral and transparent: it is the very medium and locus of conflict.

In formulating this radical notion of language, Bakhtin is also effecting a profound critique not only of linguistics and conventional stylistics but also of the history of philosophy. He sees traditional stylistics as inadequate for analyzing the novel precisely because it bypasses the heteroglossia that enables the style of the novel. Stylistics views the source of style as "the individuality of the speaking subject" (*DI*, 263–264). Stylistics, linguistics, and the philosophy of language all postulate a unitary language and a unitary relation of the speaker to language, a speaker who engages in a "monologic utterance." All these disciplines enlist the Saussurean model of language, based on the polarity of general (language system) and particular (individualized utterance) (*DI*, 269). In this respect, the historical project of literary stylistics, philosophy, and linguistics has been one. Bakhtin sees this project as deeply ideological and political: it was a project that entailed exalting certain languages over others, incorporating "barbarians and lower social strata into a unitary language of culture," canonizing ideological systems and directing attention away "from language plurality to a single proto-language." Nonetheless, insists Bakhtin, these centripetal forces are obliged to "operate in the midst of heteroglossia" (*DI*, 271). Even as various attempts are being made to undertake the project of centralization and unification, the processes of decentralization and disunification continue (*DI*, 272). This dialectic between the centripetal forces of unity and the centrifugal forces of dispersion is, for Bakhtin, a constituting characteristic of language.

What Bakhtin, like Bergson, is doing is not merely reconceiving the nature of language but the act of understanding itself: this, too, is a dialogic process. Every concrete act of understanding, says Bakhtin, is active; it is "indissolubly merged with the response, with a motivated agreement or disagreement . . . Understanding comes to fruition only in the response" (*DI*, 282). Moreover, it is not merely that language is always socially and ideologically charged and is the locus of constant tension and struggle between groups and perspectives: in its role of providing this locus, it also furnishes the very medium for the interaction of human subjects, an interaction that creates the very ground of human subjectivity. For the individual consciousness, says Bakhtin, language "lies on the borderline between oneself and the other" (*DI*, 293).

Even literary language, as Bakhtin points out, is stratified in its own ways, according to genre and profession (*DI*, 288–289). The various dialects and perspectives entering literature form "a dialogue of languages" (*DI*, 294). It is precisely this fact which, for Bakhtin, marks the characteristic difference between poetry and the novel. According to Bakhtin, most poetry is premised on the idea of a single unitary language; poetry effectively destroys heteroglossia; it strips the word of the intentions of others (*DI*, 297–298). In the novel, on the contrary, this dialogization of language "penetrates from within the very way in which the word conceives its object" (*DI*, 284). Bakhtin sees the genres of poetry and the novel as emblematic of two broad ideological tendencies, the one centralizing and conservative, the other dispersive and radical. It may even be that "poetry" and "novel" are used by Bakhtin as metaphors for these respective tendencies. The "novel" embodies certain metaphysical, ideological, and aesthetic attitudes: it rejects, intrinsically, any concept of a unified self or a unified world; it acknowledges that "the" world is actually formed as a conversation, an endless dialogue, through a series of competing and co-existing languages; it even proposes that "truth" is dialogic. Hence, truth is redefined not merely as a consensus (which by now is common in cultural theory) but as the product of verbal-ideological struggles, struggles which mark the very nature of language itself (*DI*, 300).

Roman Jakobson (1896–1982)

The work of Roman Jakobson occupies a central and seminal place in the development of formalism and structuralism. Essentially a linguist, Jakobson was born in Moscow, where he co-founded the Moscow Linguistic Circle in 1915, which also included Osip Brik and Boris Tomashevsky. Along with Victor Shklovsky and Boris Eichenbaum, he was also involved in a second Russian Formalist group, the Society for the Study of Poetic Language, formed in 1916. The Formalists were in some ways precursors of structuralism: in 1926 Jakobson founded the Prague Linguistic Circle which engaged critically with the work of Saussure. And, fleeing from Nazi occupation, he moved to America in 1941 where he became acquainted with Claude Lévi-Strauss; in 1943 he co-founded the Linguistic Circle of New York. His ideas proved to be of greatest impact first in France and then in America.

In his paper "Linguistics and Poetics" (1958) Jakobson argues that poetics is an integral part of linguistics.[7] He insists that "literary studies" must engage in "objective scholarly analysis of verbal art" (*LL*, 64). Whereas most language is concerned with the transmission of ideas, the poetic function of language focuses on the "message" for its own sake (*LL*, 69). Jakobson's essay "Two Aspects of Language and Two Types of Aphasic Disturbances" (1956) suggests that language has a bipolar structure, oscillating between the poles of metaphor and metonymy. This dichotomy, he urges, "appears to be of primal significance and consequence for all verbal behavior and for human behavior in general" (*LL*, 112). The development of any discourse takes place along two different semantic lines: one is metaphoric, where one topic leads to another through similarity or substitution. The other is metonymic, where one topic suggests another via contiguity (closeness in space, time, or psychological association). In normal behavior, says Jakobson, both processes operate, but one is usually preferred, according to cultural and personal conditions (*LL*, 110–111). In verbal art, also, while the two processes richly interact, one is often given predominance. Jakobson notes that the primacy of metaphor in literary Romanticism and symbolism has been widely acknowledged. What has been neglected, he thinks, is the predominance of metonymy in realism: the realist author often "metonymically digresses from the plot to the atmosphere and from the characters to the setting in space and time" (*LL*, 111). Jakobson notes that a competition between metaphoric and metonymic devices occurs in any symbolic process. In analyzing the structure of dreams, for example, the decisive question, he says, is "whether the symbols and the temporal sequences are based on contiguity (Freud's metonymic 'displacement' and synecdochic 'condensation') or on similarity (Freud's 'identification and symbolism')" (*LL*, 113). Here Jakobson anticipates Lacan's analysis of Freud's contrast between condensation and displacement in terms of metaphor and metonymy.

The New Criticism

In the Anglo-American world, formalistic tendencies were most clearly enshrined in the New Criticism. Some of the important features of this critical outlook originated in England during the 1920s in the work of T. S. Eliot and Ezra Pound, as well as in a further generation of professional critics who helped to rejuvenate the study of English literature. The most prominent of these, associated with the new English curriculum at Cambridge University, were I. A. Richards and his student William Empson. In his *Principles of Literary Criticism* (1924) and his *Science and Poetry* (1926), Richards attempted to establish a systematic basis for the study of literature. His *Principles of Literary Criticism* advanced literary critical notions such as irony, tension, and balance, as well as distinguishing between poetic and other uses of language. In 1929 Richards published a book, *Practical Criticism*, whose profound and pervasive influence still endures. Using samples of students' often erratic attempts to analyze poetry, he emphasized the importance of "objective" and balanced close reading which was sensitive to the figurative language of literature. The practice of close reading as established by Richards, at both Cambridge and Harvard (to which he later transferred), later had a profound impact on the New Critics who facilitated its academic institutionalization. While William Empson himself was not a New Critic, he produced a book, *Seven Types of Ambiguity* (1930), which had an impact on the New Criticism in virtue of the close attention it paid to literary texts and its stress on ambiguity as an essential characteristic of poetry.

Across the Atlantic, New Critical practices were also being pioneered by American critics, known as the Fugitives and the Southern Agrarians, who promoted the values of the Old South in reaction against the alleged dehumanization of science and technology in the industrial North. Notable among these pioneers were John Crowe Ransom and Allen Tate who developed some of the ideas of Eliot and Richards. Ransom edited the poetry magazine *The Fugitive* from 1922 to 1925 with a group of writers including Tate, Robert Penn Warren, and Donald Davidson. Other journals associated with the New Criticism included the *Southern Review*, edited by Penn Warren and Cleanth Brooks (1935–1942), the *Kenyon Review*, run by Ransom (1938–1959), and the still extant *Sewanee Review*, edited by Tate and others. During the 1940s, the New Criticism became institutionalized as the mainstream approach in academia and its influence, while pervasively undermined since the 1950s, still persists. Some of the central documents of New Criticism were written by relatively late adherents: W. K. Wimsatt and Monroe Beardsley's essays "The Intentional Fallacy" (1946) and "The Affective Fallacy" (1949) (it is worth noting, in this context, the enormous influence of E. D. Hirsch's book *Validity in Interpretation*, published in 1967, which equated a text's meaning with its author's intention); Austin Warren's *The Theory of Literature* (1949); W. K. Wimsatt's *The Verbal Icon* (1954); and Murray Krieger's *The New Apologists for Poetry* (1956).

John Crowe Ransom (1888–1974)

The seminal manifestoes of the New Criticism, however, had been proclaimed earlier by Ransom, who published a series of essays entitled *The New Criticism* (1941) and an influential essay, "Criticism, Inc.," published in *The World's Body* (1938). This essay succinctly expresses a core of New Critical principles underlying the practice of most "New Critics," whose views often differed in other respects. As Ransom acknowledges, his essay is motivated by the desire to make literary criticism "more scientific, or precise and systematic"; it must become a "serious business."[8] He urges that the emphasis of criticism must move from historical scholarship to aesthetic appreciation and understanding. Ransom characterizes both the conservative New Humanism and left-wing criticism as focusing on morality rather than aesthetics. While he accepts the value of historical and biographical information, Ransom insists that these are not ends in themselves but instrumental to the real aim of criticism, which is "to define and enjoy the aesthetic or characteristic values of literature."

In short, Ransom's position is that the critic must study literature, not *about* literature. Hence criticism should exclude: (1) personal impressions, because the critical activity should "cite the nature of the object rather than its effects upon the subject" (*WB*, 342); (2) synopsis and paraphrase, since the plot or story is an abstraction from the real content of the text; (3)

historical studies, which might include literary backgrounds, biography, literary sources, and analogues; (4) linguistic studies, which include identifying allusions and meanings of words; (5) moral content, since this is not the whole content of the text; and (6) "Any other special studies which deal with some abstract or prose content taken out of the work" (*WB*, 343–345). Ransom demands that criticism, whose proper province includes technical studies of poetry, metrics, tropes, and fictiveness, should "receive its own charter of rights and function independently" (*WB*, 346). Finally, in this essay and other works, Ransom insists on the ontological uniqueness of poetry, as distinct from prose and other uses of language, as in prose. "The critic should," he urges, "regard the poem as nothing short of a desperate ontological or metaphysical manouevre," which cannot be reduced to prose (*WB*, 347–349). All in all, he argues that literature and literary criticism should enjoy autonomy both ontologically and institutionally. His arguments have often been abbreviated into a characterization of New Criticism as focusing on "the text itself" or "the words on the page."

William K. Wimsatt, Jr. (1907–1975) and Monroe C. Beardsley (1915–1985)

In addition to their other works, the critic Wimsatt and the philosopher Beardsley produced two influential and controversial papers that propounded central positions of New Criticism, "The Intentional Fallacy" (1946) and "The Affective Fallacy" (1949). In the first of these, they lay down certain propositions that they take to be axiomatic: while acknowledging that the cause of a poem is a "designing intellect," they refuse to accept the notion of design or intention as a standard of literary critical interpretation.[9] In stating their second "axiom," they raise the question of how a critic might find out what a poet's intention was and state what is effectively their central claim: "If the poet succeeded in doing it, then the poem itself shows what he was trying to do. And if the poet did not succeed, then the poem is not adequate evidence, and the critic must go outside the poem – for evidence of an intention that did not become effective in the poem." The third axiom is the American poet Archibald MacLeish's statement that a "poem should not mean but be." Wimsatt and Beardsley explain this statement as follows: "A poem can *be* only through its *meaning* – since its medium is words – yet it *is*, simply *is*, in the sense that we have no excuse for inquiring what part is intended or meant . . . In this respect poetry differs from practical messages, which are successful if and only if we correctly infer the intention" (*VI*, 4–5). This is an effective statement of the New Critical position that the poem is an autonomous verbal structure which has its end in itself, which has no purpose beyond its own existence as an aesthetic object. It is not answerable to criteria of truth, accuracy of representation or imitation, or morality. Finally, Wimsatt and Beardsley insist that the thoughts and attitudes of a poem can be imputed only to the dramatic speaker or persona of the poem, not directly to the author (*VI*, 5).

What Wimsatt and Beardsley are opposing is what they take to be a Romantic intentional fallacy: the Romantic idea, expressed in ancient times by Longinus and more recently by figures such as the great German writer Goethe and the Italian philosopher Benedetto Croce, that a poem echoes the soul of its author, that it embodies his intentions or psychological circumstances (*VI*, 6). The most influential recent statement of intentionalism, according to the authors of this essay, is I. A. Richards' fourfold characterization of meaning as "sense," "feeling," "tone," and "intention." The passwords of the intentional school are Romantic words such as "spontaneity," "sincerity," "authenticity," and "originality." These need to be replaced, say the authors, with terms of analysis such as "integrity," "relevance," "unity," and "function," terms which they claim to be more precise (*VI*, 9).

Wimsatt and Beardsley's later essay "The Affective Fallacy" (1949) is motivated by the same presupposition, namely that literature or poetry is an autonomous object, independent not only of author psychology, biography, and history but also of the reader or audience that consumes it. The word "affection" is used by philosophers to refer to emotion, mental state, or disposition. Hence, the "affective fallacy" occurs, according to Wimsatt and Beardsley, when we attempt to explicate or interpret a poem through recourse to the emotions or mental state produced in the reader or hearer. As these authors put it, just as the intentional fallacy "is a confusion between the poem and its origins," so the affective fallacy "is a confusion between the poem and its *results* (what it *is* and what it *does*)."[10] "The outcome of either Fallacy, the Intentional or the Affective, is that the poem itself, as an object of specifically critical judgment, tends to disappear" (*VI*, 21).

There are many possible objections to the arguments of both essays. To begin with, they presuppose that we can treat a poem as an isolated artefact, torn from all of its contexts, including the circumstances of its reading or reception. Clearly, the distinction between what Wimsatt and Beardsley see as "internal" and "external" evidence cannot be absolute and will vary according to the reader's knowledge and literary education. Moreover, many interpretative disputes arise not from questions of content but rather from questions of form and tone: we may agree on the most basic meaning of a poem but disagree on the significance we attach to this meaning. For example, Horace's famous "Ode to Pyrrha" could be translated in a tone of polite urbanity or one of crude sarcasm. Broad considerations of the intention behind the poem may legitimately help us clarify such issues. Many poems, such as satires or mock-heroic poems, presuppose a reader's prior acquaintance with certain literary traditions and conventions: it is important to acknowledge, for example, that Pope's *The Rape of the Lock* is intended to employ epic conventions for the purpose of satire. Recourse to intention can yield necessary insight into the relations between form and content, as well as relations between an artist and his audience. Moreover, given that the same statement made by different speakers in differing contexts could have vastly divergent meanings, it seems implausible to attribute autonomy to any statement or group of words, whether embodied in poetic language or not. As Frank Cioffi has remarked, to refute the intentionalist, Wimsatt and Beardsley should have shown that our response to a poem is not altered by reference to intentional information; but all they have shown is that this does not always or need not happen. Perhaps the most fundamental objection is the impossibility and artificiality of somehow treating literature as a self-contained object, an object which is not somehow realized in its performance, in interaction with readers who legitimately bring to the texts their own cultural backgrounds, interests, and assumptions.

Notes

1 Irving Babbitt, *Rousseau and Romanticism* (Boston and New York: Houghton Mifflin, 1919), p. xv. Hereafter cited as *RR*.

2 Irving Babbitt, *Literature and the American College: Essays in Defense of the Humanities* (1908; rpt. Washington, DC: National Humanities Institute, 1986), pp. 86–87, 94. Hereafter cited as *LAC*.

3 Irving Babbitt, *The Masters of Modern French Criticism* (Boston and New York: Houghton Mifflin), p. 368.

4 Victor Shklovsky, "Art as Technique," in *Russian Formalist Criticism: Four Essays*, trans. Lee T. Lemon and Marion J. Reis (Lincoln: University of Nebraska Press, 1965), p. 5. Hereafter cited as AT.

5 Boris Eichenbaum, "The Theory of the 'Formal Method,'" in *Russian Formalist Criticism: Four Essays*, trans. Lee T. Lemon and Marion J. Reis (Lincoln: University of Nebraska Press, 1965), p. 103. Hereafter cited as TFM.

6 Part of this account is indebted to the valuable introduction to M. M. Bakhtin, *The Dialogic Imagination: Four Essays*, ed. Michael Holquist, trans. Caryl Emerson and Michael Holquist (Austin: University of Texas Press, 1981). Bakhtin's essay "The Dialogic Imagination" is contained in this volume, which is hereafter cited as *DI*.

7 "Linguistics and Poetics," in Roman Jakobson, *Language in Literature*, ed. Krystyna Pomorska and Stephen Rudy (London and Cambridge, MA: Harvard University Press, 1987), p. 63. Hereafter cited as *LL*.

8 John Crowe Ransom, *The World's Body* (Baton Rouge: Louisiana State University Press, 1968), p. 329. Hereafter cited as *WB*.

9 W. K. Wimsatt, Jr. and Monroe C. Beardsley, "The Intentional Fallacy," in W. K. Wimsatt, Jr., *The Verbal Icon* (Lexington: University of Kentucky Press, 1967), p. 4. Hereafter cited as *VI*.

10 W. K. Wimsatt, Jr. and Monroe C. Beardsley, "The Affective Fallacy," in *VI*, p. 21.

Chapter 2

Socially Conscious Criticism of the Earlier Twentieth Century

With the Great Depression of the 1930s and the rise of fascism, literature and criticism in both Europe and America took a turn away from formalism toward a more socially conscious mode, as in socialist and Marxist criticism, and in the work of many poets. The humanists were challenged by more liberal-minded critics such as Edmund Wilson, Allen Tate, and R. P. Blackmur, by philosophers such as George Santayana who pointed to their inconsistencies, as well as by the left-wing and Marxist critics discussed below. Other schools of criticism also rejected the New Humanism: the Chicago School, the New York Intellectuals, and the New Critics reacted against the New Humanists' subordination of aesthetic value to moral criteria and their condemnation of modern and innovative literature. Perhaps the single most important circumstance behind the eclipse of the Humanists lay in social conditions in America during the 1930s: the depression, widespread unemployment, and suffering caused by economic collapse perhaps generated a need for approaches that were more socially orientated than Humanist criticism, which had focused on perfecting the individual.

The group of critics known as the Chicago School or the Neo-Aristotelians began formulating their central ideas around the same time as the New Critics were voicing their manifestoes. In the 1930s, departments of humanities at the University of Chicago were undergoing a radical transformation in an attempt to revive them and make them institutionally more competitive with the sciences. Six of the figures later known as the Chicago critics were involved in these changes: R. S. Crane, Richard McKeon, Elder Olson, W. R. Keast, Norman Maclean, and Bernard Weinberg. These critics later produced the central manifesto of the Chicago

School, *Critics and Criticism: Ancient and Modern* (1952), which both attacked some of the important tenets of the New Criticism and elaborated an alternative formalistic method of criticism derived in part from Aristotle's *Poetics*. In an earlier essay of 1934, Crane had anticipated (and influenced) Ransom's call that professional criticism should move from a primarily historical toward an aesthetic focus. However, Crane and the Chicago School generally diverged from the New Criticism in their insistence that literary study should integrate both systematic theory of literature (being informed by the history of literary theory) and the practice of close reading and explication of literary texts. Moreover, the Chicago School drew from Aristotle's *Poetics* a number of characteristic critical concerns, such as the emphasis on literary texts as "artistic wholes," the analytical importance of locating individual texts within given genres, and the need to identify textual and generic (as opposed to authorial) intention. Whereas the New Critics had focused attention on specifically poetic uses of language, irony, metaphor, tension, and balance, the Chicago School followed Aristotle in emphasizing plot, character, and thought. In general, the Neo-Aristotelians offered an alternative formalist poetics which acknowledged the mimetic, didactic, and affective functions of literature. The influence of this school, however, was overshadowed by the widespread adoption of New Critical dispositions throughout the American education system.

The New York Intellectuals were a group of critics who produced their most significant work between the 1930s and the 1960s and who wrote extensively for radical journals such as the *Partisan Review*, the *New Republic,* the *Nation, Commentary,* and *Dissent.* Major figures in this group included Richard Chase, Irving Howe, Alfred Kazin, Philip Rahv, Lionel Trilling, Elizabeth Hardwick, Sidney Hook, Steven Marcus, Richard Poirier, Meyer Schapiro, and Susan Sontag. Taking the work of Edmund Wilson as a model, these writers considered themselves aloof from bourgeois society, commercialism, Stalinism, and mass culture; they viewed themselves as democratic socialists and wrote criticism with a social and political emphasis. They promoted literary modernism, and valued complexity, irony, and cosmopolitanism in literature. This broad critical movement (if such a diverse range of critical activity can be called such) was never institutionalized though it was continued into the 1980s, confined within small circles.

F. R. Leavis (1895–1978) and *Scrutiny*

A central figure in English literary criticism, associated with the new English at Cambridge, was F. R. Leavis, who might broadly be placed in the moralistic and humanistic tradition of Matthew Arnold. Leavis stood aloof from both the Bloomsbury Group (a position expressed during his editorship of the journal *Scrutiny* from 1932 to 1953) and the New Criticism, though he was influenced by Richards' Practical Criticism courses, which he attended. Leavis assumed both educational and critical roles. In the academy he attempted to foster an elite which might safeguard English culture against the technological and populist vulgarities of an industrial society. As a critic he attempted to foster rigorous intellectual standards informed by a sense of the moral and cultural importance of literature, as well as to revaluate the English literary tradition. His major works, *New Bearings in English Poetry* (1932), *Revaluation* (1936), and *The Great Tradition* (1948), demoted Victorian and Georgian verse and sought to increase general appreciation of Eliot, Yeats, and Pound; he argued that the mainstream of English poetry flowed through Donne, Pope, Johnson, and Eliot; and he traced the main tradition of fiction from Jane Austen, George Eliot, Henry James, and Joseph Conrad.

Leavis shared with Eliot and the New Critics the idea that literary criticism should be a separate and serious discipline. While he rejected any theory or system, he called for "a living critical inwardness with literature, and a mind trained in dealing analytically with it." He insisted that we cannot go to literature in an "external" manner, treating it merely as a social document: "literature will yield to the sociologist, or anyone else, what it has to give only if it is approached as literature," with appreciation of "the subtleties of the artist's use of language."[1] What separated him from the New Critics, however, was an equally forceful counter-insistence that literary study cannot be confined to isolated works of art nor to a realm of purely literary values. He advocated a broad study of literature which went well beyond looking at "the words on the page": the study of literature, he said, is "an intimate study of the complexities, potentialities and essential conditions of human nature." In his essay "Sociology and Literature," he affirmed that "a real literary interest is an interest in man, society and civilization, and its boundaries cannot be drawn" (*CP*, 184, 200). Leavis invoked Eliot's notion of tradition as representing "a new emphasis on the social nature of artistic achievement." This social nature, for Leavis, is grounded in what he calls an "inherent human nature." Hence, the study of literature is a study of "the complexities, potentialities and essential conditions of human nature." The apparent contradiction in Leavis' approach between viewing literature as literature and literature as inseparable from all aspects of life seems to be "resolved" by an appeal to the assimilating capacity of intuition and a maturing *experience* of literature, for which no conceptual or theoretical subtlety can substitute.

Marxist and Left-Wing Criticism

During the 1930s, a decade of economic collapse, Marxism became a significant political force. Socially and politically conscious criticism had a long heritage in America, going back to figures such as Whitman, Howells, and Emerson and running through the work of writers such as John Macy, Van Wyck Brooks, and Vernon L. Parrington. Notable Marxist critics of the 1920s and 1930s included Floyd Dell, Max Eastman, V. F. Calverton, Philip Rahv, and Granville Hicks. Eastman and Dell edited the important radical journal *The Masses* and then *The Liberator* (1918–1924). Both produced works of literary criticism, Dell relating literary history to social causes and Eastman unorthodoxically treating poetry as a distinct domain. Calverton and Hicks were perhaps the most prominent of the Marxist critics; the former founded the *Modern Quarterly: A Journal of Radical Opinion*, which later became the *Modern Monthly*. In *The Newer Spirit* (1925) he urges that aesthetic judgments are conditioned by a reader's background and that a work must be interpreted and judged in relation to the social structure which generated it. In *The Liberation of American Literature* (1932) Calverton interprets the tradition of American literature in terms of Marxist categories such as class and economic infrastructure. Granville Hicks became a Communist during the depression and his *The Great Tradition* (1933) assesses American writers in terms of their social and political awareness, their relevance to social progress, and their contribution to the development of proletarian awareness and literature. In other works, Hicks had acknowledged that literary achievement and ideological disposition were not intrinsically related. This period saw the growth of a number of other radical journals as well as the voicing of revolutionary views by non-Marxist critics such as Kenneth Burke and Edmund Wilson. The latter's most influential work, *Axel's Castle* (1931), traced the development of modern symbolist literature, identifying in this broad movement a "revolution of the word," which might open up new possibilities of thought and literature.

In Germany, a critique of modern capitalist culture was formulated by the Frankfurt School of Critical Theory, whose major figures included Theodor Adorno (1903–1969), Max Horkheimer (1895–1973), Herbert Marcuse (1898–1979), and Walter Benjamin (1892–1940). Some of these thinkers drew on Hegel, Marx, and Freud in attempting to revive the "negative dialectics" or negative, revolutionary potential of Hegelian Marxist thought. They sharply opposed the bourgeois positivism which had risen to predominance in reaction against Hegel's philosophy, and insisted, following Hegel, that consciousness in all of its cultural modes is active in creating the world. In general, these theorists saw modern mass culture as regimented and reduced to a commercial dimension; and they saw art as embodying a unique critical distance from this social and political world. Walter Benjamin argued in his "The Work of Art in the Age of Mechanical Reproduction" that modern technology has transformed the work of art, stripping it of the "aura" of uniqueness it possessed in earlier eras. Modern works are reproduced for mass consumption, and are effectively copies which relate to no original form. However, this new status of art, thought Benjamin, also gave it a revived political and subversive potential. These thinkers had a large impact on the New Left and the radical movements of the 1960s.

Socialist Criticism in Britain

The tradition of socialist criticism in Britain went back to William Morris, who first applied Marxist perspectives on the theory of labor and alienation to artistic production. In 1884 the Fabian Society was formed with the aim of substituting for Marxist revolutionary action a Fabian policy of gradually introducing socialism through influencing government policy and disseminating pamphlets to raise awareness of economic and class inequalities. The dramatist and critic George Bernard Shaw (1856–1950) was a leader of this society and produced one of its first pamphlets, *A Manifesto* (1884). Shaw edited *Fabian Essays in Socialism* (1899) and advocated women's rights, economic equality, and the abolition of private property. George Orwell (1903–1950) in his later career saw himself as a political writer and a democratic socialist, who, however, became disillusioned with Communism, as shown in his political satire *Animal Farm* (1945).

British communists did not produce any substantial works until the mid 1930s. With the menace of fascism and the threat of war, several writers began to engage in Marxist criticism. These included the art historian Anthony Blunt and the economist John Strachey, who produced two influential books, *Literature and Dialectical Materialism* (1934) and *The Coming Struggle for Power* (1933). A group of Marxist thinkers was centered around the *Left Review* (1934–1938). The poets W. H. Auden, Stephen Spender, and C. Day Lewis at various times espoused and propagated left-wing views. The most significant Marxist theorist of this generation was Christopher Caudwell (1907–1937), who died in Spain fighting in the International Brigade. Caudwell's best known work is his *Illusion and Reality: A Study of the Sources of Poetry* (1937). Here, Caudwell offers a Marxist analysis of the development of English poetry, somewhat crudely correlating the stages of this development with economic phases such as primitive accumulation, the Industrial Revolution, and the decline of capitalism. In this wide-ranging book, Caudwell addressed the origins of poetry, the connection of poetry to mythology and the unconscious as well as the future role of poetry in the struggle for socialism. Caudwell's subsequent writings included *Studies in a Dying Culture* (1938) and *Further Studies in a Dying Culture* (1949).

The Fundamental Principles of Marxism

It may be useful to provide here a brief account of the principles of Marxist thought and literary criticism. The tradition of Marxism has provided a powerful and sustained critique of capitalist institutions and ethics. Its founder, Karl Heinrich Marx (1818–1883), was a German political, economic, and philosophical theorist and revolutionist. The influence of Marx's ideas on modern world history has been vast. Until the collapse in 1991 of the Communist systems of the USSR and Eastern Europe, one-third of the world's population had been living under political administrations claiming descent from Marx's ideas. His impact on the world of thought has been equally extensive, embracing sociology, philosophy, economics, and cultural theory. Marxism has also generated a rich tradition of literary and cultural criticism. Many branches of modern criticism – including historicism, feminism, deconstruction, postcolonial and cultural criticism – are indebted to the insights of Marxism, which often originated in the philosophy of Hegel. What distinguishes Marxism is that it is not only a political, economic, and social theory but also a form of practice in all of these domains.

Marx attempted systematically to seek the structural causes behind what he saw as a system of capitalist exploitation and degradation, and to offer solutions in the spheres of economics and politics. As with all socialists, Marx's main objection to capitalism was that one particular class owned the means of economic production: "The bourgeoisie . . . has centralized means of production, and has concentrated property in a few hands." The correlative of this is the oppression and exploitation of the working classes: "In proportion as the bourgeoisie, i.e., capital, is developed, in the same proportion is the proletariat, the modern working class, developed; a class of laborers, who live only so long as they find work, and who find work only so long as their labor increases capital. These laborers, who must sell themselves piecemeal, are a commodity." Marx's third objection is the imperialistic nature of the bourgeois enterprise: in order to perpetuate itself, capitalism must spread its tentacles all over the world: "The bourgeoisie cannot exist without constantly revolutionizing the instruments of production . . . The need of a constantly expanding market . . . chases the bourgeoisie over the whole surface of the globe." Marx tells us in the next few paragraphs that the bourgeoisie must necessarily give a cosmopolitan character to production and consumption in every country; that raw material is drawn from the remotest zones; that demand for new products ever increases; that the bourgeoisie "compels all nations, on pain of extinction, to adopt the bourgeois mode of production." In short, the bourgeoisie "creates a world after its own image." Finally, capitalism reduces all human relationships to a "cash" nexus, self-interest, and egotistical calculation.[2]

The main premise of the materialist conception of history is that man's first historical act is the production of means to satisfy his material needs. The production of life, through both labor and procreation, is both natural and social: a given mode of production is combined with a given stage of social cooperation. Only after passing through these historical moments, says Marx, can we speak of men possessing "consciousness," which is itself a "social product." Hence the realms of ideology, politics, law, morality, religion, and art are not independent but are an efflux of a people's material behavior: "Life is not determined by consciousness, but consciousness by life."[3]

Marx observes that the class which is struggling for mastery must gain political power in order to represent its interest as the general interest (*GI*, 52–53). This is the germ of Marx's concept of ideology. He states that the class which is the ruling material force in society is also the ruling intellectual force. Having at its disposal the means of production, it is empowered to disseminate its ideas in the realms of law, morality, religion, and art, as possessing universal verity. Thus, dominant ideas of the aristocracy such as honor and loyalty were replaced after bourgeois ascendancy by ideas of freedom and equality, whose infrastructure is class economic imperatives (*GI*, 64–65). Marx's notion of ideology is this: the ruling class represents its own interests as the interests of the people as a whole. The modern state, as Marx says, "is but a committee for managing the common affairs of the whole bourgeoisie" (*MCP*, 45–47).

The materialistic conception of history is characterized by a number of features: (1) it is the activity and conditions of material production, not mere ideas, which determine the structure of society and the nature of individuals; law, art, religion, and morality are an efflux of these material relations, (2) the evolution of division of labor issues in the concentration of private property, a conflict between individual and communal interests (the latter assuming the status of an independent power as the state), and estrangement or alienation of social activity; (3) all struggles within the state are euphemisms for the real struggle between classes; it is this struggle which generates social change; (4) once technologically assisted capitalist accumulation, concentration, and world expansion have led to a world of sharply contrasting wealth and poverty, and working classes become conscious of their historical role, capitalism itself will yield to a communism which will do away with private property and base itself on human need rather than the greed of a minority for increasing profit; (5) the exploitation of women, an intrinsic feature of capitalist economics, will also be abolished along with private property and the family as an economic unit.

Is Marxism dead? Can we, finally, consign it to historical and political obsolescence? In addressing these questions, we need to recognize that the connection between Marx's canon and Marxism has always been dialectical: the latter has always striven to modify, extend, and adapt the former to changing circumstances rather than treating it as definitive and complete. Marxism is not somehow a finished and static system but has been continually modified according to changing historical circumstances. We should also perhaps bear in mind that most of what has passed for "communism" has had but remote connections with the doctrines of Marx, Engels, or their followers. Marx's critique of capitalism, it should be recalled, was dialectical. He regarded capitalist society as an unprecedented historical advance from centuries of benighted and superstitious feudalism. The bourgeois emphasis on reason, practicality, its technological enterprise in mastering the world, its ideals of rational law and justice, individual freedom and democracy were all hailed by Marx as historical progress. His point was not that communism would somehow displace capitalism in its entirety but that it would grow out of capitalism and retain its ideals of freedom and democracy. The essential difference is that a communist society would *realize* these ideals. For example, Marx shrewdly points out that the "individual" in capitalist society is effectively the bourgeois owner of property; individual freedom is merely economic freedom, the freedom to buy and sell. The constitution and the laws are entirely weighted in favor of large business interests and owners of property. Private property, Marx points out, is already abolished for the nine-tenths of the population in capitalist society who do not possess it. The labor of this vast majority, being commodified, is as subject to the vicissitudes of the market as any other commodity. One of the main sins of capitalism, according to Marx, was that it reduced all human relations to commercial relations. Even the family cannot escape such commodification: Marx states that, to the bourgeois man, the wife is reduced to a mere instrument of production. Moreover, once the exploitation of the laborer by the manufacturer has finished, then he is set upon, says Marx, by the other segments of the bourgeoisie: the landlord, the shopkeeper, the pawnbroker. In bourgeois society, "capital is independent and has individuality, while the living person is dependent and has no individuality" (*MCP*, 51, 53, 65–70). The aim of a communist society is to procure genuine freedom, genuine individuality and humanity, genuine democracy. As an internal critique of the tendencies of capitalism and its crises, Marxism is uniquely coherent and incisive. The influence of Marxism has been fundamental in challenging the claims of the law to be eternal, of the bourgeoisie to represent the interests of the entire nation, of individuality and freedom to be universal. It has also been important in the analysis of women's oppression as an economic factor structurally integral to capitalism. And its insights into language as a social practice with a material dimension, its awareness that truth is an interpretation based on certain kinds of consensus, its view of the world as created through human physical, intellectual, and ideological labor, its acknowledgment of the dialectical nature of all thinking, and its insistence that analysis of all phenomena must be informed by historical context, were articulated long before such ideas made their way into modern literary theory.

Marxist Literary Criticism: A Historical Overview

Marx and Engels produced no systematic theory of literature or art. Equally, the subsequent history of Marxist aesthetics has hardly comprised the cumulative unfolding of a coherent perspective. Rather, it has emerged, aptly, as a series of responses to concrete political exigencies. While these responses have sometimes collided at various theoretical planes, they achieve a dynamic and expansive coherence (rather than the static coherence of a closed, finished system) through both a general overlap of political motivation and the persistent reworking of a core of predispositions about literature and art deriving from Marx and Engels themselves.

These predispositions include: (1) the rejection, following Hegel, of the notion of "identity" and a consequent denial of the view that any object, including literature, can somehow exist independently. The aesthetic corollary of this is that literature can only be understood in the fullness of its *relations* with ideology, class, and economic substructure; (2) the view that the so-called "objective" world is actually a progressive construction out of collective human subjectivity. What passes as "truth," then, is not eternal but institutionally created. "Private property," for example, is a bourgeois reification of an abstract category; it does not necessarily possess eternal validity. Language itself, as Marx said in *The German Ideology*, must be understood not as a self-sufficient system but as social practice (*GI*, 51, 118); (3) the understanding of art itself as a commodity, sharing with other commodities an entry into material aspects of production. If, as Marx said, human beings produce themselves through labor, artistic production can be viewed as a branch of production in general; (4) a focus on the connections between class struggle as the inner dynamic of history and literature as the ideologically refracted site of such struggle. This has sometimes gone hand in hand with prescriptions for literature as an ideological ancillary to the aims and results of political revolution; and (5) an insistence that language is not a self-enclosed system of relations but must be understood as social practice, as deeply rooted in material conditions as any other practice (*GI*, 51).

To these predispositions could be added, for example, Engels' comments on "typicality," recommending that art should express what is typical about a class or a peculiar intersection of ideological circumstances. One might also include the problem raised by Engels' granting a "relative autonomy" to art, his comments that art can transcend its ideological genesis and that cultural elements are determined only in the "last instance" by economic relations: what exactly is the connection between art and the material base into which its constituting relations extend? Given the inconclusive and sometimes ambiguous nature of Marx's and Engels' scattered comments on art, the proposed solutions to such dilemmas have been as various as the political soils on which they were sown.

After Marx's death in 1883, Europe witnessed a widespread nascence of socialist political parties, together with the impact of Marxism in sociology, anthropology, history, and political science. The first generation of Marxist intellectuals included the Italian Antonio Labriola (1843–1904), who viewed the connection between economic and literary-cultural spheres as highly mediated; and Georgi Plekhanov (1856–1918), the "father of Russian

Marxism," who argued in his highly influential *Art and Social Life* (1912) that the idea of art for art's sake arises when the individual finds himself in hopeless disaccord with his society; when there is a possibility of social change, art tends to be more utilitarian, engaging in the process of larger transformation. Plekhanov also pioneered the significance of "play" as a dramatization or imitation of labor.

Vladimir Ilyich Lenin (1870–1924) occupied a central role not only in the Russian Revolution of 1917 but also in the unfolding of Marxist aesthetics toward a more politically interventionist stance. In the latter respect, Lenin's most celebrated and controversial piece is his "Party Organization and Party Literature" (1905), which, along with certain comments of Marx and Engels, was later misleadingly claimed to authorize "Socialist Realism," adopted in 1934 as the official Party aesthetic. But he is not prescribing partisanship (*partinost*) for all literature, only literature which claims to be party literature. He grants that there should be complete freedom of speech and the press. He is aware, however, that "individual" acts of reading and interpreting are conducted within parameters dictated by class interests. At a deeper level, Lenin's approach to aesthetic value, embracing as it does the totality of historical circumstances including class, preceding literary traditions, and relation to political exigency, can be seen to derive from his acknowledgment of the dialectical character of Marxism.

It can be seen from the foregoing that the early debates on art during and after the revolutionary period in Russia focused on questions such as the degree of Party control over the arts, the stance toward the bourgeois cultural legacy, and the imperative to clarify the connections between the political and the aesthetic. A related question was the possibility of creating a proletarian culture. The other major protagonist in the Russian Revolution, Leon Trotsky (1879–1940), played a crucial role in these debates. His renowned *Literature and Revolution* (1923) stressed that only in some domains can the Party offer direct leadership; the "domain of art is not one in which the Party is called upon to command. It can and must protect and help it, but can only lead it indirectly."[4] But he is against "the liberal principle of *laissez faire* and *laissez passer*, even in the field of art" (*LR*, 221). Trotsky also urges that the Party should give "its confidence" to what he calls "literary fellow-travelers," those non-Party writers sympathetic to the Revolution. What lies behind this is Trotsky's insistence that the proletariat cannot begin the construction of a new culture without absorbing and assimiliating the elements of the old cultures (*LR*, 226). In a 1938 manifesto, *Towards a Free Revolutionary Art*, drawn up in collaboration with André Breton, Trotsky urges a "*complete freedom for art*" while acknowledging that all true art is revolutionary in nature. In his speech of 1924, "Class and Art," Trotsky suggests that art has "its own laws of development" and that there is no guarantee of an organic link between artistic creativity and class interests. Moreover, such creativity "lags behind" the spirit of a class and is not subject to conscious influence. Throughout his comments on aesthetics, Trotsky seems to travel a fine line between granting art a certain autonomy while viewing it as serving, in a highly mediated fashion, an important social function.

The Communist Party's attitude toward art in this period was, in general, epiphenomenal of its economic policy. A resolution of 1925 voiced the Party's refusal to sanction any one literary faction. But later, it returned to a more committed artistic posture, crystallized in the formation of a Writers' Union. The first congress of this Union in 1934, featuring speeches by Maxim Gorky and Bukharin, officially adopted Socialist Realism, as defined primarily by A. A. Zhdanov (1896–1948). Zhdanov defined Socialist Realism as the depiction of "reality in its revolutionary development. The truthfulness . . . of the artistic image must be linked with the task of ideological transformation."[5] But, as several commentators have pointed out, despite the calls for Socialist Realism to express social values as embodied in the movement of history (rather than embracing a static naturalism), the actual aesthetic adopted was largely a return to nineteenth-century realist techniques infused with a socialist content.

Socialist Realism received its most articulate theoretical expression in the work of the Hungarian philosopher György Lukács (1885–1971), the foremost Marxist aesthetician of the twentieth century. Lukács' notion of realism collided with that of Bertolt Brecht (1898–1956). According to Lukács, modern capitalist society is riven by contradictions, by chasms between universal and particular, intelligible and sensible, part and whole. The realist artist expresses a vision of the possible totality embracing these contradictions, a totality achieved by embodying what is "typical" about various historical stages. For example, an individual character might enshrine an entire complex of historical forces. Brecht, in his notebooks, also equates realism with the ability to capture the "typical" or "historically significant." Realists also identify the contradictions in human relationships, as well as their enabling conditions. Socialist realists, moreover, view reality from the viewpoint of the proletariat. Brecht adds that realist art battles false views of reality, thereby facilitating correct views.[6] Perhaps the conflict between the two thinkers is rooted in Lukács' (arguably Stalinist-inspired) aversion to modernist and experimental art on the grounds that the ontological image of humanity it portrayed was fragmented, decadent, and politically impotent. In the 1930s, Brecht's work was viewed as tainted though later he was received into the ranks of Marxist aestheticians. In contrast, Brecht's experimentalism was crucial to his attempts to combine theory and practice in a Marxist aesthetic. Contrasting dramatic theater (which follows Aristotle's guidelines) with his own "epic" theater, Brecht avers that the audience's capacity for action must be roused and, far from undergoing catharsis, it must be forced to take decisions, partly by its standard expectations being disappointed (a procedure Brecht called "the alienation effect"). The action on stage must also implicitly point to other, alternative versions of itself. Far from being sterile, the disputes between

Lukács and Brecht display the multidimensional potential of any concept approached from Marxist viewpoints as well as the inevitable grounding of those viewpoints in political circumstances.

Mention should also be made of the Italian Marxist theorist and political activist Antonio Gramsci (1891–1937), whose main contribution to Marxism is widely thought to lie in his elaboration of the notion of hegemony. Autonomous revolutionary potential on the part of the proletariat could only be realized, argued Gramsci, through political *and* intellectual autonomy. A mass movement alone was insufficient: also, initiated through a vanguard with working-class roots and sympathies, this class "must train and educate itself in the management of society," acquiring both the culture and psychology of a dominant class through its own channels: "meetings, congresses, discussions, mutual education."[7] The transformation to a socialist state cannot be successful without the proletariat's own organic intellectuals forging an alternative hegemony. The notion of hegemony is effectively a metonymic affirmation of the dialectical connection between economic and superstructural spheres, stressing the transformative role of human agency rather than relying on the "inevitability" of economic determinism. The foregoing represent the development of Marxist aesthetics during the earlier half of the twentieth century. The later Marxist critics such as Fredric Jameson and Terry Eagleton will be considered in Chapter 4.

Early Feminist Criticism: Virginia Woolf and Simone de Beauvoir

Apart from Marxism, the other major modern critical outlook to be grounded in political practice is feminism, in all of its many currents. Feminism has antecedents going all the way back to ancient Greece, in the work of Sappho and arguably in Aristophanes' play *Lysistrata*, which depicts women as taking over the treasury in the Acropolis, a female chorus as physically and intellectually superior to the male chorus, and the use of sexuality as a weapon in an endeavor to put an end to the distinctly masculine project of the Peloponnesian War. Feminism also surfaces in Chaucer's Wife of Bath, who blatantly values "experience" over authority and was more than a match for each of her five husbands. In the Middle Ages, Christine de Pisan had the courage to enter into a debate with the predominant male critics of her day. During the Renaissance a number of women poets such as Catherine Des Roches emerged in France and England. In the seventeenth century, poets such as Aphra Behn and Anne Bradstreet were pioneers in gaining access to the literary profession. After the French Revolution, Mary Wollestonecraft argued that the ideals of the Revolution and Enlightenment should be extended to women, primarily through access to education. And the nineteenth century witnessed the flowering of numerous major female literary figures in both Europe and America, ranging from Madame de Staël, the Brontës, Jane Austen, George Eliot, and Elizabeth Barrett Browning to Margaret Fuller and Emily Dickinson. Modernist female writers included Hilda Doolittle (H.D.), Gertrude Stein, Katherine Mansfield, and Virginia Woolf.

For most of this long history women were not only deprived of education and financial independence, but also had to struggle against a male ideology condemning them to virtual silence and obedience, as well as a male literary establishment that poured scorn on their literary endeavors. Indeed, the depiction of women in male literature – as angels, goddesses, whores, obedient wives, and mother figures – was an integral means of perpetuating these ideologies of gender. It was only with women's struggles in the twentieth century for political rights that feminist criticism arose in any systematic way. Since the early twentieth century feminist criticism has grown to encompass a vast series of concerns: a rewriting of literary history so as to include the contributions of women; the tracing of a female literary tradition; theories of sexuality and sexual difference, drawing on psychoanalysis, Marxism, and the social sciences; the representation of women in male literature; the role of gender in both literary creation and literary criticism (as studied in so-called "gynocriticism"); the connection between gender and various aspects of literary form, such as genre and meter (it is clear, for example, that certain genres such as epic embody masculine values of heroism, war, and adventure, while the lyric has sometimes been seen as feminine, expressing private emotion); above all, feminist critics have displayed a persistent concern with both experience and language: is there a specifically female experience that has been communicated by women writers? And how do women confront the task of being historically coerced into using a language dominated by male concepts and values? Some feminists have urged the need for a female language, while others have advocated appropriating and modifying the inherited language of the male oppressor. The significance of language rests ultimately on its expression of male ways of thinking that go all the way back to Aristotle: the laws of logic, beginning with the law of identity, as well as the Aristotelian categories, divide up the world into strictly demarcated entities. These binary oppositions, as many modern theorists have argued, are coercive: for example, according to Aristotle's laws, *either* one is a man *or* one is a woman; a person is *either* black *or* white, *either* master *or* slave. Feminists have often rejected these divisive ways of viewing the world, stressing instead the various shades between female and male, between black and white, and indeed urging a vision of unity rather than opposition. In this process, such categories are recognized to be founded on no essence or natural distinctions, but are viewed as cultural and ideological constructions. Hence, another fundamental feminist concern has been the rejection of "theory" as such, since in its very nature it houses these masculine presuppositions. Feminism thus advocates a principled recalcitrance to definition, a conceptual fluidity and openness which laughs in the face of tyrannizing attempts to fix it as just one more category to be subsumed by the vast historical catalogue of male-generated concepts.

Indeed, one of the invaluable accomplishments of feminism has been utterly to reject the notions of objectivity and neutrality; feminists have pioneered a new honesty in acknowledging that they write from subjective positions informed by specific circumstances. This position rests largely on feminists' acknowledgment that thought is not somehow a disembodied and abstract process, but is intimately governed by the nature and situation of the body in place and time. The "body" has become a powerful meta-phor of such specificity and concreteness, which rejects the male Cartesian tradition that thinking can somehow occur on a plane of disembodied universality. The body that I inhabit will shape my thinking at the pro-foundest levels: if my body happened to be born into a rich family with political ties, my political, religious, and social affiliations will inevitably reflect this. Whether my body is male or female will initially determine my thought and experience at a far deeper level than which books I read. Notwithstanding these insights of feminism, the days are still not past in which high school students are forbidden to use the word "I" in their compositions, effectively perpetuating the pretense and self-delusion of objectivity.

It is clear, also, that feminism has potential areas of overlap with certain theories such as deconstruction and Marxism, as well as with certain phi-losophers such as Hegel (who opposed traditional logic), and Schopen-hauer and Bergson, who recognized the subjection of reason to bodily needs, and with poetic visions such as those enshrined in French symbol-ism and modernism (notwithstanding the often misogynistic leanings of male figures in these movements). Having said all of this, it should be remembered that feminism is not comprised of any one movement or set of values; it has been broadly international in scope and its disposition is dictated by many local as well as general factors. For example, writers from Arab traditions such as Fatima Mernissi and Leila Ahmed have attempted to articulate a feminist vision distinctly marked by their specific cultural concerns; the same is true of African American feminists such as Alice Walker and feminists of Asian heritage such as Gayatri Spivak. Feminism as it developed in French, American, and British traditions will be consid-ered in a later chapter. The section below will consider two of the landmark works of the early twentieth century, whose influence was disseminated through all three of these traditions, Virginia Woolf's *A Room of One's Own* (1929) and Simone de Beauvoir's *The Second Sex* (1949).

Virginia Woolf (1882–1941)

Though her views have been criticized by some feminists, Virginia Woolf was in many ways a pioneer of feminist literary criticism, raising issues –

such as the social and economic context of women's writing, the gendered nature of language, the need to go back through literary history and establish a female literary tradition, and the societal construction of gender – that remain of central importance to feminist studies. Woolf's most significant statements impinging on feminism are contained in two lectures presented at women's colleges at Cambridge University in 1928, subsequently published as *A Room of One's Own* (1929), and in *Three Guineas* (1938), an important statement concerning women's alienation from the related ethics of war and patriarchy. As seen earlier, Woolf is also known as one of the foremost modernist writers of the English-speaking world. The most famous of her many novels include *Mrs. Dalloway* (1925), *To the Lighthouse* (1927), and *Orlando* (1928).

As the daughter of the Victorian agnostic philosopher Leslie Stephen, Woolf had access to his substantial library, and it was here that she received her education. After her parents' deaths, she settled, with her brothers and sisters, in Bloomsbury, a fashionable area of London which later gave its name to the intellectual circle in which Virginia and her sister Vanessa moved, the "Bloomsbury Group," which included John Maynard Keynes, Lytton Strachey, Clive Bell, and the writer Leonard Woolf, whom Virginia was to marry in 1912. This group was unconventional in its outlooks and often in its sexuality. Woolf's own views of femininity and gender relations must have been rooted partly in her own sexuality; she was engaged in a relationship with the writer Vita Sackville-West, on whom Woolf's novel *Orlando* was based. Woolf suffered from nervous breakdowns and was acutely and sometimes debilitatingly conscious of her status as a female writer in an intellectual milieu dominated by males and masculine values. In 1941 she walked into a river, her pockets loaded with stones, and drowned herself, suffering the same fate as her imaginative character, Shakespeare's sister, who was driven to suicide on account of the overwhelming forces and institutions thwarting her female genius.

Woolf's literary criticism, like her fiction, can be approached from at least two perspectives, those of modernism and feminism. Perhaps the most fundamental point on which these overlap is their common rejection of the mainstream legacy of the bourgeois Enlightenment, which viewed the human being as a free, rational agent, enabled through progressive knowledge to subjugate the world of nature on many levels, intellectual, material, and economic. Like many Romantics, modernists, and feminists, Woolf reacted against the primacy accorded by the Enlightenment to the faculty of human reason, as well as the presumption that reason could master the world and reduce it to total intelligibility. At various points in her fiction and essays, Woolf expresses what has come to be seen as a characteristically feminist distrust of theorizing, which is seen as imbued with centuries of male values and strategies. Talking of Mary Wollstonecraft, for example, Woolf remarks that this pioneer was "no cold-blooded theorist – something was born in her that thrust aside her theories and forced her to model them afresh . . . Mary's life had been an experiment from the start."[8] In another essay, she asserts that to "know the reason of things is a poor substitute for being able to feel them" (CR, 192). She notes a tendency in modern writers that they "cannot generalise. They depend on their senses and emotions, whose testimony is trustworthy, rather than on their intellects whose message is obscure" (CR, 329–330). Indeed, in contrast with Enlightenment views of the ultimate intelligibility of the world, and of the human self, Woolf states that human nature is "infinitely mysterious" (CR, 95). Like most modernists, Woolf questioned the idea of an external reality that somehow existed independently of our minds. For Woolf the world is a construction out of a primordial and undifferentiated "vast mass," and the deeper reality that we might discern beneath appearances is not some unknowable thing in itself but our own operations, especially the operations of art, which can see a pattern and a unity in phenomena such as are inaccessible to reason or discursive thought. In her diary Woolf observes how "the creative power at once brings the whole universe to order."[9] Other diary entries confirm her view of reality as a construct. After noting another writer's charge that her characters fail, she writes: "I haven't that 'reality' gift. I insubstantise, wilfully to some extent, distrusting reality – its cheapness" (WD, 57).

Woolf's emphasis on time and change is profoundly symptomatic of a modernist perspective, and in Woolf's case it may well have been inspired by Bergson and Proust. Bergson's emphasis on the primary reality of time challenged the "spatial" disposition of mainstream Western philosophy from Plato through the Enlightenment. This mainstream tradition had effectively ignored the reality of time in its viewing of the world as laid out according to categories in space: the world had been classified and divided up into enduring entities with stable identities. The mainstream Enlightenment view of the external world as a categorizable inventory of stable objects and events persisted into Woolf's time in the form of various philosophies of realism and logical positivism, such as the realist-analytic philosophy of G. E. Moore.

The "common sense" wisdom advocated by figures such as G. E. Moore embodies certain central presuppositions of the Western philosophical tradition – the distinction between mind and reality, the independent existence of all entities, the equation of knowledge with various modes of classification of these entities – that were challenged by modernism, which insisted on reality as a productive interaction between subject and object and which stressed the reality of change and the profoundly temporal nature of all phenomena. Those same mainstream presuppositions have also been characterized as "male": the "wisdom" that figures such as G. E. Moore or Edmund Burke have equated with consensually achieved common sense has been characterized by feminists as a distinctly "male" wisdom, based on male-generated categories through which the world has been seen. In an essay on Montaigne, Woolf had lashed out against the "virtues" of common sense and non-contradiction: "let us say what comes into our heads, repeat ourselves, contradict ourselves, fling out the wildest nonsense . . . without caring what the world thinks or says" (*CR*, 94). At one level, it may well be "nonsense" that Woolf wishes to fling in the face of Moore's "common sense," and that of the entire male philosophical tradition. Whether this attitude makes her a realist or an idealist is open to debate.

What is not in question is Woolf's defiant refusal to accept "reality" as anything more than a convention, or set of conventions, which do not grasp what is most private and authentic about our experience. If Woolf is a realist, her realism seems to comprise a call for viewing things in their relatedness rather than in isolation, a fact which places her in the deepest opposition to philosophical realism. Whatever label we place on her philosophical disposition, that disposition was shared by both modernism and feminism, though it sprang from differing motivations: in the case of modernism, reality was seen as a complex and dynamic construction; in the case of feminism, the tradition of realism embodied a static and hierarchical vision of the world according to male categories founded on the notion – on the philosophy and logic – of stable identity.

In *A Room of One's Own* Woolf raised a number of issues that would remain of central concern to feminists. This book comprises two lectures, delivered by Woolf in 1928 at two women's colleges in Cambridge, on the topic of women and fiction. The "room" of the book's title is a skillfully used metaphor around which the entire text is woven: Woolf's central claim is that "a woman must have money and a room of her own if she is to write fiction."[10] The most obvious meaning of this claim is that women need financial and psychological independence in order to exercise their creative potential. But the claim itself is complex and the rest of Woolf's text effectively elaborates the metaphorical significance of "room."

At the most fundamental level, Woolf's claim situates literature within a material (economic, social, political) context. She compares fiction, for example, to a spider's web: this web is not spun in midair (literature does not arise in a vacuum) but is "attached to life at all four corners." Indeed, it is "attached to grossly material things" (*Room*, 43–44). Hence, literature cannot be produced without economic independence or backing: our "mothers," Woolf notes (talking to a female audience), were never given the chance to learn the art of making money, and it is this economic poverty that has underlain the intellectual impoverishment of women (*Room*, 21). Hence, intellectual freedom, the "power to think for oneself," rests on financial freedom (*Room*, 106). Historically, this "freedom of the mind" for women was pioneered by Aphra Behn, the first female writer to earn her living by writing. It was she who earned for women "the right to speak their minds" (*Room*, 64, 66). It was the "solid fact" of this economic basis that enabled the relative profusion of middle-class female writers in the later eighteenth century (*Room*, 65). It is also this fact which explains women's apparent silence through most of history. Even up until the beginning of the nineteenth century, Woolf notes, women were debarred from any "separate lodging" which might shelter them "from the claims and tyrannies of their families" (*Room*, 52).

But beyond the material circumstances forestalling her independence, the immaterial difficulties were much worse. Woolf relates her famous anecdote of "Shakespeare's sister" Judith, who, being "wonderfully gifted," attempts to seek her fortune in the theater like her brother. The opposition to her endeavors ranges from her father's violent anger to the laughter and exploitation of men in the theater company; such is her frustration and fragility that she kills herself (*Room*, 46–48). Woolf's point is that "genius like Shakespeare's is not born among labouring, uneducated, servile people." And if a woman had been born with potential for genius, she "would certainly have gone crazed, shot herself, or ended her days in some lonely cottage" (*Room*, 48–49). While Shakespeare's sister is fictional, her parable is extrapolated from actual circumstances: Woolf cites the examples of women such as Lady Winchilsea who were mocked for their attempts to write; many women – including Currer Bell, George Eliot, and George Sand – sought the refuge of anonymous authorship (*Room*, 50).

The metaphor of one's own "room," as embodying the ability to think independently, takes another level of significance from its resistance to the appropriation by language, history, and tradition by men. Woolf notes that most of the books on women have been written by men, defining women so as to protect men's image of their own superiority (*Room*, 27, 34). She observes a deep ambivalence and irony in male attitudes toward women: "women have burnt like beacons in all the works of all the poets." In literature, woman has been treated as full of character and importance; in reality, "she was locked up, beaten and flung about the room" (*Room*, 43).

An important task for women, as they look back through history, is to seek out the hitherto neglected and blurred outlines of a female literary tradition. "Poetry," affirms Woolf, "ought to have a mother as well as a father" (*Room*, 103). The work of the great female writers in the English tradition – including Jane Austen, the Brontës, George Eliot – was made possible by predecessors such as Aphra Behn, Fanny Burney, and others. Implied here is the need to establish a tradition of women's writing which, however closely it might be related to the male tradition, has its own emblems of distinctness in terms of both content and style. In this broader sense, the "room" might encompass a female tradition and female perspectives toward history.

A room of one's own might also represent the possibility, or ideal, of writing in a female language or at least appropriating language for female use. Woolf holds that women should not write in the same way as men do, notwithstanding the fact that many female authors have felt under enormous pressure to think and write like men. This pressure has stemmed partly from the unsuitability of language as hitherto developed to express the experience of women. The "male" language women inherited could not express their female experience; this language, habituated to showing women exclusively in their relationship to men, could not express, for example, the liking of one woman for another (*Room*, 82). Encountering the sentence "Chloe liked Olivia" in a novel by Mary Carmichael, Woolf observes that such a sentiment – the liking of one woman for another – is expressed here perhaps for the first time in literature, and, were it to find adequate expression, it might "light a torch in that vast chamber where nobody has yet been" (*Room*, 82, 84). Woolf notes how woman has been at the "centre of some different order and system of life," contrasting sharply with the world inhabited by men (*Room*, 86). Women must craft not only a sentence, a language that will grasp the rhythms of their own experience, but also a literary form that is "adapted to the body . . . women's books should be shorter, more concentrated, than those of men, and framed so that they do not need long hours of steady and uninterrupted work" (*Room*, 78). Woolf's general point – that language and thought are ultimately and irreversibly grounded in the rhythms of the body, of one's particular situation in place and time – is one that has been richly pursued by a variety of feminisms. What Woolf might have meant by a "female" use of language can perhaps be clarified by her characterization of male language: a man's writing, she said, appeared "so direct, so straightforward . . . It indicated such freedom of mind, such liberty of person, such confidence in himself." But all of these virtues – if such self-certainty and pretense to objectivity can be deemed virtues – fall, according to Woolf, under the shadow of a mighty male egotism, the shadow of the "I" that aridly dominates the male text, permeating it with an emotion incomprehensible to a woman, which Woolf associates with certain transcendental signifieds of the male world, such as "Work" and the "Flag" (*Room*, 99–102).

The mental state that Woolf sees as most creative is what she calls "unity of the mind," a unity in which the sexes are not viewed as distinct (*Room*, 97). She urges such "androgyny" on the grounds that the greatest human happiness results from the natural cooperation of the sexes. She characterizes this "theory" of androgyny (a Greek term fusing the words for "man" and "woman"; the term is taken over from Coleridge, and ultimately, from Plato) as follows: "in each of us two powers preside, one male, one female; and in the man's brain, the man predominates over the woman, and in the woman's brain, the woman predominates over the man. The normal and comfortable state of being is that when the two live in harmony together, spiritually co-operating . . . Coleridge perhaps meant this when he said that a great mind is androgynous" (*Room*, 98). Without this mixture, suggests Woolf, "the intellect seems to predominate and the other faculties of the mind harden and become barren" (*Room*, 104).

It is significant that Woolf alludes to Romantic notions of unity, as in Coleridge's view of androgyny and Blake's marriage of opposites. What her allusion brings out clearly is that the primacy of reason, advocated by the mainstream Enlightenment, against which the Romantics reacted on account of the abstractness and one-sidedness of such reason, was also a profound index and culmination of a long tradition of *male* thought and male categorization of the world. What the Romantics saw as an indeterminate deficiency of reason becomes in much feminism precisely a deficiency of male perspectives. In other words, the Romantics' perception of reason's deficiency or incompleteness was itself somewhat abstract; feminism, like Marxism, sees it as a political deficiency, ingrained in the social and economic fabric of gender relations.

Simone de Beauvoir (1908–1986)

Another classic feminist statement, *Le Deuxième Sexe* (1949; translated as *The Second Sex*, 1952), was produced by Simone de Beauvoir, a leading intellectual of her time, whose existentialist vision was forged partly in her relationship, as companion and colleague, with the existentialist philosopher Jean-Paul Sartre. De Beauvoir's text laid the foundations for much of the feminist theory and political activism that emerged during the 1960s in Western Europe and America; since then, its impact, if anything, has broadened and deepened: its basic thesis and premises continue to underlie the broad spectrum of feminist concerns. The book's central argument is that, throughout history, woman has always occupied a secondary role in relation to man, being relegated to the position of the "other," i.e., that which is adjectival upon the substantial subjectivity and existential activity of man. Whereas man has been enabled to transcend and control his environment, always furthering the domain of his physical and intellectual conquests, woman has remained imprisoned within "immanence," remaining a slave within the circle of duties imposed by her maternal and reproductive functions. In highlighting this subordination, the book explains in characteristic existentialist fashion how the so-called "essence" of woman was in fact created – at many levels, economic, political, religious – by historical developments representing the interests of men.

De Beauvoir was born in Paris. While studying at the Sorbonne, she made the acquaintance of Jean-Paul Sartre and Maurice Merleau-Ponty; with these two philosophers, she founded a literary and political journal. She belonged to a feminist collective and was politically active in feminist causes. She wrote several novels and a number of philosophical works, the most notable of which was *The Ethics of Ambiguity* (1947), articulating an existentialist ethics. Her existentialism, while influenced by Sartre, was also influenced by Marxism, psychoanalysis, and Hegel. Her view of freedom is distinguished from Sartre's view by its Hegelian emphasis on mutual recognition: it is through acknowledging another person's humanity that I confirm my own humanity and freedom. Another moment in Hegel's philosophy that underlies de Beauvoir's analyses of male–female relations through history and ideology is the master–slave relationship. According to Hegel, human consciousness strives for recognition and mastery, placing itself initially in a posture of hostility toward every other consciousness; a crucial phase in this endeavor for mastery is the willingness of one consciousness to risk everything in a life and death struggle, thereby becoming the master. But ultimately, the master is forced to recognize his own dependence on the slave, to see that his own human worth is gained in a relationship of reciprocity, of mutual recognition between himself and the slave: if he is to be recognized as human, he must acknowledge the slave's own humanity, else the latter's recognition of the master will be meaningless. In other words, humanity cannot arise in one person or in one group of people unilaterally: it is something born only of mutual recognition. This master–slave dialectic represents an important stage in Hegel's account of the development of human consciousness, and de Beauvoir skillfully bases the entire argument of her book on this intersubjective model of human consciousness and humanity. She views Hegel's master–slave dialectic as peculiarly applicable to the evolution of the male–female relationship.[11]

In her renowned introduction to *The Second Sex*, de Beauvoir points out the fundamental asymmetry of the terms "masculine" and "feminine." Masculinity is considered to be the "absolute human type," the norm or standard of humanity. A man does not typically preface his opinions with the statement "I am a man," whereas a woman's views are often held to be grounded in her femininity rather than in any objective perception of things. A man "thinks of his body as a direct and normal connection with the world, which he believes he apprehends objectively, whereas he regards the body of woman as a hindrance, a prison . . . Woman has ovaries, a uterus; these peculiarities imprison her in her subjectivity, circumscribe her within the limits of her own nature" (*SS*, xv). De Beauvoir quotes Aristotle as saying that the "female is a female by virtue of a certain *lack* of qualities," and St. Thomas as stating that the female nature is "afflicted with a natural defectiveness" (*SS*, xvi). Summarizing these long traditions of thought, de Beauvoir states: "Thus humanity is male and man defines woman not in herself but as relative to him; she is not regarded as an autonomous being . . . she is the incidental, the inessential as opposed to the essential. He is the Subject, he is the Absolute – she is the Other" (*SS*, xvi). De Beauvoir's Hegelian terminology highlights the fact that man's relegation of woman to the status of "other" violates the principle of mutual recognition, thereby threatening the very status that man has for so long jealously accorded to himself, to his own subjectivity. And yet, as de Beauvoir points out (drawing on both Hegel and Lévi-Strauss), "otherness" is a "fundamental category of human thought," as primordial as consciousness itself. Consciousness always entails positing a duality of Self and Other: indeed, no group "ever sets itself up as the One without at once setting up the Other over against itself" (*SS*, xvi–xvii). Our very conception of our identity entails consciousness of what we are not, of what stands beyond us and perhaps opposed to us.

The problem with demoting another consciousness or group to the status of "other" is that this other consciousness or ego "sets up a reciprocal claim": from *its* perspective, we are the stranger, the other. Interaction with other individuals, peoples, nations, and classes forces us to acknowledge the relativity of the notion of otherness. But this relativity and reciprocity, in the case of women, has not been recognized (*SS*, xvii). Woman's otherness seems to be absolute because, unlike the subordination of other oppressed groups such as Jews and black Americans, her subordination was not the result of a historical event or social change but is partly rooted in her anatomy and physiology. Also in contrast with these other groups, women have never formed a minority and they have never achieved cohesion as a group, since they have always lived dispersed among males: if they belong to the middle class, they identify with the males of that class rather than with working-class women; white women feel allegiance to white men rather than to black women (*SS*, xviii–xix). The "division of the sexes," de Beauvoir points out, "is a biological fact, not an event in human history . . . she is the Other in a totality of which the two components are necessary to one another." Indeed, woman has no autonomous history (*SS*, xix). Another contributing factor to women's subordination is their own reluctance to forgo the traditional advantages conferred on them by their protective male superiors: if man supports woman financially and assumes responsibility for defining her existence and purpose, then she can evade both economic risk and the metaphysical "risk" of a freedom in which she must work out her own purposes (*SS*, xxi).

Men, of course, have had their own reasons for perpetuating such a duality of Self and Other: "Legislators, priests, philosophers, writers, and scientists have striven to show that the subordinate position of woman is willed in heaven and advantageous on earth" (*SS*, xxii). A long line of thinkers stretching from Plato and Aristotle, through Augustine, Aquinas into modern bourgeois philosophers, has insisted on stabilizing woman as an object, on dooming her to immanence, to a life of subjection to given conditions, on barring her from property rights, education, and the professions (*SS*, xviii). As well as procuring the obvious economic and political benefits of such subordination, men have reaped enormous psychological reassurance: their hostility toward women conceals a fundamental desire for self-justification, as well as a fundamental insecurity (*SS*, xxii). While de Beauvoir acknowledges that by the eighteenth century certain male thinkers such as Diderot and John Stuart Mill began to champion the cause of women, she also notes that, in contradiction of its ostensible disposition toward democracy, the bourgeois class "clung to the old morality that found the guarantee of private property in the solidity of the family." Woman's liberation was thwarted all the more harshly as her entry into the industrial workforce furnished an economic basis for her claims to equality (*SS*, xxii–xxiii).

According to de Beauvoir, two essential factors paved the way for women's prospective equality: one was her ability (conferred by technology, which abrogated any innate male advantages of strength) to share in productive labor; and the second was her recently acquired freedom from the slavery of reproduction through contraception, adopted by many of the middle and then the working classes from the eighteenth century onward (*SS*, 109). And yet, a major factor retarding her freedom was the continued existence of the family, sanctioned by the various ideologies – political and religious – which aim to detain her in her traditional roles. De Beauvoir's formulation of the central problem of woman is as pertinent today as in her own era: woman's obstinate dilemma is the reconciliation of her productive and reproductive roles (*SS*, 123–124, 128).

Not least among the factors inhibiting woman's social and economic freedom is the perpetuation of certain obstinate myths of woman, in the realms of art and literature as well as in daily life. De Beauvoir examines the literary presentation of the feminine by writers such as Montherlant, D. H. Lawrence, Claudel, Breton, and Stendhal, authors whose attitudes toward women she takes to be "typical" (*SS*, 188). Montherlant, like Aristotle and St. Thomas, believes in "that vague and basic essence, femininity," defining it negatively (*SS*, 188). These writers, says de Beauvoir, reflect the "great collective myths" of woman: woman as *flesh*, as first womb then lover to the male; as nature and as the supernatural. She appears as the "*privileged Other*, through whom the subject fulfills himself" (*SS*, 233).

In an important chapter entitled "Myth and Reality," de Beauvoir observes that the myth of woman exerts an important influence not only in the world of literature but equally in everyday life. The myth *substitutes* for actual experience a transcendent idea which is timeless and unchangeable; because this idea is beyond or above the realm of actual experience, it is endowed with absolute truth. This myth of the "Eternal Feminine" is opposed to the "dispersed, contingent, and multiple existences of actual women" (*SS*, 239). Of all these myths, the one most deeply "anchored in masculine hearts" is that of the feminine "mystery." What underlies the feminine mystery is an "economic substructure" of subordination: mystery always belongs to the vassal, the colonized, the slave (*SS*, 242–243).

In the conclusion to her book, de Beauvoir argues that the age-old conflict between the sexes no longer takes the form of woman attempting to hold back man in her own prison of immanence, but rather in her own effort to emerge into the light of transcendence. Woman's situation will be transformed primarily by a change in her economic condition; but this change must also generate moral, social, cultural, and psychological transformations. Eventually, both man and woman will exist *both* for self and for the other: "mutually recognizing each other as subject, each will yet remain for the other an *other*." In this recognition, in this reciprocity, will "the slavery of half of humanity" be abolished (*SS*, 688).

Notes

1   F. R. Leavis, *The Common Pursuit* (1952; rpt. Middlesex: Penguin, 1966), p. 193. Hereafter cited as *CP*.

2   Karl Marx and Friedrich Engels, *Manifesto of the Communist Party* (1952; rpt. Moscow: Progress Publishers, 1973), pp. 11–16. Hereafter cited as *MCP*.

3   Karl Marx, *The German Ideology: Part One*, ed. C. J. Arthur (London: Lawrence and Wishart, 1982), pp. 47–51. Hereafter cited as *GI*.

4   Leon Trotsky, *Literature and Revolution* (New York: Russell and Russell, 1957), p. 218. Hereafter cited as *LR*.

5   A. A. Zhdanov, *Essays on Literature, Philosophy, and Music* (New York: International Publishers, 1950), p. 15.

6   *Marxism and Art: Writings in Aesthetics and Criticism*, ed. Berel Lang and Forrest Williams (New York: McKay, 1972), pp. 226–227.

7   Antonio Gramsci, *Selections from Political Writings*, trans. J. Mathews, ed. Q. Hoare (New York: International Publishers, 1977), p. 171.

8   Virginia Woolf, *The Common Reader: First and Second Series* (New York, 1948), p. 172. Hereafter cited as *CR*.

9   *A Writer's Diary: Being Extracts from the Diary of Virginia Woolf*, ed. Leonard Woolf (London: Hogarth Press, 1953), p. 220. Hereafter cited as *WD*.

10 Virginia Woolf, *A Room of One's Own* (1929; rpt. San Diego, New York, London: Harvest/Harcourt Brace Jovanovich, 1989), p. 4. Hereafter cited as *Room*.

11 Simone de Beauvoir, *The Second Sex*, trans. H. M. Parshley (New York: Bantam/Alfred A. Knopf, 1961), p. 59. Hereafter cited as *SS*.

Chapter 3

Criticism and Theory After the Second World War

The conclusion of the Second World War formalized the opposition between the Western powers and the Soviet bloc of nations. While some literature participated in the ideological implications of this conflict, much writing retreated into a longer-term contextualization of the confrontation as futile and resting on debased values. This retreat from an "objective" reality reached a climax in philosophies such as phenomenology (which parenthesized the objective world, viewing it as a function of perception) and existentialism, which called into question all forms of authority and belief, as well as literary developments such as the Theater of the Absurd, whose proponents such as Samuel Beckett and Eugene Ionesco dramatized the existential absurdity, anguish, and ultimate isolation of human existence. The Italian thinker Benedetto Croce formulated an aesthetic which revived Hegelian idealist principles as against the tradition of bourgeois positivism and scientism. The German existentialist philosopher Martin Heidegger (1889–1976) increasingly saw poetry as transcending the discursive and rational limitations of philosophy. In France, the philosopher Gaston Bachelard (1884–1962) formulated a phenomenological and surrealist account of poetry, while the existentialist Jean-Paul Sartre (1905–1980) advocated a literature of political engagement. The phenomenological emphasis was further elaborated by Georges Poulet (b. 1902), Jean-Pierre Richard (b. 1922), and Georges Bataille, and given a linguistic orientation in the work of Maurice Blanchot (1907–2003). It was in the 1950s that structuralism – another tendency which parenthesized or diminished the agency of the human subject by situating it within a broad linguistic and semiological structure – began to thrive through figures such as the anthropologist Claude Lévi-Strauss and the narratologist A. J. Greimas, who drew upon Saussure and the earlier Russian Formalism. Roland Barthes analyzed the new myths of Western culture and proposed a revolutionary opposi- tional discourse which was aware of its own mythical status. Barthes proclaimed the "death of the author," and his later works moved in post- structuralist directions. Notable among the formalist thinkers of this period were Roman Jakobson, Emile Benveniste, Tzvetan Todorov, and Gerard Genette. The following sections will examine phenomenology as formu- lated by Husserl, existentialism as expounded by Heidegger, the heterology of Georges Bataille, and structuralism as expressed in its foundations by Saussure and in its later phases by Barthes.

Edmund Husserl (1859–1938) and Phenomenology

One of the foremost philosophies of this period, in which much reader- response theory had its philosophical origins, was the doctrine known as phenomenology, whose foundations were laid by the German philosopher Edmund Husserl. The Greek word *phainomenon* means "appearance." Hence, as a philosophical attitude, phenomenology shifts our emphasis of study away from the "external" world of objects toward examining the ways in which these objects *appear* to the human subject, and the subjective contribution to this process of appearing. Husserl gives the name "phe- nomenological reduction" to this "bracketing" of the external world, which underlies his attempt to achieve certainty in philosophy. He argues that we cannot be sure of the nature of the outside world, but we can have certainty about the nature of our own perception and about the ways in which we construct the world, the ways in which that world appears to our subjective apparatus. This emphasis on subjectivity proved to be enormously influ- ential; it provided the foundations of the Geneva School of phenomeno- logical criticism (including figures such as Georges Poulet and Jean Starobinski) which read literature as embodying the consciousness of its author; it exerted a considerable impact on the reception theories of Wolf- gang Iser and Hans Robert Jauss; and it provided a starting point against which Martin Heidegger's thought reacted.

Husserl wished to establish philosophy on a rational and scientific basis. He gives a fairly succinct account of his own philosophical position in a lecture of 1917 entitled "Pure Phenomenology, its Method and its Field of Investigation."[1] Here, Husserl announces that, in response to an urgent need, a "new fundamental science, pure phenomenology," has developed, and he defines this as "the science of pure phenomena" ("PP," 4–5). One of Husserl's accomplishments in this lecture is to define and refine the concept of "phenomenon," which in its simplest meaning refers to "some- thing which appears" (to the subject or observer). Husserl's most general claim is that "objects would be nothing at all for the cognizing subject if they did not 'appear' to him, if he had of them no 'phenomenon.' Here, therefore, 'phenomenon' signifies a certain content that intrinsically inhabits the intuitive consciousness" ("PP," 7). Husserl is not only claiming, as Kant did, that we can know the object only as it appears to us, regardless of what it might be in itself; he is also urging that the object is *nothing* in itself, and its very constitution as an object, as a phenomenon or object which appears, is grounded on the subjective apparatus which intuits it as an object. In a sense, what Husserl is doing is removing the Kantian notion of noumenon which acts as a constraint or limitation upon the constitution of phenomena by the mind: for Husserl, there is nothing beyond the sphere and status of phenomena. The phenomenal world is not merely the only reality we can know; it *is* the only reality.

Husserl points out the complexity of the term "phenomenon" as it is used in his thought. When we perceive an object (i.e., when an object "appears" to us), this is not a single or simple operation: the object might be given to us, or appear to us, in differing ways. We might look at it from above, below, near, far, past, and present. So we in fact have several single intuitions of the "same" object. And these single intuitions are combined and integrated into "the unity of one continuous consciousness of one and the same object." Hence, "one unitary 'phenomenon' permeates all the manifolds of phenomenal presentation." In other words, what we call a phenomenon, or object as it appears to us, is in fact an intuited unity of a *series of perceptions* of an object ("PP," 8). On the other side, consciousness itself is a unity of a variety of processes that are performed upon phenomena, such as remembering, referring, combining, contrasting, and ultimately, theorizing. So we have a situation where the "unity of one consciousness . . . constitutes intrinsically a single synthetic objectivity" ("PP," 9). Again, this situation seems similar to that outlined in Kant's description of the transcendental ego, which unifies the individual perceptions of the empirical ego; but again, Husserl's emphasis is different: the entire world of phenomena, ranging from the simplest designations of objectivity to complex groupings and sub-groupings of objects, is constituted by acts of consciousness, by a variety and hierarchy of such acts which themselves must form part of a pattern of ordered unity. The point here is that it is consciousness that determines objectivity, that classifies and arranges the world of objects and phenomena: without this activity, there simply would be no objects as such. By way of example, Husserl suggests that no object in the category "work of art" could occur in the world of someone who was "devoid of all aesthetic sensibility" ("PP," 13–14). The implication, clearly, is that a work of art (like any other phenomenon) cannot somehow exist prior to its reception; it is *constituted* by the sensibility which receives it as such, *as* a work of art.

The task of phenomenology, then, is to examine not the world of objects "in itself" but how this world is constituted by a vast range of acts of consciousness. As Husserl says, a phenomenological investigation will address "the intrinsic nature . . . of the perceiving itself," i.e., the thinking itself, as well as the object that is thought about ("PP," 15). As such, phenomenology will be a "science of consciousness" ("PP," 16).

Husserl insists on making a distinction between "phenomena" and "objects." Objects, such as all natural objects, are "foreign to consciousness," whereas phenomena comprise the processes and constituents of consciousness itself. This distinction indicates a sharp contrast, says Husserl, between phenomenology and the so-called "objective" sciences ("PP," 17–18). Husserl sees his "phenomenological reduction" as a development of Descartes' *cogito ergo sum* toward non-Cartesian aims: "phenomenological reduction is the method for effecting radical purification of the phenomenological field of consciousness from all obtrusions from Objective actualities" ("PP," 30). What does such a reduction involve? First of all, it entails suspending or bracketing or "putting out of action" the whole of "material Nature," and the entire corporeal world, including one's own body, the "body of the cognizing subject" ("PP," 32). Secondly, we must exclude "all psychological experience," all consideration of conscious processes being grounded in the body or nature. Hence, "the Objective world," as comprehending both nature and the psyche, "is as if it were placed in brackets" ("PP," 33–34).

Once we have done this, what is left over? What is left for phenomenological analysis? Husserl's answer is "the totality of the phenomena of the world . . . Consciousness and what it is conscious of . . . is what is left over as field for pure reflection" ("PP," 34–35). The difference is that, in our phenomenological investigation, we will treat objects not as independent entities but as "correlates of consciousness." We can still examine everything that we would have done prior to the advent of this wondrous phenomenological science; only, now, we will not regard these as "actualities" but will view them in relation to the consciousness that constitutes them ("PP," 35). Hence, in examining pure consciousness, we are examining not only the structures of thought and perception that are immanent in consciousness but also the entire range of "external" phenomena as they *appear* to, and are structured by, consciousness.

Following Brentano, Husserl sees acts of consciousness as *intentional*: consciousness is always conscious *of* something, and it posits or intends the objects toward which it is directed. Such objects are therefore "immanent" in the thinking process of the subject; and, since such immanent objectivity is ideal (certain qualities being abstracted from an object and recognized as its essence), it is an objectivity that is valid for all subjects ("PP," 43). In short, Husserl replaces the notion of objectivity with a model of intersubjectivity: coherence is found no longer in nature itself or in objects themselves but in the patterns of our perceptions of objects. Husserl ends his paper with a confident prediction that phenomenology will "overcome all resistance and stupidity and will enjoy enormous development"

("PP," 44). While it may not have overcome all stupidity, phenomenology has certainly inaugurated, and has been symptomatic of, an enormous shift, discernible in many fields, including modernist literature, existentialism, deconstruction, and many branches of psychoanalytic and feminist theory, toward examining the world as integrally related to the apparatus of human subjectivity. Where the modern world has left Husserl behind, however, is his Cartesian insistence on isolating the mind from the body and conceiving the mind in an individualistic and atomistic way; subsequent thinkers have indeed built on Husserl's insights but have tended to ground human subjectivity in a social and historical framework, after the model of Hegel rather than that of Descartes.

Husserl himself, however, saw his "scientific" method of philosophy as answering to a much-needed exigency of the modern world. His inaugural lecture, just examined, was delivered in 1917, while Europe was still being devastated by the First World War. In a subsequent lecture, "Philosophy and the Crisis of European Man" (1935), Husserl stated that the "European nations are sick" because the humanistic sciences, blinded by naturalism, have neglected to seek a "pure science of the spirit."[2]

Husserl traces the spiritual unity of Europe to a new kind of attitude that arose in the ancient Greek world: instead of being concerned solely with survival and practical needs, the Greeks acquired interest in systematic and universal knowledge that transcended any immediate application: in knowledge for its own sake, in the concept of a universal truth, and universal standards of morality (PCP, 160). This theoretical attitude is unique to European culture (though it has been exported and imitated), and contrasts sharply with the "natural attitude," with the "naively direct living immersed in the world" that has characterized other cultures (PCP, 166). Husserl urges that theoria is "called upon . . . to serve humanity in a new way," by offering "a universal critique of all life and of its goals" (PCP, 169). He urges Europeans to rise like the phoenix from "the annihilating conflagration of disbelief" and to engage once again in "the West's mission to humanity" (PCP, 192). His words have echoed loudly through the mouths of politicians speaking into the twenty-first century.

Martin Heidegger (1889–1976) and Existentialism

Husserl's student Martin Heidegger proved to be one of the most influential philosophers of the twentieth century, and the major modern exponent of existentialism. His impact extends not only to existentialist philosophers such as Merleau-Ponty, Sartre, and Simone de Beauvoir but also to psychiatrists such as Ludwig Binswanger and to theologians such as Rudolph Bultmann, Paul Tillich, Martin Buber, and Karl Barth, as well as to poststructuralist thinkers such as Jacques Derrida. Influenced by the phenomenological method of his mentor as well as by writers in the hermeneutic tradition of Friedrich Schleiermacher and Wilhelm Dilthey, Heidegger's central project consisted in a radical re-examination of the notion of "being," in its intrinsic relationship with time. His major work, *Sein und Zeit* (*Being and Time*), was published in 1927, making an immediate impact in both the halls of professional philosophy and the educated reading public. Heidegger argued that our answer to the question of what Being is would determine the future of humankind. Moreover, he developed his own hermeneutic or method of interpretation of texts; his later work focuses increasingly on the analysis of poetry and language.

Heidegger was appointed Professor of Philosophy at the University of Marburg in 1923; he was subsequently, in 1929, elected Husserl's successor to the Chair of Philosophy at Freiburg and then elected Rector in 1933 under Hitler's recently inaugurated regime. It was in this year that Heidegger joined the National Socialist Party; in his inaugural address at the university, "The Role of the University in the New Reich," he decried freedom of speech in the interests of national unity, and lauded the advent of a glorious new Germany. He resigned his position as Rector in early 1934. Did these events represent merely a brief flirtation on Heidegger's part with Nazism or an enduring collaboration and commitment? The controversy remains.

In *Being and Time* Heidegger insisted that philosophers to date had still failed to answer the question raised by Plato and Aristotle: what is being?[3] In this work, Heidegger analyzes what he terms *dasein* or *human* being. What characterizes human being is its "thrownness" into the world or "facticity": a human being is already cast into a series of relationships and surroundings that constitute his or her "world" (*BT*, 82–83). A second feature is "existentiality" or "transcendence," whereby a human being appropriates her world, impressing on it the unique image of her own existence and potential. In other words, she uses the various elements of her world as given to realize herself (*BT*, 235–236). Yet this positive feature is accompanied by a third characteristic, that of "fallenness": in attempting to create herself, the human being falls from true Being, becoming immersed instead in the distractions of day to day living, becoming entangled in particular beings (*BT*, 220). The authentic being, the authentic self, is thus buried beneath the cares and distractions of life (*BT*, 166–168).

How does a human being overcome such inauthentic existence, such loss of true being? Heidegger's answers to this question comprise one of the classic statements of existentialism. Inauthenticity consists in losing sight of the unity of human being, of human existence, caused by attention to the practical interests and cares of daily existence; human being is thereby prescinded and experienced as a series of desultory phenomena. Heidegger suggests that there is one particular state of mind which is unique: "dread" or *angst* (*BT*, 227–235). This refers to a sense of nothingness, of loss, of the emptiness, when we look at life or existence in its totality, as essentially orientated toward death. In such a mood, the human self attains knowledge of itself as a whole, as "being-to-death." In other words, death is the fundamental fact that shapes our existence and the course of our life. And the mental state of "dread" enables us to rise above our immanence, our dispersion in the immediate and transitory affairs of the world, to reflect upon our life as a whole, in the fullest glare of its finitude and its potential to lack meaning (*BT*, 293–299). The vehicle through which we acknowledge this responsibility to ourselves is "conscience," which acknowledges both our facticity, our being placed within a world, and our obligation actively to fashion our selves in relation to this very world. Conscience makes us aware of this guilt or obligation (*BT*, 313, 317–319).

Like Bergson, Heidegger views time as integral to the constitution of the self or human being. As in Bergson's concept of *durée* or "internal" time (as opposed to mechanical "clock" time which merely spatializes time), time for Heidegger is the profoundest substratum of human existence (*BT*, 466–472). What Heidegger calls existential time is time that is unique to a particular person's consciousness; a person's life, her traversing of the journey between birth and death, is most fundamentally constituted by time (*BT*, 376). Hence, her sense of existential responsibility is a temporal notion, lying in the ability to view her life from beginning to end (to a projected end) (*BT*, 395–396). This ability to situate my present (immersed inauthentically in temporary distractions) within a broader context of past and future, this attempt actively to engage in the world into which I have been cast, this assertion of my freedom in the midst of determination, is seen by Heidegger as living out one's "destiny" (*BT*, 416–417, 436–437).

In his later works, such as *Introduction to Metaphysics* (1953), Heidegger warns that we have fallen away from Being and have lost ourselves in the distractions of worldly and proximate aims, as well as in technology and gadgetry. In tones which are reminiscent of Husserl, Heidegger wishes to save Western man from this dire fate. Ironically, like humanists such as Arnold, he attaches overwhelming importance to poetry in this salvific enterprise. The works of Heidegger which directly concern literary theory and criticism include "The Origin of the Work of Art" (1935), "Hölderlin and the Essence of Poetry" (1936), and "Language" (1950). In these later works, Heidegger appeals increasingly to the power of poetry to express the truths of authentic being.

Indeed, in his essay "The Origin of the Work of Art," Heidegger states that the origin of a work of art is art itself: "art is by nature an origin: a distinctive way in which truth comes into being, that is, becomes histori-cal."[4] We can attempt to follow Heidegger's elaboration of these general statements. He defines art as "the setting-into-work of truth." This process has two aspects: art fixes truth in place within a particular figure, and it also preserves truth. Heidegger broadens his definition of art to "the creative preserving of truth in the work. *Art then is the becoming and happening of truth*" (*PLT*, 71). What Heidegger seems to be indicating here is that art does not simply express prior or ready-made truths: rather, it both *creates* truths and *preserves* them, the latter being a historical function, for, as Heidegger says, art grounds history (*PLT*, 77). Heidegger proceeds to say that, in the midst of ordinary objects, art "breaks open an open place, in whose openness everything is other than usual . . . everything ordinary and hitherto existing becomes an unbeing" (*PLT*, 72). Hence, art has the power to transform our earlier and "ordinary" conceptions of truth, exposing the unreality of the arrangements of our ordinary life, releasing us from the closure and rigidity of conventional perception. Heidegger states that the "truth that discloses itself in the work [of art] can never be proved or derived from what went before" (*PLT*, 75).

Like many twentieth-century theorists, Heidegger insists that language has an important role beyond its merely communicative function: "language alone brings what is . . . into the Open for the first time . . . Language, by naming beings for the first time, first brings beings to word and to appearance" (*PLT*, 73). The emphasis here is characteristic of Heidegger's later, somewhat mystically orientated, writing: language not only creates but reveals the true being that is already there, bringing this being to the light of expression. In this sense, language "itself is poetry." Poetry "takes place in language because language preserves the original nature of poetry" (*PLT*, 74).

In his epilogue, Heidegger quotes Hegel's statement that in the modern era, art is no longer the highest expression of truth, this function having been assumed by philosophy. Heidegger states: "the beautiful belongs to the advent of truth" (*PLT*, 81). In other words, Heidegger views beauty as intrinsic to the expression of truth in art, perhaps echoing Platonic and even medieval conceptions of the connection between being, truth, and beauty.

In "Hölderlin and the Essence of Poetry," Heidegger develops certain insights of the poet Hölderlin. The first of these is that poetry is the "most innocent of all occupations."[5] Heidegger takes this to refer to poetry's unfettered invention of a world of images, in the guise of "play" (*EB*, 272). Hölderlin's line "We have been a conversation" is analyzed by Heidegger as indicating that only in conversation is language realized, and that the single, unitary "conversation" of man grounds his historical existence: "it is precisely in the naming of the gods, and in the transmutation of the world into word, that the real conversation, which we ourselves are, consists" (*EB*, 279). Language is indeed "the supreme event of human existence," and poetry is "the establishing of being by means of the word" (*EB*, 280–281). In the language of Hölderlin, the poet interprets the signs of the gods and is also the voice of the people, and it is these two tendencies in himself that mark his position of "betweenness" (*EB*, 288–289).

This notion of "betweenness" is developed and imbued with further associations is Heidegger's subsequent essay "Language." Here, Heidegger analyzes a poem entitled "*Ein Winterabend*" ("A Winter Evening") by

Georg Trakl in order to arrive at certain insights into the nature of language. Heidegger's "analysis," like much of his later work, is itself written poetically and presents the kind of difficulties that we might encounter in a complex and obscure poem. The style and the insights of this piece anticipate Derrida's prose, as well as Derrida's rejection of a distinction between philosophy and literature, between prose and poetry, and between literal and figurative language. Heidegger begins by reaffirming his view that "only speech enables man to be the living being he is as man" (*PLT*, 189). He notes that certain broad views of language have persisted for two and a half millennia. These are: language as expression (whereby something internal is externalized); language as an activity of man; and, finally, language as the presentation or representation of reality or unreality. But these views, says Heidegger, fail to confront language *as* language. By this, he appears to indicate that language cannot be treated merely as an appendage or adjective of the "human," an instrument of human communication and self-definition. It is not man, says Heidegger, but language, which speaks: "It is language that first brings man about, brings him into existence." In this sense, man is "bespoken by language" (*PLT*, 192–193).

Heidegger's "explication" of Trakl's poem anticipates some of the central positions of much reception and reader-response theory. The language of Trakl's poem, says Heidegger, does not merely name familiar objects such as "snow," "bell," "window," "falling," and "ringing." Rather, it "calls into the word . . . The calling calls into itself," into a "presence sheltered in absence" (*PLT*, 199). Inasmuch as we can "explain" this statement, we might take it to indicate that language does not name things which are somehow already there, waiting to be named. They achieve their very status as "things" only by being called into the word, only by being given a status, a position, a situation, in language. The status they enjoy in the uniqueness of their current combination in language is different from that which they occupied prior to this combination, this current "calling" of language. Moreover, they are called into the act of calling itself: they achieve their very thinghood only in the process of this calling, of which they are an integral element. As things they are called into "presence"; but this is not a literal or immediate presence: the "falling snow" of which the poem speaks is not actually present in the immediate world of the listener or reader: it is called into presence in her mind, hence it is a "presence sheltered in absence."

The various images of the poem, according to Heidegger, such as snowfall, the vesper bell, house, and table set with bread and wine, evoke respectively the sky, the divine, mortals, and earth. Heidegger refers to this combination as the "unitary fourfold" which makes up the "world" (*PLT*, 199). It is this "world" that is called into being by the things that are named in the poem: "In the naming, the things named are called into their thinging. Thinging, they unfold world, in which things abide . . . The world grants to things their presence. Things bear world." Language speaks by "bidding things come to world, and world to things . . . For world and things do not subsist alongside one another. They penetrate each other" (*PLT*, 199–200, 202). If "world" expresses the core elements of a vision of unity or totality (sky, earth, mortals, divinities), and "things" express isolated features within that world (such as snowfall, or the ringing of a bell), the language that names these things does not merely name them in their isolation previous to the poem; rather, it names them *as* things in their current mutual combination, and as such, it is language which brings into visibility – into being – the bearing by each thing of its participation in a larger scheme, the self-gesturing of each thing toward its own essential relatedness, its implication of its own environment. In other words, language allows things to achieve their thinghood by bringing to light the "world" borne by them or implicitly contained within them. A thing becomes a thing only by release, through the power of language, from its bare immediate particular existence (a condition that can be only hypothetical) and access into its own mediation by more general categories, access into the fullness of its thinghood as part of a relational complex through the naming of it in language.

Heidegger's further explication of this situation appears to anticipate certain features of Derrida's notion of difference. He states that the "intimacy of world and thing is not a fusion." There is a persistent separation between the two. Between world and thing prevails a condition of "betweenness," or what Heidegger calls *difference* where the latter part of this noun may refer to the "bearing" or "carrying" of world by thing. The intimacy of world and thing, says Heidegger, "is present in the separation of the between; it is present in the difference. The word dif-ference is now removed from its usual and customary usage. What it now names is not a generic concept for various kinds of differences. It exists only as this single difference" (*PLT*, 202). This formulation anticipates Derrida's hypostatization of difference – his treating of it as a primordial essence, a linguistic primum mobile, an aseitic first cause prescinded from the very relationality into which it plunges all else. But what can Heidegger possibly intend? He has told us that it is language which speaks, language which brings together world and things *in their intimacy which is a relation of absolute difference.* He proceeds to tell us that the "dif-ference carries out world in its worlding, carries out things in their thinging. Thus carrying them out, it carries them toward one another" (*PLT*, 202). The neologisms "thinging" and "worlding" represent an extension of the gerund verbal form to the nouns "thing" and "world." In everyday language, the gerund form (which has the form of the present participle, such as "singing") could be used as the subject of a sentence ("singing is healthy") or as an object ("she likes singing"). What is thereby emphasized, by the ending "ing," is not a noun (such as "song") but the *act* of singing. Hence, Heidegger's extension of this *verbal* form to a noun such as "world," transforming this into "worlding," draws attention to the world not as a thing but as an act; to be more accurate, it stresses the nature of the world or thing *as* an act. Hence, it is language, language that speaks, which brings the processes of world-composition and thing-composition into the mutuality in which alone either can be realized.

Heidegger proceeds to explain that the "dif-ference does not mediate after the fact by connecting world and things through a middle added on to them. Being in the middle, it first determines world and things in their presence, i.e. in their being toward one another, whose unity it carries out" (*PLT*, 202). In other words, dif-ference is not an external relation that connects two entities (world and thing) that are already there: rather, dif-ference is internal to their relation, shaping the very entities themselves. Heidegger insists, then, that the word is not merely our way of representing a distinction between objects; nor is it merely a relation between world and thing. If language speaks by bidding, by calling "thing and world, what is really called is: the dif-ference" (*PLT*, 203). Language speaks by bidding "thing-world and world-thing, to come to the between of the dif-ference. What is so bidden is commanded to arrive from out of the dif-ference into the dif-ference" (*PLT*, 206). If dif-ference primordially pre-exists identity, if dif-ference is prior to the constitution of world and thing, then language is the vehicle by which world and thing are called into being, through mutual relation, from this primordial dif-ference into the dif-ference which is language itself. "Language goes on as the taking place or occurring of the dif-ference for world and things" (*PLT*, 207). What ultimately takes place in the speaking of language is the creation of what is human: "mortals live in the speaking of language" (*PLT*, 210).

While much of what Heidegger says in these later works leans toward mysticism, his insights into language overlap with those of many modern theorists such as Barthes and even Lacan. Heidegger indicates that not only is the human being "thrown" into the world (his or her particular world) but also that the human is characterized by a thrownness into language. It is the language that we are born into (not this or that particular language but language in general) that speaks through us and that speaks to us. At the core of language is dif-ference, the irreducible relation between world and thing, the irreducible self-transcendence of all of the elements of our world in a larger unity toward which they point; it is language that constitutes the human; all of our attempts to understand and act upon the world and thereby to create ourselves are mediated by the speaking of language, a speaking in which we must enter to find our own voice. In other words, it is when we arrive at a dialogue with language that we truly speak.

Georges Bataille (1897–1962) and Heterology

Loosely associated with the surrealist movement in the first half of the twentieth century, Bataille – whose writings of the 1930s and 1940s emerged into a renewed significance in the 1960s – was a radical thinker whose works spanned philosophy, poetry, economics, and pornography. His major works include *La Part maudite* (1949; *The Accursed Share*) and *La Littérature et le Mal* (1975; *Literature and Evil*). Sometimes called the "metaphysician of evil," and condemned as an "excremental philosopher" by the leading surrealist André Breton,[6] Bataille engaged in what he himself called "intellectual violence" to produce writings which were often designed to shock and appall, advancing his endeavor to write a "heterology," a science of the other, of the heterogeneous, of all that had been excreted and rejected as waste matter or undesirable by conventional thought: sacrifice, excrement, violence, blood, incest, all of this comprising the "accursed share," pertaining to the bodily and material part of us that has been suppressed and subordinated. All of these are constituents of forbidden and tabooed realms whose repudiation and expulsion are integral to the formation of the tradition of rationalism (as superordinate to the body), and the structures of transcendence (religious, social, political) through which order and meaning are imposed and created. Bataille's work heavily influenced poststructuralist thinkers such as Derrida and Kristeva, as well as theorists of postmodernism such as Lyotard and Baudrillard.

Bataille drew inspiration from "deviant" figures such as the Marquis de Sade, who saw the very notion of reason as coercive and violent. The concept of reason, since at least the time of Plato, has been used to control and suppress the desires and appetites of the body in the interests of political order and communal benefit. In the era of capitalism, desires must be subordinated to the principle of utility and the requirements of the market such as economy and efficiency. It should be remembered, however, that Bataille's project of heterology was hardly altogether new; he was continuing, with perhaps a more scatological emphasis, a heterological tradition that had already been richly articulated by a series of thinkers from Schopenhauer and Nietzsche through Bergson, Freud, Heidegger, and many feminist writers, who had drawn attention to the role of the body, of survival instincts, and ideological formations of subjectivity in the very processes of perception and cognition.

In his paper entitled "The Use Value of D. A. F. de Sade," Bataille observes that the insights of the Marquis de Sade – which should be seen as the basis of an entire way of living and thinking – have been domesticated and confined even by his so-called admirers (*VE*, 92, 94). Inspired by de Sade's mentality, Bataille suggests that there are two polarized human impulses, appropriation and excretion. Appropriation is characterized by homogeneity whereas excretion is the result of heterogeneity (*VE*, 94–95). The elementary form of appropriation is oral consumption. Man appropriates not only his food but also the various products of his activity such as clothes, furniture, dwelling, instruments of production, and land. Such appropriation is based on a homogeneity or identity between the possessor and the object possessed (*VE*, 95). But this homogeneity is merely one aspect of a much larger homogeneity which man has imposed on the external world by means of classification through conceptions and ideas. This effective identification or assimilation of all the world's elements is pursued with a "constant obstinacy," and has been effected by philosophy, religion, and poetry, as well as by "common sense" (*VE*, 96).

Bataille asks, what are the waste products of this operation? In other words, what elements have had to be excreted or expelled in order to arrive at such a homogeneous view of the world? Philosophy has envisaged these waste products – elements that would threaten its homogenizing operation – in merely abstract and negative terms such as nothingness, infinity, the absolute, to which it can assign no positive content. It is thereby freed to identify the unknowable world with the known world and an endless world with a finite world. In other words, what philosophy cannot know, it assimilates into the form of what is known (*VE*, 96). An example might be the notion of God, which, being unknowable, is invested with attributes of the human, such as mercy, love, and wrath. In a different form of the same homogenizing operation, religion divides the sacred domain into a superior celestial world and an inferior, demoniacal, decaying world. The former is homogeneous, using God as the paternal "sign of universal homogeneity," while the latter resists all attempts at appropriation, being consigned to an irremediable multiplicity. The excretion or expulsion effected by religion applies to the lower portion of human nature, which is subjected to various prohibitions and obligations (*VE*, 96).

In contrast with philosophy and religion, poetry appears to allow access to a heterogeneous world (presumably because it exercises some autonomy in its presentation of life). But, Bataille argues, poetry has "always been at the mercy of the great historical systems of appropriation." In other words, poetry does not subsist in a vacuum and is dependent on factors such as patronage and later the capitalist market. Moreover, poetry's very autonomy leads it into various aesthetic homogeneities. And the practical unreality of its heterogeneous worlds, which it sees as superior to vulgar reality, actually perpetuates the process of excretion or expulsion of what is viewed as undesirable, lower, or vulgar (*VE*, 97).

What is the purpose of these varied coercive movements toward homogenization? Their goal, as characterized by Bataille, is "the development of a servile human species, fit only for the fabrication, rational consumption, and conservation of products" (*VE*, 97). As against the forces of homogenization and exploitation, Bataille advances "heterology," which he defines as "the science of what is completely other" (*VE*, 102); heterology scientifically considers heterogeneity and "leads to the complete reversal of the philosophical process," which becomes an instrument of excretion instead of appropriation, introducing the demand for "violent gratification" (*VE*, 97). The heterogeneous, being resistant to assimilation and appropriation, can be determined only through negation, and cannot be incorporated into any homogeneous intellectual system; it is accessible only in concrete form, in gratification, ecstatic trance, orgasm, and violence (*VE*, 98–99). It is precisely what is excreted or expelled as unassimilable. Excretion "is not simply a middle term between two appropriations": Bataille may be thinking here of the Hegelian dialectic where what is presented as simple identity in the first phase is externalized (or, in Bataille's terminology, excreted or expelled) in the second phase into the diversity of its relations with everything else, to be reintegrated in the third phase into a higher unity.

What is expelled or excreted must be used practically, against the exploitative, appropriative mentality which accumulates products, regularizes the circulation of goods for profit, and crushes people under the yoke of morality. Acting under the principles of practical heterology, man "acquires the capacity to link overtly not only his intellect and his virtue but his *raison d'être* to the violence and incongruity of his excretory organs, as well as to his ability to become excited and entranced by heterogeneous elements, commonly starting with debauchery" (*VE*, 99). Bataille links the practical development of heterology to "the overturning of the established order" (*VE*, 100). We may well wonder how such apparently antisocial impulses and violent gratifications could achieve anything, let alone a revolution. But Bataille assures us that such impulses, as directed against a stagnant society where the submerged masses are "doomed to an obscure and impotent life," are directed toward "social revolution," liberating force with a long-restrained violence. The violence of such revolution will first separate and then excrete or exclude the group that has hitherto possessed power (*VE*, 100). Revolution requires such "sadistic understanding" which comprehends the need for destruction of the social edifice, as well as the "erotic bond" which links us to death and physical pain (*VE*, 100). Bataille seems to be urging that we draw upon our long repressed libidinal energies, on those parts of our nature that have been suppressed or excreted as undesirable, antisocial, or aggressive, to achieve the "violent excitation" associated with the heterogeneous, with the ability to resist assimilation, in order to engage in the destructive activities necessary for today's "fiery and bloody" revolution, based on a "heterological conception of human life" (*VE*, 102).

Clearly, Bataille's call is in some sense fundamental: to overturn the very project of philosophy, religion, and art as they have hitherto existed, exerting as they have a coercive and falsifying homogeneity over both the world and human nature; to redeem what has been excreted or expelled as lower, as evil, as depraved; to restore heterogeneity and difference from its degraded and condemned state; and, perhaps, to realize, more fully, the full extent of our nature. Unfortunately, he tends to formulate with insufficient precision and detail the kind of revolution he desires. A naive realist might argue that it is difficult to know how any of his terms – notwithstanding their scatological charm – could be transposed or applied to the actual world of political practice, beyond a vaguely articulated call to revaluate the Western tradition. And a skeptic might argue that the scatological tendencies that Bataille wishes to unleash already permeate the capitalist world and are in fact one of the important directions in which it has extended its markets and deepened its conditioning of human subjectivity.

Structuralism

Much criticism since the 1950s can be regarded as an implicit impugnment of widely institutionalized New Critical practices. A sustained challenge came from structuralism and some of its descendants such as deconstruction. In the West, the influx of structuralism was to some extent anticipated in the work of the Canadian Northrop Frye, who was the most influential theorist in America of what is called Myth Criticism, which was in vogue from the 1940s to the mid-1960s and whose practitioners included Richard Chase, Leslie Fiedler, Daniel Hoffman, and Philip Wheelwright. Drawing on the findings of anthropology and psychology regarding universal myths, rituals, and folk tales, these critics were intent on restoring spiritual content to a world they saw as alienated, fragmented, and ruled by scientism, empiricism, positivism, and technology. They wished to redeem the role of myth, which might comprehend magic, imagination, dreams, intuition, and the unconscious. They viewed the creation of myth as integral to human thought, and believed that literature emerges out of a core of myth, where "myth" is understood as a collective attempt on the part of various cultures and groups to establish a meaningful context for human existence. Frye's *Anatomy of Criticism* (1957) continued the formalist emphasis of the New Criticism but insisted even more strongly that criticism should be a scientific, objective, and systematic discipline. Moreover, Frye held that such literary criticism views literature itself as a system. For example, the mythoi of Spring, Summer, Autumn, and Winter gave rise to fundamental literary modes such as comedy, tragedy, irony, and romance. Given the recurrence of basic symbolic motifs, literary history is a repetitive and self-contained cycle. Hence the historical element ostensibly informing Frye's formalism is effectively abrogated, literature being viewed as a timeless, static, and autonomous construct.

Frye's static model, exhibiting recurrent patterns, is a feature shared by structuralist views of language and literature. The foundations of structuralism were laid in the work of the Swiss linguist Ferdinand de Saussure, whose insights were developed by the French anthropologist Claude Lévi-Strauss, Roland Barthes, and others. In his *Course in General Linguistics* (1916), Saussure saw language as a system of signs, constructed by convention, which lent itself to synchronic structural analysis. Meaning itself is relational, being produced by interaction of various signifiers and signifieds within that system. In addition to these insights, what Claude Lévi-Strauss and others took from Saussure was an emphasis on linguistic features described as structures; they also stressed the deep structures underlying various phenomena and sometimes referred these structures to basic characteristics of the human mind.

Also entailed in structuralist analyses was the anti-humanist view that, since language is an institution, individual human agency is unprivileged, neither human beings nor social phenomena having essences. Hence, structuralism diverged sharply from the Romantic notion of the author as the source of meaning, and shifts emphasis away from authorial intention toward the broader and impersonal linguistic structure in which the author's text participates, and which indeed enables that text.

Many of these principles underlay the methods of American structuralists. Structuralism was imported into America from France during the 1960s and its leading exponents included Roman Jakobson, Jonathan Culler, Michael Riffaterre, Claudio Guillen, Gerald Prince, and Robert Scholes. Other American thinkers working in the field of semiotics have included C. S. Peirce, Charles Morris, and Noam Chomsky. In his renowned study *Structuralist Poetics* (1975), Jonathan Culler explained that structuralist investigations of literature would seek to identify the systems of conventions underlying literature. Robert Scholes, in *Structuralism in Literature: An Introduction* (1974), sought a scientific basis for the study of literature as an interconnected system of various texts. Other key texts of structuralism in America included a special issue of *Yale French Studies* (1966), and volumes entitled *Structuralism* (1970), edited by Jacques Ehrmann, and *The Structuralist Controversy* (1970), edited by Richard Macksey and Eugenio Donato. Also influential in America was the work of Roman Jakobson, who taught for many years at various American universities and who worked out an influential model of communication as well as a distinction between metaphor and metonymy in the analysis of narratives. The major principles of structuralism can now be examined in more detail in the work of Saussure and Roland Barthes.

Ferdinand de Saussure (1857–1913)

Ferdinand de Saussure was effectively the founder of modern linguistics, as well as of structuralism; and, while much poststructuralism arose in partial reaction against his thought, it nonetheless presupposed his theoretical advances in linguistics. Born into a Swiss family, Saussure taught, in Paris and later at the University of Geneva, a wide range of subjects including Gothic, Old German, Latin, and Persian. It was, however, his lectures in general linguistics, posthumously compiled by his colleagues as *Course in General Linguistics* (1916), that proved to be of seminal influence in a broad range of fields, including anthropology, as in the work of Lévi-Strauss; the semiological work of Roland Barthes; the literary-philosophical notions of Derrida; the analyses of ideology by structuralist Marxists such as Louis Althusser; the psychoanalytic theories of Jacques Lacan; and the analyses of language conducted by feminists such as Julia Kristeva.

Prior to Saussure, the predominant modes of analyzing language were historical and philological. As opposed to a diachronic approach which studies changes in language over a period of time, Saussure undertook a synchronic approach which saw language as a structure that could be studied in its entirety at a given point in time. Saussure pioneered a number of further influential and radical insights. Firstly, he denied that there is somehow a natural connection between words and things, urging that this connection is conventional. This view of language also challenges the view of reality as somehow independent and existing outside of language, reducing language to merely a "name-giving system." Saussure's view implies that we build up an understanding of our world by means of language and view the world *through* language. Secondly, Saussure argued that language is a system of signs in relation: no sign has meaning in isolation; rather, its signification depends on its difference from other signs and generally on its situation within the entire network of signs. Finally, Saussure made a distinction between two dimensions of language: *langue*, which refers to language as a structured system, grounded on certain rules, and *parole*, the specific acts of speech or utterance which are based on those rules.

In his *Course in General Linguistics* Saussure explains that it is *langue*, not the acts of speech, which must be the object of scientific investigation. Indeed, the "science of language" is possible only if many elements of speech are excluded.[7] Understood in this sense, language (as opposed to speech) is "outside of the individual who can never create nor modify it by himself." It exists through an implicit contract between the members of a community, and it must be learned in order for a person to communicate through speech (*CGL*, 14). Saussure points out other differences between language and speech. Whereas speech is homogeneous, language is heterogeneous: "It is a system of signs in which the only essential thing is the union of meanings and sound-images, and in which both parts of the sign are psychological." Moreover, language is no less concrete than speech: language is constituted by linguistic signs which are collectively approved, and these signs "are realities that have their seat in the brain." Finally, unlike speech, language can be classified among human phenomena: it is a social institution, with unique features that distinguish it from other, political and legal, institutions (*CGL*, 15).

Saussure suggests that the study of language should be situated within a larger investigative province, which he names semiology, from the Greek word *semeion* meaning "sign." Semiology, he explains, "would show what constitutes signs, what laws govern them . . . Linguistics is only a part of the general science of semiology; the laws discovered by semiology will be applicable to linguistics" (*CGL*, 16). Saussure proposes that semiology be "recognized as an independent science with its own object like all the other sciences." Language needs to be studied "in itself" (*CGL*, 17).

Saussure's exposition in his *Course* of the "Nature of the Linguistic Sign" is worth considering in some detail since it provides a reference point for much subsequent literary and cultural theory. Especially important is his use of the terms "sign," "signifier," and "signified." He attacks the conventional correspondence theory of meaning whereby language is viewed as a naming process, each word corresponding to the thing it names (*CGL*, 65).

As against this conventional view, Saussure urges that *both* terms of the linguistic sign are psychological in nature; the sign unites not a thing and a name but a *concept* and *sound-image*. The latter is not the material sound but the "psychological imprint of the sound," the impression it makes on our senses; hence it too is psychological (*CGL*, 66). To avoid ambiguity, Saussure suggests a new terminology: *sign* designates the whole construct; *signified* designates the *concept*; and *signifier* designates the *sound-image*. As Saussure states, the linguistic sign in its totality is "a two-sided psychological entity," consisting of both signifier and signified. The sign as a whole refers to the actual object in the world, as displayed in the following diagram:

Signifier (the word or sound-image "table")

                                               Sign > Actual object: table

Signified (the concept of "table")

The sign has two primordial characteristics: firstly, the bond between signifier and signified is *arbitrary*: by this, Saussure means that the concept (e.g., "sister") is not linked by any inner relationship to the succession of sounds which serves as its signifier (in French, s-o-r). Saussure offers another clarification: the bond is not *natural* but unmotivated, based on collective behavior or convention, fixed by rules. Signifiers and gestures do not have any intrinsic value. Saussure is careful to suggest that "arbitrary" does not imply that the choice of the signifier is left entirely to the speaker: the individual has no power to change a sign in any way once it has become established in the linguistic community (*CGL*, 69).

Roland Barthes (1915–1980)

Roland Barthes' theoretical development is often seen as embodying a transition from structuralist to poststructuralist perspectives, though certain of his works are characterized by a Marxian perspective. Barthes effectively extended structural analysis and semiology (the study of signs) to broad cultural phenomena, and it was he also who confronted the limits of structuralism, pointing the way to freer and more relativistic assessments of texts and their role in culture. It was Barthes who made famous the notion of the "death of the author," the idea of the text as a site of free play or pleasure, and differences such as those between "work" and "text," and "writerly" and "readerly" works of art. As such, he anticipates many facets of poststructuralism, including certain elements of deconstruction, cultural studies, and queer studies.

Notwithstanding his suffering from tuberculosis, his homosexuality, and his esoteric and eclectic world view, Barthes was at times affiliated with certain mainstream French institutions, such as the National Center for Scientific Research (CNRS) and the Collège de France. His first works derived inspiration from Saussure, Sartre, and Marxist writers such as Brecht: *Writing Degree Zero* (1953) and *Mythologies* (1957). Then came a number of influential works in the structuralist vein, such as *Elements of Semiology* (1964) and his seminal essay, "Introduction to the Structural Analysis of Narrative" (1966). His renowned essay "The Death of the Author" appeared in 1968. Barthes' multivalent analysis of Balzac's novella *Sarrasine* in his *S/Z* (1970) marks the point of transition between his earlier structuralism and his later poststructuralist dispositions. These dispositions were elaborated in his essay "From Work to Text" (1971) and books such as *The Pleasure of the Text* (1973).

In his book *Mythologies*, Barthes undertook an ideological critique of various products of mass bourgeois culture (ranging from soap to advertising to images of Rome), attempting to account for this mystification of culture or history into a "universal nature."[8] He argued that such mystification is explained by the notion of "myth," and he devotes the second part of his book to a theoretical analysis of myth.

Barthes' most fundamental suggestion is that myth is not an object, a concept, or an idea but a language, a type of speech. It is a mode of signification (*Myth.*, 109). In explaining the nature of myth, Barthes reiterates Saussure's view that semiology is comprised of three (rather than two) terms: the *signifier*, which is an acoustic (mental) image, the *signified*, which is a concept, and the *sign*, which is a word and which consists of the combination of signifier and signified. In other words, the sign is a *relation* (*Myth.*, 113). The structure of myth repeats this tridimensional pattern: myth is a second-order semiological system. An entire sign in the first system becomes a mere signifier (only one component of the sign) in the second system. Barthes cites an example: on the cover of a Parisian magazine, "a young Negro in a French uniform is saluting, with his eyes uplifted," probably gazing at the French flag (*Myth.*, 116). In the first semiological system, that of language, the signifier is the black soldier giving the French salute, and this signifies perhaps a "mixture of Frenchness and militariness." But on the mythological level, the original meaning of the picture and its entire history are left behind: we are no longer concerned with the black soldier, his peculiar biography or location. We are now confronted with a new signification: "that France is a great Empire, that all her sons, without any colour discrimination, faithfully serve under her flag, and that there is no better answer to the detractors of an alleged colonialism than the zeal shown by this Negro in serving his so-called oppressors" (*Myth.*, 116). The new signifier, the new form, then, signifies nothing personal about the black soldier but the ideal of French imperiality in general (*Myth.*, 117).

Other examples of mythical concepts might be democracy, freedom, and American imperiality, signifiers which are often wrenched from their actual history and made to signify concepts such as peace, world order, and security. Hence myth naturalizes these concepts, and this in fact is "the very principle of myth: it transforms history into nature" (*Myth.*, 129). Barthes adds that the function of myth is to "empty reality" and that "*myth is depoliticized speech*" (*Myth.*, 143). Myth establishes a world "without depth," a world of "blissful clarity" where things "appear to mean something by themselves" (*Myth.*, 143). Or, a world where the meaning of things lies no deeper than their isolated existence.

What has been most influential in Barthes' account of myth is his equation of the process of myth-making with the process of bourgeois ideology. After the French Revolution of 1789 which marked the rise to power of the bourgeoisie, this class underwent what Barthes calls an ex-nominating operation: "the bourgeoisie is defined as *the class which does not want to be named*" (*Myth.*, 138). This ex-nominating phenomenon, says Barthes, was effected through the idea of the "nation": the bourgeoisie as a class merges into the concept of "nation," thereby presenting bourgeois values and interests as in the national interest, through such pre-emptive identification. Through this depoliticizing and "universalistic effort" of its vocabulary, the bourgeoisie was able to postulate its own definitions of justice, truth, and law as universal; it was able to postulate its own definition of humanity as comprising "human nature"; and "bourgeois norms are experienced as the evident laws of a natural order" (*Myth.*, 138–140). According to Barthes, there are two basic ways in which myth can be opposed or undermined. The first is to mythify it in its turn so as to produce an artificial myth, highlighting its mythical status, or to use speech in an explicitly political manner (*Myth.*, 135–136, 145–146).

In his classic essay "Introduction to the Structuralist Analysis of Narratives" (1966), Barthes had talked of the "problem" of the subject, insisting on viewing an author or persona as a grammatical function rather than a psychological subject. Barthes' most well-known formulation of this problem occurs in his essay "The Death of the Author" (1968), a phrase which has come to be associated with both Barthes and structuralism, just as the phrase "God is dead" had been attributed to Nietzsche (though in fact it had first occurred in Hegel's *Phenomenology*). Barthes' argument is that as soon as narration occurs without the practical purpose of acting on reality, as soon as narrative occurs as an end in itself, "this disconnection occurs, the voice loses its origin, the author enters into his own death, writing begins."[9] The modern, individual author, says Barthes, was "a product of our society insofar as, emerging from the Middle Ages with English empiricism, French rationalism and the personal faith of the Reformation, it discovered the prestige of the individual . . . It is thus logical that in literature it should be this positivism, the epitome and culmination of capitalist ideology, which has greatest importance to the 'person' of the author." Even in the present, says Barthes, our studies of literature and literary history are "tyrannically centred on the author" (*IMT*, 143).

Recently, as Barthes observes, many writers, such as Mallarmé, Valéry, and Proust, have challenged this centrality of the author. Linguistics, moreover, has shown that enunciation "is an empty process . . . the author is never more than the instance writing . . . language knows a 'subject', not a 'person', and this subject [is] empty outside of the very enunciation which defines it" (*IMT*, 145). This removal of the author, explains Barthes, transforms the modern text: previously, the author was conceived as the past of his own book, the pre-existing cause and explanation. In contrast, "the modern scriptor is born simultaneously with the text . . . there is no other time than that of the enunciation and every text is eternally written *here* and *now*." Hence we can no longer think of writing in the classical ways, as recording, representing, or depicting. Rather, it is a "performative" act (*IMT*, 145–146).

What is more, a text can no longer be viewed as releasing in a linear fashion a single "theological" meaning, as the message of the "Author-God." Rather, it is "a multi-dimensional space in which a variety of writings, none of them original, blend and clash. The text is a tissue of quotations drawn from the innumerable centres of culture" (*IMT*, 146). The writer has only the power to mix writings. Hence Literature, by refusing to assign an "ultimate meaning . . . to the text (and to the world as text)," facilitates an "anti-theological" activity which is revolutionary since "to refuse to fix meaning is, in the end, to refuse God and his hypostases – reason, science, law" (*IMT*, 147).

A text's unity, says Barthes, "lies not in its origin but in its destination," in the reader. Yet Barthes cautions that the humanism we have rejected via removal of the author should not be reintroduced through any conception of the reader as a personal and complete entity. The reader of which Barthes speaks is a reader "without history, biography, psychology; he is simply that *someone* who holds together in a single field all the traces by which the written text is constituted." In other words, the reader, like the author, is a function of the text. In this sense "the birth of the reader must be at the cost of the death of the Author" (*IMT*, 148).

In a subsequent essay, "From Work to Text" (1971), Barthes provides a succinct statement of a poststructuralist perspective. Barthes notes that in recent decades conceptions of language and literature, influenced by developments in linguistics, anthropology, Marxism, and psychoanalysis, have been marked by an increasing tendency toward interdisciplinarity. The object of linguistic and literary studies accordingly has been changed: it is no longer the stable, fixed object enclosed within one discipline but an object that is fluid, has many levels of meaning, and ranges across disciplinary boundaries. The former is the "work" and the latter is the "text."

Whereas a work offers up to analysis a closed signified or definite meaning, a text can never allow investigation to halt at some signified, some concept which represents the ultimate meaning of a work. Like language, the text "is structured but off-centred, without closure" (*IMT*, 159).

Barthes states an important feature of poststructuralist analysis when he says that the text is held in "intertextuality," in a network of signifiers (*IMT*, 160–161). And, whereas the work is consumed more or less passively, the text makes the process of reading active, productive, and constitutive. It asks of the reader a "practical collaboration" in the production of the work (*IMT*, 162–163). The implication here is that the text invites participation in its own play, its subversion of hierarchies, and its endless deferment of the definite (*IMT*, 164).

Notes

1   In *Husserl: Shorter Works*, ed. Peter McCormick and Frederick A. Elliston (Notre Dame, IN: University of Notre Dame Press, 1981). Hereafter cited as "PP." Numbers refer to paragraphs.

2   Edmund Husserl, *Phenomenology and the Crisis of Philosophy*, trans. Quentin Lauer (New York: Harper and Row, 1965), p. 155. Hereafter cited as *PCP*.

3   Martin Heidegger, *Being and Time*, trans. John Macquarrie and Edward Robinson (New York: Harper and Row, 1962), pp. 19, 21–23. Hereafter cited as *BT*. Given the necessarily brief nature of my account, I have referred the reader to passages that provide useful summaries or definitions of important terms.

4   "The Origin of the Work of Art," in Martin Heidegger, *Poetry, Language, Thought*, trans. Albert Hofstadter (New York and London: Harper and Row, 1975), p. 78. Hereafter cited as *PLT*.

5   "Hölderlin and the Essence of Poetry," trans. Douglass Scott, in Martin Heidegger, *Existence and Being*, ed. Werner Brock (Indiana: Gateway, 1949), p. 270. Hereafter cited as *EB*.

6   Quoted in introd., Georges Bataille, *Visions of Excess: Selected Writings 1927–1939*, ed. Allan Stoekl (Minneapolis: University of Minnesota Press, 1985), pp. x–xi. Hereafter cited as *VE*.

7   Ferdinand de Saussure, *Course in General Linguistics*, ed. Charles Bally, Albert Sechehaye, and Albert Reidlinger, trans. Wade Baskin (New York: Philosophical Library, 1959), p. 15. Hereafter cited as *CGL*.

8   Roland Barthes, *Mythologies*, trans. Annette Lavers (London: Collins, 1973), p. 9. Hereafter cited as *Myth*.

9   Roland Barthes, *Image: Music: Text*, trans. Stephen Heath (Glasgow: Fontana, 1982), p. 142. Hereafter cited as *IMT*.

Chapter 4

The Era of Poststructuralism (I): Later Marxism, Psychoanalysis, Deconstruction

The broad term "poststructuralism" denotes a range of critical approaches emerging after the 1960s which took from structuralism its insights into language as a system of signs, and the construction of identity, subjects, and objects through language. It rejected, however, the centrality of structure, the use of binary oppositions, and structuralism's ahistorical approach, emphasizing instead the indeterminate and polysemic nature of semiotic codes and the arbitrary and constructed nature of the foundations of knowledge. These subsequent movements, born in a politically more volatile climate, laid greater emphasis on the operations of ideology and power in the construction of human subjectivity, which they described in gendered, racial, and economic terms. While Marxism itself cannot be classified as poststructuralist, Marxist thinking in this era interacted richly with other approaches and itself registered the impact of certain poststructuralist insights.

It was, ironically, the period of relative economic prosperity after the Second World War that eventually gave impetus to the Civil Rights movements and the women's movement. The revolutionary fervor of the 1960s gave Marxist criticism a revived impetus. A group of Marxist critics was centered around the *New Left Review*, founded in 1960 and edited first by Stuart Hall and then by Perry Anderson. Its contributors included E. P. Thompson, Raymond Williams, and Terry Eagleton. This was also the period in which the radical journal *Tel Quel*, established in 1960 in France, fostered an intellectual milieu in which the writings of Derrida, the founder of deconstruction, Lacan, who reinterpreted Freudian concepts in linguistic terms, and several major feminist thinkers such as Julia Kristeva were fomented, eventually displacing the prominence of French existentialism.

77

Drawing on the insights of Bachelard, Barthes, and others, *Tel Quel* moved from an initial aesthetic emphasis toward activism. Its general aim was to draw on literary texts and new critical approaches to redeem the revolutionary power of language. Significantly, many of the thinkers associated with the journal challenged the categories and binary oppositions which had acted as the foundation of much Western thought since Plato and Aristotle, oppositions which represented political and social hierarchies. Lacan's understanding of the unconscious as linguistic was seen by some as having revolutionary implications, though some feminists, notably Luce Irigaray and Hélène Cixous, indicted both Freud and Lacan's own discourse, which they saw as privileging the male and even as misogynistic. Feminists such as Monique Wittig and Julia Kristeva reflected on the possibility of an *écriture féminine*.

These movements drew on the previous challenges to binary oppositions and on the "textual" nature of all phenomena, viewing even history and economics as interpretive narratives. Marxist critics in this era, notably Terry Eagleton and Fredric Jameson, have been obliged to define the connections and divergences between their own stances and the various other branches of criticism; they have drawn on the analyses of Althusser as well as Adorno, Horkheimer, and Benjamin in attempting to account for various phenomena of a mass consumer society and the spectrum of ideas falling under the labels of poststructuralism and postmodernism. Writers such as Gilles Deleuze and Félix Guattari and Jean Baudrillard have variously offered powerful analyses of capitalist society in terms of psychological categories and drives, as well as of the symbolic processes that structure consciousness, and the lack of foundations for arriving at intellectual or moral judgment. More recent thinkers such as Clément Rosset, Jacques Bouveresse, and Richard Rorty have turned away from the tenets of poststructuralism, such as its reductive view of reality as ultimately linguistic. Rorty attempts to impugn the very notion of a perspective rooted in fixed foundations. Feminists such as Nancy Chodorow and Jessica Benjamin have reacted against the predominant Freudian-Lacanian accounts of sexuality, seeking instead to trace the formation of gender to the infant's pre-Oedipal connections with the mother. Vincent Descombes has returned to the principles of early twentieth-century analytical philosophers such as Wittgenstein, and whereas many poststructuralists drew heavily on Hegelian notions, thinkers such as Jean-François Lyotard have turned instead to Kant. Lyotard has theorized influentially about the "postmodern condition," seeing it as marked by an absence of totalizing schemes of explanation, and the dissolution of human subjectivity.

Most of the literary critical tendencies cited above saw themselves as "oppositional," as undermining and challenging the prevailing power structures and ideologies of late capitalism and, in some cases, of Communism. In philosophy, this tradition of "heterological" thought can be traced back to Schopenhauer's critique of Enlightenment philosophy and of a totalizing Hegelian vision, a critique that has continued through Nietzsche, Freud, Bergson, Wittgenstein, Saussure, Heidegger, and Sartre to modern literary and cultural theory. An important influence on many of these oppositional thinkers was the thought of Friedrich Nietzsche (1844–1900), who occupies a prominent place in the spectrum of resistance to mainstream Western thought as embodied in Platonic philosophy, Christianity, and the bourgeois Enlightenment. Influenced by the German philosopher Arthur Schopenhauer (1788–1860) who, as mentioned, reacted archetypally against the systematizing and historicizing philosophy of Hegel, Nietzsche's own thought refuses to present itself in the mold of any system; it challenges the authority of reason and conventional morality, both Christian and utilitarian; it stresses the Dionysian side of human nature, fueled by unconscious impulses and excess, as a counter to the Apollonian side, which is conscious, rational, and individuated; it suggests that what we call reality, truth, the world, are constructions, projections of human needs and interests, through the medium of human senses, human faculties, and human language; and it undermines modern liberal political visions of democracy. Effectively, it challenges the fundamental assumptions of Western philosophy at epistemological, moral, political, and spiritual levels. For these reasons, as well as for his style – poetic, ironic, discontinuous, intimate – Nietzsche has exerted an enormous influence on modernism, existentialism, the Frankfurt School of Marxism, the philosophy of science, and various branches of poststructuralism, such as those associated with Derrida and Foucault.

Later Marxist Criticism

From the 1960s, Marxist critics continued to reinterpret and develop the insights of Marx and Engels. Louis Althusser, Lucien Goldmann, and Pierre Macherey turned away from Hegel and were heavily influenced by the structuralist movements of the earlier twentieth century, which stressed the role of larger signifying systems and institutional structures over individual agency and intention. Louis Althusser emphasized the later Marx's "epistemological break" from his own earlier humanism, and Marx's scientificity and his departure from, rather than his debt to, Hegel. Althusser's structuralist Marxism – as stated in his *Pour Marx* (*For Marx*, 1965) and his often-cited "Ideology and Ideological State Apparatuses," rejected earlier humanist and historicist readings of Marx, as well as literary critical emphases on authorial intention and subjective agency. Goldmann rejected the Romantic-humanist notion of individual creativity and held that texts are productions of larger mental structures representing the mentality of particular social classes. He stressed the operation of larger forces and doctrines in literary texts, and developed the notion of "homology" to register the parallels between artistic and social forms. Pierre Macherey's

A Theory of Literary Production (1966) saw the literary text as the product of the artist's reworking of linguistic and ideological raw material, unwittingly exposing, through its lacunae and contradictions, ideological elements which the author had attempted to suppress into a false coherence. In this way, a critique of ideology could emerge through the literary text.

In the Anglo-American world a "cultural materialist" criticism was first revived by Raymond Williams (1921–1988), notably in *Culture and Society 1780–1950*, which analyzes the cultural critique of capitalism in English literary tradition. Williams rejected a simplistic explanation of culture as the efflux of material conditions, but stressed the contribution of cultural forms to economic and political development. *The Long Revolution* (1961) continued and refined this project using categories such as dominant, residual, and emergent cultures mediated by what Williams called "structures of feeling." Williams' work became overtly Marxist with the publication in 1977 of *Marxism and Literature*. In this work Williams undertook a critical review of earlier Marxist theories and offered his own analyses of fundamental Marxist notions such as ideology, hegemony, base, and superstructure. His own cultural materialism as set forth here attempts to integrate Marxist conceptions of language and literature. *Keywords* (1976) examines the history of fundamental concepts and categories. In general, Williams' work analyzed the history of language, the role of the media, mass communications, and the cultural connections between the country and the city. Another dimension of Williams' work will be considered under the rubric of cultural studies (see chapter 7).

The major American Marxist critic Fredric Jameson (b. 1934) outlined a dialectical theory of literary criticism in his *Marxism and Form* (1971), drawing on Hegelian categories such as the notion of totality and the connection of abstract and concrete. Such criticism recognizes the need to see its objects of analysis within a broad historical context, acknowledges its own history and perspective, and seeks the profound inner form of a literary text. Jameson's *The Political Unconscious* (1981) attempts to integrate this dialectical thinking with insights from structuralism and Freud, using the Freudian notion of repression to analyze the function of ideology, the status of literary texts, and the epistemological function of literary form. In subsequent work such as *Postmodernism, or the Cultural Logic of Late Capitalism* (1991), Jameson performed the valuable task of extending Marx's insights into the central role of postmodernism in determining the very form of our artistic and intellectual experience.

Terry Eagleton (b. 1943)

In Britain, the most prominent Marxist critic has been Terry Eagleton, who has outlined the categories of a Marxist analysis of literature, and has persistently rearticulated the terms of communication, as well as the differences, between Marxism and much of modern literary theory. Eagleton has insisted that there are at least two fundamental premises in Marx from which any Marxist criticism must begin. In the first place all forms of consciousness – religious, moral, philosophical, legal, as well as language itself – have no independent history and arise from the material activity of men. Eagleton identifies a twofold specificity of Marxist criticism: material production is regarded as the ultimate determining factor of social existence, and class struggle is viewed as the central dynamic of historical development. Eagleton adds a third, Marxist-Leninist, imperative, namely a commitment to the theory and practice of political revolution.[1] Eagleton is aware of the highly mediated and complex relation between base and superstructure,[2] but his aptly Marxist insistence on the primacy of material production can be seen to be the basis of virtually all his attacks on non-Marxist literary theory.

In defining ideology, Marx had affirmed that the class which is the ruling material force is also the ruling intellectual force: it owns the means of production both materially and mentally. In the light of this we can better understand Eagleton's statement of the tasks of a "revolutionary literary criticism." Such a criticism would

> dismantle the ruling concepts of "literature," reinserting "literary" texts into the whole field of cultural practices. It would strive to relate such "cultural" practices to other forms of social activity, and to transform the cultural apparatuses themselves. It would articulate its "cultural" analyses with a consistent political intervention. It would deconstruct the received hierarchies of "literature" and transvaluate received judgments and assumptions; engage with the language and "unconscious" of literary texts, to reveal their role in the ideological construction of the subject; and mobilize such texts . . . in a struggle to transform those subjects within a wider political context.[3]

But all of this subserves the "primary task" of Marxist criticism, which is "to actively participate in and help direct the cultural emancipation of the masses" (WB, 97). Eagleton repeatedly stresses that the starting point of theory must be a practical, political purpose and that any theory which will contribute to human emancipation through the socialist transformation of society is acceptable.[4] He effectively develops Marx's insight above when he emphasizes that the "means of production" includes the means of production of human subjectivity, which embraces a range of institutions such as "literature." Eagleton regards the most difficult emancipation as that of the "space of subjectivity," colonized as it is by the dominant political order. The humanities as a whole serve an ideological function that helps to perpetuate certain forms of subjectivity. Eagleton's views here imply that for Marxist criticism, "ideology" is a crucial focus of the link between material and mental means of production.

Eagleton affirms that, unlike the case of deconstruction, the "negation" entailed by Marxist criticism must have an affirmative material basis. There is an internal, not merely epiphenomenal, connection between practical goal and theoretical method. Hence the similarities between Marxism and "negative" non-Marxist theories are purely superstructural: which is itself an impossible contradiction since no Marxist insight can be "purely" superstructural. Whatever "threat" a radical theory such as structuralism may pose to received ideology is thwarted by its complicity. As Eagleton shrewdly observes, the reactionary nature of structuralism lies in the very concept of "structure" (*LT*, 141), in the very positing of this received ideological notion as a basis of enquiry. It is only at this expense that structuralism dismantles the ruling ideologies of subjectivity. The general point here is that whatever non-Marxist theory postulates as a base or infrastructure of investigation is in fact an aspect of superstructure. Inasmuch as these theories fail to articulate their connections with the material infrastructure, they lapse into an effective, if sometimes undesired, complicity with ruling ideologies.

This is why Eagleton views non-Marxist theories as both subversive and complicit with capitalism, a contradiction inherent in their superstructural status. He arraigns, for example, structuralism's static ahistorical view of society, as well as its reduction of labor, sexuality, and politics to "language." Structuralism, moreover, ignores both literature and language as forms of social practice and production. Its anti-humanism brackets the human subject, thereby abolishing the subject's potential as a political agent. These factors, Eagleton observes, contributed to a certain integration of structuralism into the orthodox academy (*LT*, 110–115). Similarly, in Eagleton's eyes, the insights of psychoanalysis are not necessarily politically radical. For example, he asserts that the political correlative of Julia Kristeva's theories, which disrupt all fixed structures, is anarchism. And her dismantling of the unified subject is not in itself revolutionary (*LT*, 189–193).

Eagleton acknowledges the radical potential of deconstruction. But he is also aware that this potential is already contained in the dialectical character of Marxism. What is original to Derrida and his followers is their remorseless insistence on "difference" as a basis of impugnment of literary and philosophical texts. Eagleton says of the "negative": "only a powerless petty-bourgeois intelligentsia would raise it to the solemn dignity of a philosophy" (*WB*, 142). The bases of Derrida's insights are already contained, according to Eagleton, in the context of a far vaster historically self-conscious vision, in the writings of Hegel and Marx. In fact, Eagleton's latest work, *After Theory*, suggests that we need to return in some respects to a "plain realism." He cautions that "If cultural theory is to engage with an ambitious global history, it must have answerable resources of its own, equal in depth and scope to the situation it confronts. It cannot afford simply to keep on recounting the same narratives of class, race and gender, indispensable as these topics are."[5]

Psychoanalysis: Freud and Lacan

Like Marxist criticism, psychoanalysis has its roots in the nineteenth century, and has interacted richly with many streams of poststructuralist thought. The psychology of literature is hardly a new concern: ever since Aristotle, critics, rhetoricians, and philosophers have examined the psychological dimensions of literature, ranging from an author's motivation and intentions to the effect of texts and performances on an audience. The application of psychoanalytic principles to the study of literature, however, is a relatively recent phenomenon, initiated primarily by Freud and, in other directions, by Alfred Adler and Carl Jung. The notion of the "unconscious" was not in itself new, and it can be found in many thinkers prior to Freud, notably in some of the Romantics such as Schlegel, in Schopenhauer, and in Nietzsche. Freud's fundamental contribution was to open up the entire realm of the unconscious to systematic study, and to provide a language and terminology in which the operations of the unconscious could be expressed. The positing of an unconscious as the ultimate source and explanation of human thought and behavior represented a radical disruption of the main streams of Western thought which, since Aristotle, had held that man was essentially a rational being, capable of making free choices in the spheres of intellection and morality. To say that the unconscious governs our behavior is to problematize all of the notions on which philosophy, theology, and even literary criticism have conventionally rested: the ideal of self-knowledge, the ability to know others, the capacity to make moral judgments, the belief that we can act according to reason, that we can overcome our passions and instincts, the ideas of moral and political agency, intentionality, and the notion – held for centuries – that literary creation can be a rational process. In a sense, Freud postulated that we bear a form of "otherness" within ourselves: we cannot claim fully to comprehend even ourselves, why we act as we do, why we make certain moral and political decisions, why we harbor given religious dispositions and intellectual orientations. Even when we think we are acting from a given motive, we may be deluding ourselves; and much of our thought and action are not freely determined by us but driven by unconscious forces which we can barely fathom. Moreover, far from being based on reason, our thinking is intimately dependent upon the body, upon its instincts of survival and aggression, as well as obstinate features that cannot be dismissed (as in the Cartesian tradition where the mind is treated as a disembodied phenomenon) such as its size, color, gender, and social situation. The fact that I am a black working-class female will determine my world view just as much, and perhaps far more, than anything I consciously learn in the realm of ideas.

Clearly, this general problematization of conventional notions extends to literature: if the unconscious is a founding factor of our psyche, we can no longer talk unequivocally of an author's intention, or take for granted, as Aristotle did, that a drama structured according to certain rules will produce a precise effect upon its audience. We cannot assume that we are fully in control of what we say or that readers are fully in control of their responses. We cannot presume that our intended meanings will be conveyed, or that our conscious purposes represent our true aims. Neither can we presume that language is a transparent medium of communication, of either thought or emotion.

Freud was aware of the problematic nature of language itself, its opaqueness and materiality, its resistance to clarity and its refusal to be reduced to any one-dimensional "literal" meaning. His own writings contain many literary allusions, and some of his major concepts, such as the Oedipus complex, were founded on literary models such as *Oedipus Rex* and *Hamlet*. Freud's own literary analyses tend to apply his models of dream interpretation to literary texts, viewing the latter as expressions of wish fulfillment and gratifying projections of the ego of an author. Subsequent psychologists and literary critics, developing Freud's ideas, have extended the field of psychoanalytic criticism to encompass: analysis of the motives of an author, of readers, and fictional characters, relating a text to features of the author's biography such as childhood memories, relationship to parents; the nature of the creative process; the psychology of reader's responses to literary texts; interpretation of symbols in a text, to unearth latent meanings; analysis of the connections between various authors in a literary tradition; examination of gender roles and stereotypes; and the functioning of language in the constitution of the conscious and unconscious. What underlies nearly all of these endeavors is the perception of a broad analogy, fostered by Freud himself, between the psychoanalytic process and the production of a narrative. In a sense, the psychoanalyst himself creates a fiction: triggered by a patient's neurosis and recollection of traumatic events, the psychoanalyst creates a coherent narrative about the patient within which the traumatic event can take its place and be understood.

After Freud, psychoanalytic criticism was continued by his biographer Ernest Jones (1879–1958), whose book *Hamlet and Oedipus* (1948) interpreted Hamlet's indecisive behavior in killing his uncle in terms of his ambivalent feelings toward his mother. Another of Freud's disciples, Otto Rank (1884–1939), produced *The Myth of the Birth of the Hero* (1909), which reaffirmed Freud's notions of the artist producing fantasies of wish fulfillment, and which compiled numerous myths on subjects such as incest and on the notion of the hero. Ella Freeman Sharpe (1875–1947) treated language and metaphor from a psychoanalytic perspective. Marie Bonaparte (1882–1962) wrote a large study of Edgar Allen Poe, attributing much of his creative disposition to the loss of his mother when he was a child. Melanie Klein (1882–1960) modified Freudian theory of sexuality, rejecting the primacy of the Oedipus complex and elaborating a theory of the drive.

Another generation of literary critics – not necessarily Freudians – drew upon psychoanalysis in their interpretations of literary texts. These included I. A. Richards, William Empson, Lionel Trilling, Kenneth Burke, and Edmund Wilson, who in various ways searched texts for latent content. Harold Bloom's theory of literary influence as mediated through "anxiety" drew upon Freud's account of the Oedipus complex. Poets and critics such as Robert Graves and W. H. Auden (who wrote a poem in memory of Freud) also had recourse to Freudian concepts in their prose writings. Indeed, the influence of Freud's ideas was so pervasive that it can be seen in the very conception of character in many modern novelists, such as William Faulkner and James Joyce. Interestingly, D. H. Lawrence appears to have arrived independently at ideas very similar to Freud's, as for example in his novel *Sons and Lovers*, where Oedipal feelings figure powerfully.

The influence of psychoanalysis has extended into nearly all dimensions of modern literary theory. Simon O. Lesser (1909–1979) furnished a psychoanalytic account of the reading process. Influenced by Lesser, Norman Holland (b. 1927) used ego psychology and the notion of the literary text as fantasy to elaborate his version of reader-response criticism, studying the manner in which texts appeal to the repressed fantasies of readers. Feminist critics such as Juliet Mitchell have used Freud's ideas in their explanations of the operations of patriarchy; others, such as Julia Kristeva, have modified his notions in undertaking their analyses of language and gender. Members of the Frankfurt School of Marxist thinkers, such as Herbert Marcuse, have enlisted Freudian concepts in their analyses of mass culture and ideology. Other significant theorists include Norman O. Brown (b. 1913), D. W. Winnicott, and Gilles Deleuze and Félix Guattari, who have explored the ideological bases of psychoanalysis; and Jacques Lacan, whose ideas will be examined later in this chapter. The following account of Freud's own literary analyses places them in the context of his theories as a whole.

Sigmund Freud (1856–1939)

Sigmund Freud was born to Jewish parents in Moravia, a small town in what is now the Czech Republic.[6] His father was somewhat aloof and authoritarian while his mother was a warmer and more accessible figure. When Freud was 4 years old, his family moved to Vienna where he received all of his education. When he first began his medical studies at the University of Vienna in 1873, Freud found himself somewhat excluded from the academic community and looked down upon, on account of his Jewish origins. He saw this period, where he was forced into the role of outsider, as furnishing the foundation for his independence of thought. We can briefly look at some of the important themes in Freud's work. Among these are repression, whereby thoughts and impulses which are viewed as alarming, painful, or shameful are expunged or repressed from the conscious memory. Freud also pioneered the notion of infantile sexuality: contravening conventional notions of childhood innocence, he viewed normal adult sexual life as the result of a long and complicated development of the sexual function in an individual since infancy.

Perhaps the most important of Freud's notions was the Oedipus complex: after the first stage of auto-eroticism, the first love-object for both sexes is the mother, who is not yet perceived as distinct from the child's own body. As infancy progresses, sexual development undergoes the Oedipus complex: the boy focuses his sexual wishes upon his mother and develops hostile impulses toward his father. At this stage, Freud thought that girls underwent an analogous development but his views on this changed drastically. Again in the face of established beliefs, Freud saw the constitution of the human being as "innately bisexual." Only later was sexuality differentiated in terms of gender, children being initially unclear as to the differences between the sexes. Under the threat of castration, the male child represses his desire for the mother and accepts the rules laid down by the father. Freud's continuing observations led him to believe that the Oedipus complex was the nucleus of the neuroses. It was both the climax of infantile sexual life and the foundation for all of the later developments of sexuality. This in turn brought Freud to believe that neurotics failed to overcome difficulties that were resolved by normal people.

Freud effectively extended the meaning of sexuality to encompass not merely genital satisfaction but a broader bodily function, having pleasure as its goal and only subsequently serving a reproductive function. Secondly, sexuality now encompassed all of the emotions of affection and friendliness traditionally subsumed under the word "love" (*Freud*, 23). This extension of the realm of sexuality, Freud thought, would allow for a greater understanding, rather than merely dismissal or moral condemnation of, the sexuality of children and perverts, which had hitherto been neglected. Homosexuality, in particular, was hardly a perversion; rather, it could be traced back to the constitutional bisexuality of *all* human beings. Indeed, sexuality is restricted in Western civilization, where object-choice is narrowed to allow only the opposite sex and where there is basically one standard of sexual life for all (*Freud*, 746).

Also central to Freud's work is his interpretation of dreams, claiming that psychoanalysis could offer a scientific analysis. From the associations produced by the dreamer, the analyst could infer a thought-structure, composed of *latent dream-thoughts*. These were expressed not directly but only as translated and distorted into the *manifest* dream, which was composed largely of visual images. In his study *The Interpretation of Dreams* (1900), Freud argued that the latent dream-thoughts are obliged to undergo alteration, a process Freud called *dream-distortion*, so that the forbidden meaning of the dream is unrecognizable. Freud defined a dream as the disguised fulfillment of a repressed wish (*Freud*, 28). The *dream-work*, or process by which the latent thoughts are converted into the manifest or explicit content of the dream, occurs through a number of functions: *condensation* of the component parts of the preconscious material of the dream; *displacement* of the psychical emphasis of the dream; and *dramatization* of the entire dream by translation into visual images.

Freud and Culture

Around 1907 Freud's interests in the implications of psychoanalysis began to extend over the entire domain of culture. He sought to apply psychoanalytic principles to the study of art, religion, and primitive cultures. In his studies of religion, Freud viewed obsessional neurosis as a distorted private religion and religion itself as a universal obsessional neurosis. In studies such as *Totem and Taboo* (1912–1913), Freud explored taboos or prohibitions in primitive cultures, and analogized the various postulates of primitive beliefs with neurosis. In works such as *Civilization and its Discontents* (1930), Freud suggested the extension of the analysis of neurosis in individuals to the examination of the imaginative and cultural creations of social groups and peoples. Some of Freud's disciples, such as Ernest Jones and Otto Rank, followed through the implications of psychoanalytic theory in the realms of literary analysis, mythology, and symbolism. All in all, Freud hoped that psychoanalysis, while yet underdeveloped, might offer valuable contributions in the most varied regions of knowledge.

Freud's Literary Analyses

Even in his earlier work, Freud had appealed to literary texts – notably *Oedipus Rex* and *Hamlet* – not only to exemplify and illuminate, but even to ground some of his theoretical notions. He saw Sophocles' play *Oedipus Rex* as expressing a "universal law of mental life," and interpreted fate in that play as the materialization of an "internal necessity." He also saw the Oedipus complex as governing the tragedy of *Hamlet*, though he later altered his views on this play. As for poetic and artistic creation in general, Freud wrote a paper, "Creative Writers and Daydreaming" (1907), which viewed works of art as the imaginary satisfactions of unconscious wishes, just as dreams were. What the psychoanalyst can do is to piece together the various elements of an artist's life and his works, and to construct from these the artist's mental constitution and his instinctual impulses. Freud conducted such an analysis of Leonardo da Vinci's picture of "The Madonna and Child with St. Anne" (1910). His lengthy examination of Leonardo da Vinci's character generated a prototype for psychoanalytic biography. In 1914 he published (anonymously) an acute reading of the "meaning" of

Michelangelo's statue of Moses in Rome. Notwithstanding his own readings of literary and artistic texts, Freud never claimed that psychoanalysis could adequately explain the process of artistic creation. In his paper "Dostoevsky and Parricide" (1928), he stated: "Before the problem of the creative artist analysis must, alas, lay down its arms."[7]

We can obtain a sense of Freud's psychoanalytic "literary critical" procedure by looking at his paper "Creative Writers and Day-Dreaming." Freud suggests that, like the child who fantasizes, the creative writer also engages in a kind of play: "He creates a world of phantasy which he takes very seriously – that is, which he invests with large amounts of emotion – while separating it sharply from reality" (Freud, 437). Freud here opens up certain pathways of literary critical analysis. He observes that popular stories typically have "a hero who is the centre of interest," a hero whom the writer appears to "place under the protection of a special Providence." No matter what dangers and adventures he undergoes, he is invulnerable: knowing that he will eventually survive allows the reader to follow his journey with a feeling of security, which Freud describes as "the true heroic feeling." Through "this revealing characteristic of invulnerability," says Freud, "we can immediately recognize His Majesty the Ego, the hero alike of every day-dream and of every story" (Freud, 441). Freud's point here is that the fiction is not a "portrayal of reality" but has all the constituents of a phantasy or day dream: the hero is invulnerable, women invariably fall in love with him, and the other characters in the story are "sharply divided into good and bad" in a manner that contravenes the more subtle variations found in real life (Freud, 441). Hence the story expresses a phantasy on the part of the creative writer, who can indulge in this parading and projection of his ego.

Freud points out that his emphasis on a writer's childhood memories derives from his assumption that a creative work is "a continuation of, and a substitute for, what was once the play of childhood" (Freud, 442). It might be remarked that while Freud's notion of "play" is not quite the same as the concept of "play" or "free play" in the work of Barthes, Lacan, Derrida, Kristeva, and others, there are perhaps continuities between all of these uses, which might usefully be pursued. For example, Freud's understanding of play implies a self-created world of language, a language that reconfigures the conventional idioms that are held to express reality; it also lays stress on the writer's highly subjective entry into the system of language, an entry marked by psychological make-up as well as by social and political circumstances; it implies, like much of Bakhtin's thought, that language is appropriated by the artist for her own ends; it implies a kind of "return" to a Lacanian imaginary realm of infantile security and satisfying wholeness, a realm where everything is ordered just as we might wish it; and that, whatever the author's explicit aims or intentions, there is an underlying subtext, working unconsciously, whose motivations may be different.

In this brief paper, Freud opens up a number of literary critical avenues: the linking of a creative work to an in-depth study of an author's psychology, using a vastly altered conception of human subjectivity; the tracing in art of primal psychological tendencies and conflicts; and the understanding of art and literature as integrally related to deeper, unconscious, impulses that lie hidden in recurring human obsessions, fears, and anxieties. Such paths will be further explored by Carl Jung, Northrop Frye, Lacan, and others.

Freud on History and Civilization

In later works such as *Civilization and its Discontents*, Freud dealt with social and religious phenomena as expressed in collective, as well as individual, psychology. He situates the human psyche within the fabric of social institutions: what we call civilization is to some extent the cumulative product of our psychology, its intrinsic character and the ways in which it reacts upon its environments; civilization is also in some ways analogous to the human psyche, exhibiting a collective psychology that develops according to similar rules. It is in this text that Freud situates the production and enjoyment of creative art and other forms of sublimation within the contexts of broader questions such as the purpose of human life, the pursuit of happiness, and the functions of culture and religion.

Here, as in his earlier essay about creative writers, Freud sees the entire realm of art as arising from a psychical constitution on the part of human beings that allows them a channel of escape or release from the harsh demands of reality; in this view, art is of the same order as phantasy, issuing from the demands of wish-fulfillment, and by its very nature opposed to reality. Freud's brief comments on beauty are in the same vein: when we adopt an "aesthetic attitude to the goal of life," we seek happiness predominantly in the enjoyment of beauty, even though beauty "has no obvious uses" and even though there is no "clear cultural necessity" for it (*Freud*, 733).

Freud's argument concerning art is fundamental: the human psyche, frustrated in its attempts to mold the world in a self-comforting image, resorts to art to create its world in phantasy. Art – in a broad sense that includes science, philosophy, and religion – is the highest form of such an impulse, and is the embodiment of civilization itself, whose foundations are erected on the graveyard of repressed instincts. Indeed, Freud views religion as one of the schemes of human thought that regard "reality as the sole enemy," and encourage a turning away from the world, as is embodied in the delusive behavior of hermits or madmen. The "religions of mankind," exclaims Freud, "must be classed among the mass-delusions of this kind" (*Freud*, 732). By arresting people in a state of "psychical infantilism . . . religion succeeds in sparing many people an individual neurosis. But hardly anything more" (*Freud*, 734–735).

Civilization checks both aggression and sexuality by fostering their internalization into the superego. The resulting tension between the superego and the ego is characterized by Freud as the sense of guilt (*Freud*, 759). The place of the father or of both parents, says Freud, is taken by the larger human community (*Freud*, 756–757). Freud states that aggressiveness "is an original, self-subsisting instinctual disposition in man," which "constitutes the greatest impediment to civilization." Since civilization develops by restricting sexuality and aggression, the evolution of culture is a struggle between *eros* and *thanatos* (*Freud*, 755–756). The sense of guilt, he says, arises from precisely this primordial ambivalence, and is the expression of this "eternal struggle" (*Freud*, 763). What is interesting is Freud's statement that the demands of an individual's superego will "coincide with the precepts of the prevailing cultural super-ego" (*Freud*, 769). This is an implicit acknowledgment that the content of the superego is not somehow patterned on some primal or timeless myth but that it is profoundly and locally rooted in an individual's ethical environment. Like Schopenhauer and Nietzsche, Freud has no illusions about where our ideas ultimately derive from: "man's judgments of value follow directly his wishes for happiness – that, accordingly, they are an attempt to support his illusions with arguments" (*Freud*, 771). In general, "civilization is built up upon a renunciation of instinct" (*Freud*, 742).

Clearly, Freud challenges many of the central impulses of Enlightenment thought: the (Cartesian) view of the human self as an independent unit; the view – extending through many Enlightenment thinkers into the work of Kant – of the ego as autonomous and rational agent; the idea (culminating in the philosophy of Hegel) of human progress in history; the notion that the external world and nature can be subjugated both intellectually and materially; and, perhaps above all, the view deriving from Plato and Aristotle and reaching into the later nineteenth century, that human beings can understand themselves. But neither is Freud part of the Romantic reaction against Enlightenment thought. He is indeed a rationalist, and wishes to extend the domain of science over the terrain of the human mind itself. But, like Schopenhauer, Nietzsche, and Bergson, he sees human reason as intrinsically practical and self-preservative in its orientation, and ultimately involved in an intense struggle with our sexual and aggressive instincts. What Freud gives to, and shares with, much cultural and literary theory is a view of the human self as constructed to a large extent by its environment, as a product of familial and larger social forces; a profound sense of the limitations of reason and of language itself; an intense awareness of the closure effected by conventional systems of thought and behavior, of the severe constraints imposed upon human sexuality; a view of art and religion as issuing from broader patterns of human need; and an acknowledgment that truth-value and moral value are not somehow absolute or universal but are motivated by the economic and ideological demands of civilization.

Jacques Lacan (1901–1981)

The work of the French psychoanalyst Jacques Lacan centers around his extensive re-reading of Freud in the light of insights furnished by linguistics and structuralism. Lacan's project was not merely to apply these discourses to psychoanalysis, but rather to enable the mutual reinterpretation of all of these areas of inquiry. He effectively employed these disciplines, as well as mathematics and logic, to reformulate Freud's account of the unconscious and his own account of human subjectivity in a (somewhat altered) Saussurean terminology of the connections between signifier and signified. Lacan was born in Paris to Roman Catholic parents who gave him the name "Jacques-Marie." It is arguable that his (anti-nominalist) views of language and subjectivity found their initial inspiration here, in reaction against this moment of primordial naming. He later de-nominated himself, removing the appellation "Marie," and went on to study medicine, after which he undertook training in psychiatry.

Apart from Freud, the main influences on Lacan's work were Saussure, Roman Jakobson, and Hegel (Alexandre Kojève's famous lectures on whom Lacan had attended). Lacan's reputation was established by his publication of *Écrits* (1966), a large collection of essays and papers, which were translated into English in a much abbreviated format in 1977. Like Derrida, Julia Kristeva, Louis Althusser, and other notable French thinkers, Lacan participated in a landmark conference in 1966 at Johns Hopkins University. Lacan's influence has extended not only over the field of psychoanalysis but also reaches into the work of Marxists such as Louis Althusser (whose theories were influenced by Lacan and who, ironically, became Lacan's patient, after which, even more ironically, he killed his wife) and feminists such as Julia Kristeva and Jane Gallop, as well as deconstructive thinkers such as Barbara Johnson. Other feminists have reacted strongly against the phallocentric thrust (a not altogether inapt expression) of Lacan's own work.

Before examining Lacan's most influential texts, it may be useful to outline some of his pivotal views. As stated earlier, Lacan rewrites Freud's account of the unconscious using linguistic terminology and concepts. Lacan posits three orders or states of human mental disposition: the *imaginary* order, the *symbolic* order, and the *real*. The imaginary order is a pre-Oedipal phase where an infant is as yet unable to distinguish itself from its mother's body or to recognize the lines of demarcation between itself and objects in the world; indeed, it does not as yet know itself as a coherent entity or self. Hence, the imaginary phase is one of unity (between the child and its surroundings), as well as of immediate possession (of the mother and objects), a condition of reassuring plenitude, a world consisting wholly of images (hence "imaginary") that is not fragmented or mediated by difference, by categories, in a word, by language and signs. The mirror phase – the point at which the child can recognize itself and its environment in the mirror – marks the point at which this comforting imaginary condition breaks down, pushing the child into the symbolic order, which is the world of predefined social roles and gender differences, the world of subjects and objects, the world of language.

In this way, Lacan effectively reformulates in linguistic terms Freud's account of the Oedipus complex. Freud had posited that the infant's desire for its mother is prohibited by the father, who threatens the infant with castration. Faced with this threat, the infant represses his desire, thereby opening up the dimension of the unconscious, which is for Lacan (and Freud as seen through Lacan) not a "place" but a relation to the social world of law, morality, religion, and conscience. According to Freud, the child internalizes through the father's commands (what Lacan calls the Law of the Father) the appropriate standards of socially acceptable thought and behavior. Freud calls these standards internalized as conscience the child's "superego." The child now identifies with the father, sliding into his own gendered role, in the knowledge that he too is destined for fatherhood. Of course, the repressed desire(s) continue to exert their influence on conscious life. As Lacan rewrites this process, the child, in passing from the imaginary to the symbolic order, continues to long for the security and wholeness it previously felt: it is now no longer in full possession of its mother and of entities in the world; rather, it is distinguished from them in and through a network of signification. The child's desire, as Lacan explains it, passes in an unceasing movement along an infinite chain of signifiers, in search of unity, security, of ultimate meaning, in an ever elusive signified, and immaturely clinging to the fictive notion of unitary selfhood that began in the imaginary phase. The child exists in an alienated condition, its relationships with objects always highly mediated and controlled by social structures at the heart of whose operations is language. For Lacan, the phallus is a privileged signifier, signifying both sexual distinction and its arbitrariness. Lacan never accurately describes the "real": he seems to think of it as what lies beyond the world of signification, perhaps a primordial immediacy of experience prior to language or a chaotic condition of mere thinghood prior to objectivity. For Lacan, the real is the impossible: that which occurs beyond the entire framework of signification. The real is a sign of its own absence, pointing to itself as mere signifier. Lacan rejects any notion that the mind of either child or adult has any intrinsic psychical unity; it is merely a "subject" rather than a self or ego, merely the occupant of an always moving position in the networks of signification; hence, for Lacan, as he indicates in a famous statement, even "the Unconscious is structured like a language." The unconscious is as much a product of signifying systems, and indeed is itself as much a signifying system, as the conscious mind: both are like language in their openness, their constant deferral of meaning, their susceptibility to changing definition and their constitution as a system of relations (rather than existing as entities in their own right). In Lacan's view, the subject is empty, fluid, and without an axis or center, and is always recreated in his encounter with the other, with what exceeds his own nature and grasp. Influenced by Hegel's master–slave dialectic, as well as by his account of objectivity, Lacan sees the individual's relation to objects as mediated by desire and by struggle.

Lacan elaborates his most renowned concept, that of the "mirror stage," in a 1949 paper of that title.[8] When does the mirror stage occur? Lacan locates it in the development of a child between the ages of 6 and 18 months. Such a child can "recognize as such his own image in a mirror." Lacan states that the child exhibits a "jubilant assumption of his specular image" [*speculum* meaning "mirror"] (*Écrits*, 2). The child is "jubilant" because the image reflected in the mirror is what Lacan calls "the Ideal-I," an idealized, coherent, and unified version of itself. The child's ego is precipitated into the symbolic matrix of language, the symbolic order: the word "primordial" indicates that the experience of the child is somewhat premature, anticipating its entry into language, and into the entire relation of subject and object which will govern its engagement in the world. In other words, the mirror stage occurs prior to the child's actual acquisition of a sense of self, a sense of itself as subject in distinction from objects in the world: the child experiences, as projected in its mirror image, itself and its surroundings as an integrated unity.

What is also important, however, is that this present experience of illusory unity is not entirely left behind even when the child grows beyond the mirror stage. The illusion of unity and enduring identity that occurs in the mirror phase also anticipates the life-long alienation of the ego, not only from the objects that surround it, objects of its desire, but also from itself (*Écrits*, 2). The passing of the mirror stage marks the transition from the child's jubilant and comforting assumption of his satisfying total image or "I" in the mirror to his entry into the social world (*Écrits*, 5). The child has effectively passed from the imaginary order to the symbolic order. What Lacan seems to be suggesting is that from this point onward, the child's knowledge or awareness will never be immediate, will never be based on a somehow pure experience which precedes identity formation and the categories of subject and object; rather, it will enter a "socially elaborated" system where all knowledge will be relational and highly mediated (through social, educational, and ideological structures), and where the child as "subject" will confront elements of the world as "objects," as forms of otherness or foreignness to his identity; his relation to these objects will assume the form of desire, which is according to Hegel the form of consciousness itself (since it is desire of a subject for an object that defines their mutual relation as one of mutual demarcation, separation, and definition).

Lacan suggests that the ego, far from being the coherent, unified, and rational agency that has been bequeathed by Descartes and by

Enlightenment philosophy, is characterized by its very failure to achieve unity, by its very failure to achieve self-understanding, by its perpetual propensity to misprision. At the end of his article, Lacan seems to imply that the very process of the formation of the "I," of which the mirror stage is a founding moment, itself harbors "the most extensive definition of neurosis" (*Écrits*, 7). Is Lacan, like Freud, redefining the human being as the "neurotic animal"? If so, he hints at certain historical conditions underlying our general neurosis: his opposition to existentialism is based in part on its failure to explain the "subjective impasses" arising from a society based primarily on utilitarian functions and a lack of true freedom (*Écrits*, 6).

Lacan's theories of language and the unconscious are formulated in a widely known paper called "The Agency/Insistence of the Letter in the Unconscious since Freud" (1957). In the first part of his paper, entitled "The Meaning of the Letter," Lacan urges that psychoanalysis "discovers in the unconscious . . . the whole structure of language" (*Écrits*, 147). Language and its structure exist prior to the moment at which the speaking subject makes his entry into it (*Écrits*, 148). Lacan talks of the subject as "the slave of language," whose place is already "inscribed at birth" (*Écrits*, 148).

Lacan observes that the current reclassification of the sciences around linguistics is tantamount to "a revolution in knowledge" (*Écrits*, 149). The constitutive moment of the emergence of linguistics, the founding moment of this science, is contained in an algorithm:

S   (Signifier)
s   (Signified)

This algorithm is essentially Saussure's formulation. But the position of Saussurean linguistics, says Lacan, is suspended at this precise distinction between two orders "separated initially by a barrier resisting signification" (*Écrits*, 149). What Lacan seems to be pointing out is that the bar or barrier, in Saussure's scheme, is itself outside of the structure of language, imposed, as it were, from without. In sum, no signification can be sustained other than by reference to another signification. There is no language (*langue*) which cannot cover the whole field of the signified. If we grasp in language the constitution of an object, this constitution is found at the level of a concept (which is very different from simple naming). To grasp an object in language, we find the object constituted only at the level of the concept, not as a thing. In other words, it is an illusion that "the signifier answers to the function of representing the signified," or to search for the final signified (treating this as the actual thing or entity) to which the signifier points, excluding the apparatus of interpretation (*Écrits*, 150). The relation between signifier and signified is not one of parallelism.

Lacan suggests that Saussure's diagram of TREE/Picture of tree (as an illustration of the connection between signifier and signified) could be replaced, to better illustrate this connection, with two identical doors over which, respectively, are inscribed "Ladies" and "Gentlemen." This, says Lacan, illustrates how "the signifier enters the signified" (*Écrits*, 151). In other words, the signifier or sound-image "Ladies" does not merely *point* to a signified or concept that somehow is already there, outside of it: it *enters* the signified, it alters or creates the meaning or concept. The bathroom doors are identical but they do not have the same meaning; this meaning is structured or "entered" by the signifier (*Écrits*, 153). If a train arrives at a station and a little brother and sister are sitting face to face in a compartment, one of them will see the sign "Ladies," and the other, "Gentlemen." They will disagree on what they are seeing. This signifier (seen differently) will become subject to "the unbridled power of ideological warfare." For these children, "ladies" and "gentlemen" will henceforth be "two countries towards which each of their souls will strive on divergent wings" (*Écrits*, 152). Another way of putting this might be to say that each signified is the "same" country, traversed from different points of view; the difference in point of view, however, creates a difference in the signified.

No signifier alone has meaning. As Lacan has it, "it is in the chain of the signifier that the meaning 'insists' but that none of its elements 'consists' in the signification of which it is at the moment capable" (*Écrits*, 153). In other words, meaning does settle or halt at any one element in the signification chain: none of these elements in itself consists of meaning. Rather, meaning pauses, or stands upon, elements in the chain, always moving from one to another, none of the elements, therefore, being stable. Lacan characterizes the chain of signifiers as "rings of a necklace that is a ring in another necklace made of rings" (*Écrits*, 152–153).

We are forced then, says Lacan, in a statement that was to become widely cited, "to accept the notion of an incessant sliding of the signified under the signifier" (*Écrits*, 154). What he appears to mean by this is that (1) we can never reach the pure signified; (2) the realm of the signifier is far more extensive, both structuring and controlling the realm of the signified; the latter realm can never somehow extend or protrude beyond the domains of the signifier since that would imply that concepts (and ultimately things, entities) can exist prior to, and independently of, the process of signification; (3) the relation between the two realms, contrary to Saussure's formulation of it, is not linear (*Écrits*, 154). Lacan sees all discourse as marked by polyphony. As an example of this polyphonic process, of the sliding of the signified under the signifier, of the crossing of the bar (*barre*) of Saussure's algorithm, he looks again at the word "tree" (pointing out that *arbre* is an anagram of *barre*). The signifier "tree" can bring to mind a range of significations, from the strength and majesty of nature, through Biblical connotations (the shadow of the cross), to various pagan symbolisms: what these multiple significations show is that an element in the signifying chain can be used "to signify *something quite other* than what it says" (as "tree" was used to refer to the cross, etc.). And this function of speech is also the "function of indicating the place of this subject in the search for the true" (*Écrits*, 155). Hence, in the very process of using signification, the subject or speaker is herself inserted at a specific point into the signifying chain. This "properly signifying function . . . in language," this process whereby one word is used to mean something else, has a name (that Lacan purports vaguely to recall from Quintilian): this name is metonymy (*Écrits*, 156). Lacan cites an example of metonymy: when "thirty sails" is used to refer to "ship"; in other words, when the part is taken for the whole (*Écrits*, 156). Metonymy, then, the core of the signifying process, is a connection between signifiers, between words, and not between signifiers and signifieds.

Lacan states: "I shall designate as metonymy, then, the one side (*versant*) of the effective field constituted by the signifier, so that meaning can emerge there . . . The other side is *metaphor*" (*Écrits*, 156). Lacan acknowledges his debt to Roman Jakobson in viewing metonymy and metaphor as lying at the heart of the signifying process. Lacan urges that metaphor does not spring from the presentation of two images, i.e., of "two signifiers equally actualized." Rather, the creative spark of metaphor "flashes between two signifiers one of which has taken the place of the other in the signifying chain, the occulted signifier remaining present through its (metonymic) connexion with the rest of the chain . . . *One word for another*: that is the formula for metaphor" (*Écrits*, 157). Hence, in Lacan's eyes, the "occulted" or displaced word remains, though reduced to the same level of metonymic presence as other signifiers (*Écrits*, 158). It was "none other than Freud who had this revelation, and he called his discovery the unconscious" (*Écrits*, 159). By the end of this section, Lacan has, with several forms of wordplay, discussed the "meaning of the letter," laying down his basic positions regarding language and the signifying process, viewing the notions of truth, subjectivity, and objectivity as immanent in this process (created within it rather than assuming any externality or independence from it). His final sentence, concerning Freud's revelation, anticipates his forthcoming examination of structuring of the unconscious by the operations of the linguistic process.

Lacan now turns to the function and place of the subject in the signifying process. Descartes' statement "I think, therefore I am" assumes that the human self is "transcendental": it exists as a unity prior to its empirical experience. It is transparent because, in principle, everything is knowable about it, and it provides a clear, detached, perspective onto the world, being uncolored or smeared by the opacity of a specific historically conditioned subjectivity. This transparent self affirms its own existence, locating this in its very ability to think. In other words, its "being" is equated or identified with its "thought" in an unmediated relationship. Lacan cites a more modern, and perhaps less impugnable, version of Descartes' formula: " '*cogito ergo sum*,' *ubi cogito, ibi sum*" (I think, therefore I am, where I think, there I am) (*Écrits*, 165).

It was Freud's "Copernican Revolution" (which we might see as a second such revolution, Kant having claimed the first) that created "the Freudian universe," in which was questioned for a second time "the place man assigns to himself at the centre of a universe." According to Lacan, the place that I occupy as signifier will be a place in language, a grammatical function; the place that I occupy as a signified will be a concept that is also situated within the networks of language. The "I" which speaks (known to linguists as the "subject of enunciating," the actual person pronouncing a sentence about herself) is not definable as a coherent unity and cannot be adequately represented or signified by the "I" which is the subject of the sentence (the "subject of enunciation"). Language, as a network of signifiers, displaces and redistributes the world of immediate existence, a world that can be known only as it is mediated by language. We might recall that the self that emerged from the imaginary stage was a split subject, with its repressed desire opening up the field of its unconscious; hence the child is split between unconscious desire (for the mother, for wholeness, for unity, for absolute meaning, all vestiges of the imaginary stage) and its conscious obligations in the symbolic order. It might be said that certain of Lacan's insights here, such as the distinction between the ontological and semiotic dimensions of any entity, had already been formulated by Hegel and a number of neo-Hegelian philosophers on a somewhat higher intellectual plane.

After the mirror phase, the subject is on an endless quest for unity, for wholeness, for security, a quest that must take place metonymically along a chain of signifiers, one being displaced for another (*Écrits*, 167). The desire that comprises the unconscious, a desire that mocks philosophy and the infinite, a desire that associates knowing and dominating with *jouissance*, is an endless journey through an infinite chain of signifiers. The subject is "caught in the rails – eternally stretching forth towards the *desire for something else* – of metonymy" (*Écrits*, 167).

The third section of Lacan's paper is called "The Letter, Being and the Other." His concern here is to show how psychoanalysis has been bypassing the "truth discovered by Freud," which affirms, in Lacan's words, "the self's radical ex-centricity to itself with which man is confronted" (*Écrits*, 171). The notion of the unconscious indicates that the self bears an otherness within itself; or, rather, the self's otherness can be seen as external, as alien, to itself. Psychoanalysis has "compromised" this insight, which is contained in both the letter and spirit of Freud's works. The psychoanalytic institution has fallen prey to a humanism long prevalent in Western thought, one of its tenets being the idea of a unified personality, an idea that has persisted through Descartes' *cogito* and Enlightenment philosophy into the present: the idea of the human being as a rational, autonomous, free agent. Psychoanalysis has fallen under this general disposition, engaging in "moralistic tartufferies" and talking endlessly about the "total personality" (*Écrits*, 172). The underlying idea being that neurosis can be cured once placed in the totalizing narrative of the coherent conscious life of the patient.

But this, insists Lacan, is to compromise and domesticate Freud's radical discovery: the unconscious cannot be treated as simply an aberration that must somehow be reintegrated into the total, normal personality, into the customary bourgeois-Enlightenment conception of the ego. The unconscious, as constituted by desire, is not only structured like a language in its operations through mechanisms such as metaphor and metonymy, but thereby extends the nature of its operations, fueled by desire – including the endless search for unity along an infinite chain of signifiers, the deferment and displacement of meaning, the inability to accede to reality other than through language – into the realm of the conscious, there in fact being no sharp demarcation between these. Freud taught us that we witness our nature "as much and more in our whims, our aberrations, our phobias and fetishes, as in our more or less civilized personalities" (*Écrits*, 174). We cannot simply place the unconscious alongside our rational selves as inherited from the Renaissance and the Enlightenment: our conception of the operations of reason itself must be transformed; madness has been used by the philosopher to adorn the "impregnable burrow of his fear . . . the supreme agent forever at work digging its tunnels is none other than reason, the very Logos that he serves" (*Écrits*, 174). Reason has been used to hide and define madness, an operation inspired by fear rather than love of knowledge. Since Freud's discovery, however, of a "radical heteronomy . . . gaping within man," this gap can never be hidden over again. Repeating his famous statement, Lacan reminds us that the "unconscious is the discourse of the Other (with a capital O)" (*Écrits*, 172). It is with the appearance of language that "the dimension of truth emerges" and the existence of subjects can be recognized in "the manifested presence of intersubjectivity" (*Écrits*, 172). The slightest alteration "in the relation between man and the signifier . . . changes the whole course of history by modifying the moorings that anchor his being" (*Écrits*, 174). It is precisely in this, says Lacan, that Freudianism has "founded an intangible but radical revolution . . . everything has been affected" (*Écrits*, 174). What Lacan is calling for, then, is a return to Freud, a return to the letter (and spirit) of the Freudian text, a return to the truly radical nature of his discovery of the unconscious, as well as an endeavor to formulate this discovery – and to realize its radical potential – in linguistic terms. Lacan reminds us that the patient's symptom is indeed a metaphor, and that man's desire is a metonymy: it is the concept of humanistic man, man as a total, integrated being, that has stood in the way, through "many centuries of religious hypocrisy and philosophical bravado," of our being able to articulate the connection between metaphor and the question of being, and between metonymy and a lack of being (*Écrits*, 175).

In insisting on the self's "radical ex-centricity" to itself, what does it mean to say that the self in these ways is external to itself? The unconscious is not somehow beneath or external to the conscious mind. Rather, the unconscious is engaged in a dialectically uneven series of connections with the conscious mind whereby *it* structures the conscious mind somewhat and the conscious mind thus structured in turn exerts its influence on the unconscious. In answering the questions just posed, we need to be careful not to think of the conscious mind itself as some sort of unity – this is precisely what Lacan is rejecting – any more than the unconscious is a unity. The two notions do not stand in binary opposition. The point is that by viewing the unconscious as radically exterior and "other," Lacan forces into visibility the notion that the unconscious is not somehow tucked away, hidden and protected from the social structures which govern the world, a world they construct and define through language. Rather, the unconscious is *part of* that world; it is subject to, and constituted by, the same fundamental linguistic processes as is the conscious mind; as such, like the conscious mind, it is without a center, without an essence, without a psychological substratum; it is nothing more than the series of positions it occupies in language, a series of positions that can only artificially and for convenience be coerced into identity as a "subject," and, with even more coercion, molded into the coherence of an ego or self.

In this way, Lacan, through "insisting" on the agency of the "letter" in the unconscious, brings out the truly radical and subversive nature of the otherness discovered by Freud: the unconscious. In Freud's work (in spite of its actually radical implications), the unconscious – often treated as one controllable and aberrational element in a broader overall and normalizable structure of the mind – is in danger of being tamed and domesticated, of subserving the very notion of a coherent ego or self, descended through centuries of theology, humanism, and Enlightenment, that it set out to subvert. By dethroning the unconscious from this unwitting disposition toward transcendence in Freud's work, by immanentalizing it within the vast networks of signification into which the child is born and which in effect constitute the child's psychology as a network of significations, by resituating the unconscious within language, by redefining it *as* and *through* language, Lacan returns us to the startling and revolutionary nature of the Freudian discovery. This extension of the genuine implications of Freud's theories was furthered by the structuralist Marxist Louis Althusser, who adapted Lacan's insights in his account of the workings of the ideological apparatus of the political state, thereby exploring the connections – which are merely latent in Freud – between the unconscious and social structures.

Jacques Derrida (1930–2004) and Deconstruction

The term "poststructuralism" is often identified with "deconstruction," a pervasive phenomenon in modern literary and cultural theory originated by the French thinker Jacques Derrida. While Derrida himself has insisted that deconstruction is not a theory unified by any set of consistent rules or procedures, it has been variously regarded as a way of reading, a mode of writing, and, above all, a way of challenging interpretations of texts based upon conventional notions of the stability of the human self, the external world, and of language and meaning.

Derrida was born in Algeria to a Jewish family and suffered intensely the experience of being an outsider. While in Algeria he undertook a study of several major philosophers, including Søren Kierkegaard and Martin Heidegger. He then studied at various prestigious institutions in Paris, eventually becoming a teacher of philosophy. He also worked at Harvard and, in 1975, began teaching at Yale University. More recently, he gave lectures at various American institutions, in particular at the University of California at Irvine. He established a reputation in France during the 1960s, a reputation which crossed to the United States in the 1970s. Derrida's transatlantic influence can be traced to an important seminar held at Johns Hopkins University in 1966. A number of leading French theorists, such as Roland Barthes, Jacques Lacan, and Lucien Goldmann, spoke at this conference. Derrida himself presented what was quickly recognized as a pioneering paper entitled "Structure, Sign, and Play in the Discourse of the Human Sciences."

The following year, 1967, marked Derrida's explosive entry onto the international stage of literary and cultural theory, with the publication of his first three books: *La Voix et le phénomène* (*Speech and Phenomena*), concerning Edmund Husserl's theory of signs; *De la grammatologie* (*Of Grammatology*), whose subject was the "science" of writing; and *L'Écriture et la différence* (*Writing and Difference*), which contained important essays on Hegel, Freud, and Michel Foucault. Later works included *La Dissemination* (*Dissemination*) (1972), which included a lengthy engagement with Plato's views of writing and sophistry; *Marges de la philosophie* (*Margins of Philosophy*) (1982), which included essays on Hegel's semiology and the use of metaphor in philosophy; *Positions* (1972), containing three illuminating interviews with Derrida, touching on his attitude to Marxism, Hegel, and other issues; *Circumfessions* (1991), an autobiographical work that engages with the text of Augustine's *Confessions*; and *Spectres de Marx* (*Specters of Marx*) (1994), which looks at the various legacies of Marx.

Proponents of deconstruction often point out that it is not amenable to any static definition or systematization because the meaning of the terms it employs is always shifting and fluid, taking its color from the localized contexts and texts with which it engages. Indeed, deconstruction is often regarded as undermining all tendency toward systematization. However, there are a number of concerns, and certain heuristic terms, that can be said to characterize deconstruction. The most fundamental project of deconstruction is to display the operations of "logocentrism" in any "text" (where the meaning of "text" is broadened to include not merely written treatises in a variety of disciplines but the entire range of their political, theological, social, and intellectual contexts, as manifested primarily in their use of language).

What is logocentrism? Etymologically and historically, this term refers to any system of thought which is founded on the stability and authority of the *Logos*, the divine Word. The various meanings accumulated by this word in the Hebrew, ancient pagan, and early Christian worlds are complex. The scholar C. H. Dodd explains that *Logos* is both a thought and a word, and the two are inseparable: the *Logos* is the word as determined by and conveying a meaning. He also observes that the root of the Hebrew equivalent for *Logos* means "to speak," and that this expression is used of God's self-revelation. Moreover, in Hebrew culture, the word once spoken was held to have a substantive existence. The word and concept *Logos* may have derived in part from the Greek thinker Heracleitus and the Jewish philosopher Philo of Alexandria (ca. 20 BC–50 AD); in its simplest meaning it can signify "statement," "saying," "discourse," or science.[9] In the Gospel of John, the plural *logoi* refers to the words spoken by Jesus or others; but the singular *Logos* signifies the whole of what Jesus said, his message as both revelation and command. The life of Jesus is the *Logos* incarnate, and events in this life are signs of eternal realities. And the Gospel in general is the record of a life that expresses the eternal thought of God, the meaning of the universe (Dodd, 204–205). Dodd states that all of these senses accord with the fundamental Greek connotation of *Logos* as the spoken word *together* with its meaning or rational content. A further sense of *logos* in the fourth Gospel is the "Word of God," his self-revelation to man; it denotes the eternal truth revealed to men by God. Hence the *Logos* is not simply an uttered word; it *is* truth itself, it has a rational content of thought corresponding to the ultimate reality of the universe. And this reality is revealed *as spoken and heard* (Dodd, 266–267). As such, the *Logos* is the thought of God which is the "transcendent design of the universe and its immanent meaning" (Dodd, 285). In its ancient Greek philosophical and Judeo-Christian meaning, then, the *Logos* referred both to the Word of God which created the universe and to the rational order of creation itself. In other words, it is in the spoken *Logos* that language and reality ultimately coincide, in an identity that is invested with absolute authority, absolute origin, and absolute purpose or teleology. If we think of the orders of language and reality as follows, it is clear that one of the functions of the *Logos* is to preserve the stability and closure of the entire system:

LOGOS

Language		Reality
Signifier 1 -*a*- Signified 1	——————*b*——————	Object 1
Signifier 2 – Signified 2	—————————————	Object 2
Signifier 3 – Signified 3	—————————————	Object 3
Signifier 4 – Signified 4	—————————————	Object 4

Ad Infinitum

101

It is because the *Logos* holds together the orders of language and reality that the relation between signifier (word) and signified (concept), i.e., relation *a*, is stable and fixed; so too is relation *b*, the connection between the sign as a whole and the object to which it refers in the world. For example, in a Christian scheme, the signifier "love" might refer to the concept of "self-sacrifice" in relation to God. And this sign as a whole, the word "love" as meaning "self-sacrifice," would refer to object 1, which might be a system of social or ecclesiastical relationships institutionally embodied in a given society, enshrining the ideal of self-sacrifice. In other words, the meaning of "love" is sanctioned by a hierarchy of authority, stretching back through institutional church practice, theology, philosophy, as well as political and economic theory, to the authority of the scriptures and the Word of God Himself. In the same way, all of the other signifiers and signifieds in language would be constrained in their significance, making for a stable and closed system in terms of which the world and the human self could be interpreted in terms of their origins, their meaning and purpose in life, what counts as good and evil, what kind of government is legitimate, and so forth. The *Logos* thereby authorizes an entire world view, sanctioned by a theological and philosophical system and by an entire political, religious, and social order.

If, now, the *Logos* is *removed* from this picture, what happens? The entire order will become destabilized; historically, of course, this disintegration does not happen all at once but takes centuries, as indeed does the undermining of the *Logos*. Once the *Logos* vanishes from the picture, there is nothing to hold together the orders of language and reality, which now threaten to fly apart from each other. The relations *a* and *b* both become destabilized: if we are not constrained by a Christian perspective, we might attribute *other* meanings to the word "love," meanings which may even conflict with the previously given Christian signification. Moreover, various groups might give different meanings to the word so that a general consensus is lost. In this way, signifier 1 may be defined by a meaning attributed to signified 1. But since there is no authoritative closure to this process, it could go on ad infinitum: signified 1 will itself need to be defined, and so this signified will itself become a signifier of something else; this process might regress indefinitely so that we never arrive at a conclusive signified but are always moving along an endless chain of signifiers. Derrida attributes the name of "metaphor" to this endless substitution of one signifier for another: in describing or attempting to understand our world, we can no longer use "literal" language, i.e., language that actually describes the object or reality. We can only use metaphor, hence language in its very nature is metaphorical. Hence there cannot be a sharp distinction between, say, the spheres of philosophy and science, on the one hand, which are often presumed to use a "literal" language based on reason, and literature and the arts, on the other hand, which are characterized as using metaphorical and figurative language in a manner inaccessible to reason.

Even the languages of mathematics, science, and philosophy are ultimately metaphorical, and cannot claim any natural and referential connection with the world they purport to describe.

Logocentrism, however, is not uniform but takes a variety of guises: for example, the stabilizing function of the *Logos* might be replaced by other notions. For Plato, this notion might be *eidos* or the Forms; what holds Aristotle's metaphysics together, as its foundation, is the concept of substance; similarly, we could cite Hegel's "Absolute Idea" or Kant's categories of the understanding. Modern equivalents in Western society might be concepts such as freedom or democracy. All of these terms function as what Derrida calls "transcendental signifieds," or concepts invested with absolute authority, which places them beyond questioning or examination. An important endeavor of deconstruction, then, is to show the operation of logocentrism in all of its forms, and to bring back these various transcendental signifieds within the province of language and textuality, within the province of their relatability to other concepts.

Hence, in one sense, the most fundamental project of deconstruction is to reinstate *language* within the connections of the various terms that have conventionally dominated Western thought: the connections between thought and reality, self and world, subject and object. In deconstructive thought, these connections are not viewed as already existing prior to language, with language merely being the instrument of their expression or representation. Rather, all of these terms are linguistic to begin with: they are enabled by language. We do not simply have thought which is then expressed by language; thought takes place in, and is made possible by, language. The notion of language that is thereby reinstituted by deconstruction is partly influenced by Saussure: it is a notion of language as a system of relations; the terms which are related have no semantic value outside of the network of relations in which they subsist; they *depend* on those relations for their meaning and significance. Also implicit in this view of language is the arbitrary and conventional nature of the sign: there is no natural connection between the sign "table" and an actual table in the world. Equally arbitrary and conventional is the connection between the signifier "table" and the concept of a "table" to which it points. Moreover, there is no "truth" or "reality" which somehow stands outside or behind language: truth is a relation of linguistic terms, and reality is a construct, ultimately religious, social, political, and economic, but always of language, of various linguistic registers. Even the human self, in this view, has no pregiven essence but is a linguistic construct or narrative. Derrida's much-quoted statement that "il n'y a pas de hors-texte," often translated as "there is nothing outside the text," or "there is no outside of the text," means precisely this: that the aforementioned features of language, which together comprise "textuality," are all-embracing; textuality governs all interpretative operations. For example, there is no history outside of language or textuality: history itself is a linguistic and textual construct. At its deepest level, the insistence on viewing language (as a system of relations and differences) as lying at the core of any world view issues a challenge to the notion of *identity*, a notion installed at the heart of Western metaphysics since Aristotle. Identity, whether of the human self or of objects in the world, is no longer viewed as having a stable, fixed, or pregiven essence, but is seen as fluid and dependent, like linguistic terms, on a variety of contexts. Hence a deconstructive analysis tends to prioritize language and linguistic operations in analyzing texts and contexts.

While this prioritization of language is the main way in which deconstruction exhibits and undermines logocentrism, deconstructive analysis enlists other strategies and terms toward the same general endeavor. One of these strategies is the unraveling and undermining of certain oppositions which have enjoyed a privileged place in Western metaphysics. Derrida points out that oppositions, such as those between intellect and sense, soul and body, master and slave, male and female, inside and outside, center and margin, do not represent a state of equivalence between two terms. Rather, each of these oppositions is a "violent hierarchy" in which one term has been conventionally subordinated, in gestures that embody a host of religious, social, and political valencies. Intellect, for example, has usually been superordinated over sense; soul has been exalted above body; male has been defined as superior in numerous respects to female. Derrida's project is not simply to reverse these hierarchies, for such a procedure would remain imprisoned within the framework of binary oppositional thinking represented by those hierarchies. Rather, he attempts to show that these hierarchies represent privileged relationships, relationships that have been lifted above any possible engagement with, and answerability to, the network of concepts in general.

Perhaps the most significant opposition treated by Derrida, an opposition which comprehends many of the other hierarchies, is that between speech and writing. According to Derrida, Western philosophy has privileged speech over writing, viewing speech as embodying an immediate presence of meaning, and writing as a mere substitute or secondary representation of the spoken word. Speech implies, as will be seen shortly, an immediate connection with the *Logos*, a direct relation to that which sanctions and constrains it; while writing threatens to depart from the *Logos*, the living source of speech and authority, and to assert its independence. The very centrality of this opposition generates the importance of certain deconstructive strategies: Derrida imputes a meaning to "writing" that far exceeds the notion of "graphic signifier" or "inscription" of letters and words. For him, "writing" designates the totality of what makes inscription possible: all of the differences by which language is constituted. Writing refers to the diffusion of identity (of self, object, signifier, signified) through a vast network of relations and differences. Writing expresses the movement of difference itself. Indeed, it is in an attempt to subvert the conventional priority of speech over writing that Derrida both extends the meaning of "writing" and coins a term that many regard as central to his thought: *différance*. The significance of this term derives partly from Saussure's concept of "difference" as the constituting principle of language: a term is defined by what it is *not*, by its differences from other terms. Also, however, Derrida incorporates into his term an ambivalence in the French word *différer*, which can mean both "to differ" and "to defer" in time. Hence Derrida adds a temporal dimension to the notion of difference. Moreover, the substitution of *a* for *e* in the word *différance* cannot be *heard* in French: it is a silent displacement that can only be discerned in writing, as if to counter the superior value previously accorded to speech. The terms that recur in Derrida's texts – their meanings often changing according to contexts – are usually related to the extended significance that Derrida accords to "writing." Such terms include "trace," "supplement," "text," "presence," "absence," and "play."

Logocentrism, then, is sanctioned and structured in a multitude of ways, all of which are called into question by deconstruction. The privileging of speech over writing, for example, has perpetuated what Derrida calls a "metaphysics of presence," a systematization of thought and interpretation that relies on the stability and self-presence of meaning, effecting a closure and disabling any "free play" of thought which might threaten or question the overall structure. Another way of explaining the term "metaphysics of presence" might be as follows: conventionally, philosophers have made a distinction between the "thisness" or haecceity of an entity and its "whatness" or quiddity. The term "whatness" refers to the *content* of something, while "thisness" refers to the *fact* that it exists in a particular place and time. A metaphysics of "presence" would be a metaphysics of complete self-identity: an entity's content is viewed as coinciding completely with its existence. For example, an isolated entity such as a piece of chalk would be regarded as having its meaning completely within itself, completely in its immediate "presence." Even if the rest of the world did not exist, we could say what the piece of chalk was, what its function and constitution were. Such absolute self-containment of meaning must be sanctioned by a higher authority, a *Logos* or transcendental signified, which ensured that all things in the world had specific and designated meanings. If, however, we were to challenge such a "metaphysics of presence," we might argue that in fact the meaning of the chalk does *not* coincide with, and is not confinable within, its immediate existence; that its meaning and purpose actually lie in relations that extend far beyond its immediate existence; its meaning would depend, for example, upon the concept of a "blackboard" on which it was designed to write; in turn, the relationship of chalk and blackboard derives its meaning from increasingly broader contexts such as a classroom, an institution of learning, associated industries and technologies, as well as political and educational programs. Hence the meaning of "chalk" would extend through a vast network of relations far beyond the actual isolated existence of that item; moreover, its meaning would be viewed as relative to a given social and cultural framework, rather than sanctioned by the presence of a *Logos*. In this sense, the chalk is *not* self-identical since its identity is *dispersed* through its relations with numerous other objects and concepts. Viewed in this light, "chalk" is not a name for a self-subsistent, self-enclosed entity; rather, it names the provisional focal point of a complex set of relations. It can be seen, then, that a metaphysics of "presence" refers to the *self-presence*, the immediate presence, of meaning, as resting on a complete self-identity that is sanctioned and preserved by the "presence" of a *Logos*.

A deconstructive reading of a text, then, as practiced by Derrida, will be a multifaceted project: in general, it will attempt to display logocentric operations in the text, by focusing on a close reading of the text's language, its use of presuppositions or transcendental signifieds, its reliance on binary oppositions, its self-contradictions, its *aporiai* or points of conceptual impasse, and the ways in which it effects closure and resists free play. Hence deconstruction, true to its name (which derives from Heidegger's term *Destruktion*), will examine all of the features that went into the *construction* of text, down to its very foundations. Derrida has been criticized for his lack of clarity, his oblique and refractive style: his adherents have argued that his engagement with the history of Western thought is not one of mere confrontation but necessarily one of inevitable complicity (where he is obliged to use the very terms he impugns) as well as of critique. This dual gesture must necessarily entail play on words, convolution of language that accommodates its fluid nature, and divergence from conventional norms of essayistic writing. It might also be argued that the very form of his texts, not merely their content, is integral to his overall project.

Derrida's style and approach might be illustrated by examining his seminal work, "Structure, Sign, and Play," which exhibits some of the persistent concerns of deconstruction and reveals both what he owes to structuralism and his divergence from it. In this paper, Derrida's endeavor might be seen as threefold: (1) to characterize certain features of the history of Western metaphysics, as issuing from the fundamental concepts of "structure" and "center"; (2) to announce an "event" – in effect, a complex series of historical movements – whereby these central notions were challenged, using the work of the structuralist anthropologist Lévi-Strauss as an example; and (3) to suggest the ways in which current and future modes of thought and language might deploy and adapt Lévi-Strauss' insights in articulating their own relation to metaphysics.

According to Derrida, the concept of structure that has dominated Western science and philosophy has always been referred to as a "center or . . . a point of presence, a fixed origin."[10] The function of such a center has been both to organize the structure and to limit the *free play* of terms and concepts within it, in other words, to foreclose such play. The center, says Derrida, is the point at which any substitution or permutation of elements or terms is no longer possible. Although the structure thereby depends on the center, the center itself is fixed and "escapes structurality," since it is beyond the transformative reach of other elements in the structure. Hence the center is, paradoxically, *outside* the structure, and the very concept of a centered structure is only "contradictorily coherent" (*WD*, 279). What it expresses is a desire for a "reassuring certitude" which stands beyond the subversive or threatening reach of any play which might disrupt the structure. The center, that which gives stability, unity, and closure to the structure, can be conceived as an "origin" or a "purpose," terms which invoke the notion of a "full presence" (such as the *Logos*) that can guarantee such stability and closure (*WD*, 279).

Derrida suggests that the history of Western metaphysics can be viewed as the history of this concept of structure, with various philosophies substituting one center for another. These successive centers have received different metaphorical names, all of which are grounded on "the determination of Being as *presence*." The names of this presence have included *eidos* (the Platonic Form), *arche* (the concept of an absolute beginning), *telos* (the, often providential, purpose and direction attributed to human existence), *ousia* (the Aristotelian concept of "substance" or "essence" as the underlying reality of things), as well as the concepts of truth, God, and man. Each of these concepts has served as a center, as a transcendental signified, stabilizing a given system of thought or world view.

Derrida announces an "event" which has begun to disrupt this system of Western metaphysics. The "event" metaphorically refers to a complex network of historical processes. Most fundamentally, the "event" signifies the "moment when language invaded the universal problematic, the moment when, in the absence of a center or origin, everything became discourse" (*WD*, 280). Here, Derrida refers to a phase in modern intellectual history when central problems in a variety of fields – such as the connection between thought and reality, self and world – were reposited or newly posed as problems of language, where "language" was understood as a system of differences. For example, where previously the term "God" was held to refer to an actual entity independent of language, this term was now seen as one signifier among many others, a signifier which took its meaning and function from its *relation* to a vast system of signifiers; the term was no longer exalted above such relational status in a posture of absolute privilege and authority. Hence, the term "God," which once acted as a "center" (or origin or purpose) of many systems of thought, was brought back within the province of relatability to other elements of language, being dethroned from its status as a transcendental signified to one more signifier on the same level as other signifiers. In this sense, the concept of God moves from being a reality beyond language to a concept *within* language: it becomes discourse. And the systems of thought that depended on the understanding of God as a reality become "decentered," losing their former stability and authority.

When did such a process of decentering occur in Western thought? Derrida suggests that certain names can be associated with this process: Nietzsche, for example, undertook a radical critique of metaphysics, especially of the concepts of being and truth (and, we might add to Derrida's list, of space and time), regarding these as convenient fictions; Freud engaged in a critique of consciousness and the self-identity of the human subject; again, Heidegger re-examined the conventional metaphysics of being and time. The discourses of each of these thinkers put into question some of the central concepts and categories that have dominated Western thought since Plato and Aristotle. Yet Derrida is careful to point out that each of these newer, radical discourses, while attempting to break free of the traditional metaphysical enclosure, is nonetheless trapped in a circle of its own. The critique of metaphysics is inevitably a dual gesture, one which involves not only confrontation and destruction of traditional concepts but also a necessary complicity with them: we must employ the very language of metaphysics to criticize it, a duality that extends even to our discussion of the sign itself (*WD*, 280–281). We might cite as a further example the dilemma of some modern feminists who wish to break free of "male" language: we cannot simply create from nothing a "female" language, and are obliged to use in our critique terms and concepts from the very language that we wish to undermine. However, as Derrida acknowledges, there are "several ways of being caught in this circle," and it is these differences between the radical discourses that often lead them into mutual confrontation and destruction (*WD*, 281).

The examples of "radical" discourses given by Derrida suggest that the "event" or process of "decentering" was initiated in the nineteenth century. Apart from the critiques advanced by thinkers such as Nietzsche, Freud, and Heidegger (Derrida might equally have mentioned Schopenhauer, Hegel, Marx, and Bergson), there was, according to Derrida, a profounder, structural shift in the orientation of Western thinking, as pertaining to the "human sciences" in general. In the nineteenth century, a decentering occurred in European culture, and consequently in European metaphysics and science: for a complex of political, economic, and philosophical reasons, European culture was "forced to stop considering itself as the culture of reference" (*WD*, 282). In other words, Europe was obliged to retreat from its conception of itself as the political and cultural "center" of the world stage. It was at this moment, says Derrida, this moment of retreat from ethnocentrism, that the "science" of ethnology emerged; while this science undertook a critique of ethnocentrism and the conventional categories of thought underlying it, it was obliged to borrow the very terms and concepts of that heritage itself (*WD*, 282).

In order to illustrate this dual posture of ethnology, Derrida chooses the work of the French structural anthropologist Claude Lévi-Strauss. He begins with Lévi-Strauss' treatment of an opposition – between nature and culture – that is "congenital to philosophy," an opposition that predates Plato and goes back at least at far as the Sophists of the fifth century BC. In fact, this opposition encompasses "a whole historical chain which opposes 'nature' to law, to education, to art, to technics – but also to liberty, to the arbitrary, to history, to the mind, and so on" (*WD*, 283). Derrida points out that Lévi-Strauss' research has entailed both the need to use this opposition and the "impossibility of accepting it." In his first book, *The Elemetary Structures of Kinship*, Lévi-Strauss defines "nature" as encompassing that which is universal and spontaneous, whereas "culture" comprehends what is relative, variable, and dependent on a system of social norms (*WD*, 282). However, as Derrida recounts, Lévi-Strauss encounters a "scandalous" threat to this opposition in the notion of "incest-prohibition." This notion, says Lévi-Strauss, refuses to conform to either side of the opposition, since it is both a norm *and* universal, thereby combining characteristics of both culture and nature. Derrida extends the significance of this recalcitrance to conventional categories to the entire conceptual system of philosophy, in which the nature–culture opposition operates systematically. He cites this as an example of the fact that "language bears within itself the necessity of its own critique" (*WD*, 284).

In general, this critique, suggests Derrida, can follow two broad paths. The first would be systematically to question the "founding concepts of the entire history of philosophy, to deconstitute them." This would indeed be the most daring way to take "a step outside of philosophy," but it would be an enormously difficult, if not impossible, task. The second path would be that effectively taken by Lévi-Strauss: to conserve all the old concepts while recognizing their limits, to refrain from attributing any truth-value to them while using them as tools or instruments (*WD*, 284). In this way, Lévi-Strauss points toward a direction beyond conventional philosophical discourse. Yet Derrida cautions that "the passage beyond philosophy does not consist in turning the page of philosophy . . . but in continuing to read philosophers *in a certain way*" (*WD*, 288). We cannot, that is, simply dispense with previous philosophy and start anew: that would be a project of engineering, whereas we are obliged to engage in *bricolage*, to use the materials already at our disposal to read philosophy in a more radical manner.

In conclusion, Derrida states that there are "two interpretations of interpretation, of structure, of sign, of play." The one dreams of arriving at a truth or origin which "escapes play and the order of the sign . . . The other, which is no longer turned toward the origin, affirms play and tries to pass beyond man and humanism," man being he who has "dreamed of full presence, the reassuring foundation, the origin and the end of play." These two interpretations, he thinks, are "absolutely irreconcilable," and our current task is to chart both the common ground and the *différance* of their irreducible difference, in the interests of the "as yet unnameable which is proclaiming itself" (*WD*, 293).

Derrida's influence in America and Europe was unparalleled in the latter twentieth century. His American disciples included the Yale critics Paul de Man, J. Hillis Miller, Geoffrey Hartman as well as Barbara Johnson and, arguably, Harold Bloom. These critics applied and richly extended Derridean techniques such as searching for impasses or *aporiai* in various texts, displaying the hidden presuppositions and contradictions of literary and philosophical works, and demonstrating how their central claims and oppositions undermined themselves. In *Blindness and Insight* (1971), for example, de Man argues that the insights produced by critics are intrinsically linked to certain blindnesses, the critics invariably affirming something other than what they intended. De Man's *Allegories of Reading* (1979) explores the theory of tropes or figurative language, affirming that language is intrinsically metaphorical and that literary texts above all are highly self-conscious of their status as such and are self-deconstructing. Hence criticism inevitably misreads a text, given that figurative language mediates between literary and critical text. Harold Bloom, also centrally concerned with the function of tropes in literature, is best known for his assessment of poetic tradition on the basis of the "anxiety of influence." Each writer, asserts Bloom, attempts to carve out an imaginative space free from overt domination by his or predecessors; to this end, as Bloom argues in *A Map of Misreading* (1975), the writer assumes an Oedipal disposition, creatively misreading those predecessors or "fathers" by way of certain tropes such as irony, synecdoche, and metonymy.

A number of critics have explored the implications of deconstruction for other fields of study and other literary and cultural perspectives. Barbara Johnson's *A World of Difference* (1987) furnished powerful examples of deconstructive criticism in the context of broader issues of gender, race, and the institution of literary criticism. Gayatri Spivak has brought deconstructive insights to bear on her feminist and postcolonial concerns. Michael Ryan's *Marxism and Deconstruction* (1982) explores the commensurability and sharp contrasts between Marxist and deconstructive perspectives. Shoshana Felman and Stephen W. Melville have related Derrida's work to psychoanalysis.

It is clear that deconstruction has had a profound influence in a wide range of disciplines. Its remorseless insistence on exposing the foundations of and assumptions behind important concepts is a strategy that can be valuably enlisted by many forms of thought which endeavor to scrutinize conventional ways of thinking. It is also true, however, that deconstruction has met with substantial criticism on a number of accounts. One of the sharpest objections, voiced by Marxist critics such as Terry Eagleton, is that deconstruction exhibits a merely destructive or "negative" capability, whereby it criticizes various systems and institutions without offering any alternatives. Hence, its critique is abstract, leaving everything as it was. Scholars such as Jean-Michel Rabaté have pointed out that in his more recent writings Derrida resisted this characterization of his endeavor as "negative." Moreover, Derrida's later work ventured into areas such as politics, law, and the academy. A case in point is his *Specters of Marx* (1994), written in response to the concerns of various scholars over the fate of Marxism after the collapse of Communism.[11] Derrida aligns the deconstructive spirit with certain legacies of Marx; even in his earlier work, he had acknowledged his debt to the same Hegelian dialectic that shaped Marx's thought.

Nonetheless, Derrida's thought is nonetheless open to further substantive criticisms. The notions of "difference" and *différance* on which so much of Derrida's thought rests are abstract. The notion of difference is an abstraction from the logical movement of the Hegelian dialectic. The notion of *différance* is a dual abstraction from the logical and historical movement of the dialectic, and involves a third abstraction from the progressive unity of logic and history. It suspends the entry into itself of all relations, logical or historical; it freezes the second phase of the dialectic into a self-bounded immunity from movement. Thus the movement of difference is nothing other than pure stasis. It coerces the movement from logic to ontology, as well as the ontological differences between past, present, and future, into one uniform ideal plane, of textuality. Having no past or future, nor acknowledging *itself* as a result or product of previous thought, it usurps the place of movement, situating itself as an absolute beginning, a beginning not defined by its subsequent extension or emergence as such through various relations but by the very suppression of relations between itself and all else: by an act of willful self-positing, willful return to itself as the undiluted principle of beginning. It does not endure process but rather imprisons itself within an eternal circle of beginning which, for that very reason, is no beginning at all because nothing develops from it except its own uniform priority. Whatever might genuinely develop and differ from it is coerced into the shadow of its indiscriminate determination. It abolishes not only historical specificity but also all possibility of logical precedence leading up to it. It is simply inserted into logic from the outside; it is not shown to be an inner development of any logic whatsoever or of any history. It is simply textuality abstracting into its own self-identical structure all the endless variety of true historical relation; it dissolves actual relations into a principle of abstract relationality. For Derrida, *différance* is effectively elevated to the status of a transcendental signified. Given that this notion underlies Derrida's critiques of philosophical systems which vary widely from one another, it is evident that he coerces all of these systems into a uniform assailability: they all suffer from the same defects, the same kinds of *aporiai* or impasses. And it is only against a simplistic and positivistic understanding of truth, meaning, presence, and subjectivity that his notions of trace, difference, and writing can articulate themselves.

Finally, there has been a tendency to overestimate Derrida's originality (though he himself was well aware of his debt to other thinkers). The relational and arbitrary nature of language has been perceived by many thinkers, ranging from Hellenistic philosophers and rhetoricians through Locke and Hume to Hegel, Marx, the French symbolists and Saussure. The notions that "reality" is a construction, that "truth" is an interpretation, that human subjectivity is not essentially fixed, and that there are no ultimate transcendent foundations of our thought and practice are as old as the Sophists of Athens in the fifth century BC. Many of the *aporiai* "revealed" by Derrida were encountered as such long ago by the neo-Hegelian philosophers in connecting phenomena to their various absolutes. And whether Derrida has added anything to our understanding of time or of logic – both important in his thought – is uncertain. What is certain is that we can benefit from a detailed reading of Derrida's texts, one which situates them in a balanced manner within the history of thought rather than merely using them as a privileged lens to view that history.

Notes

1 Terry Eagleton, *Against the Grain: Essays 1975–1985* (London: New Left Books, 1986), pp. 81–82.
2 Terry Eagleton, *Marxism and Literary Criticism* (London: New Left Books, 1976), pp. 8–10.
3 Terry Eagleton, *Walter Benjamin or Towards a Revolutionary Criticism* (London: New Left Books, 1981), p. 98. Hereafter cited as *WB*.
4 Terry Eagleton, *Literary Theory: An Introduction* (Oxford and Minnesota: Blackwell/University of Minnesota Press, 1983), p. 211. Hereafter cited as *LT*.
5 Terry Eagleton, *After Theory* (Harmondsworth: Allen Lane and Penguin, 2003), pp. 221–222.
6 This treatment of Freud's life and work is based on his own account as offered in "An Autobiographical Study" (1925). It is included in *The Freud Reader*, ed. Peter Gay (New York and London: W. W. Norton, 1989). The following accounts of Freud's various works draw upon some of Peter Gay's insights, and all further citations of Freud's works refer to this excellent and easily accessible collection. Hereafter cited as *Freud*.
7 Quoted by Peter Gay in *Freud*, p. 444.
8 Reprinted in Jacques Lacan, *Écrits: A Selection*, trans. Alan Sheridan (London: Tavistock Publications, 1977). Hereafter citations from this volume are given in the text.
9 C. H. Dodd, *The Interpretation of the Fourth Gospel* (Cambridge: Cambridge University Press, 1953), pp. 263–265. Hereafter cited as Dodd.
10 "Structure, Sign, and Play in the Discourse of the Human Sciences," in *Writing and Difference*, trans. Alan Bass (Chicago: University of Chicago Press, 1978), p. 278. Hereafter cited as *WD*.
11 Jacques Derrida, *Specters of Marx: The State of the Debt, the Work of Mourning, and the New International*, trans. Peggy Kamuf (New York and London: Routledge, 1994).

Chapter 5

The Era of Poststructuralism (II): Postmodernism, Modern Feminism, Gender Studies

Postmodernism

The term "postmodernism" resonates in at least three registers: firstly, in terms of historical development, the term appears as "postmodernity," designating the latest phase in the broad evolution of capitalist economics and culture, especially since the latter part of the twentieth century. This historical phenomenon has generated two further registers: that of postmodern theory, which has attempted to account for and explain it, and that of literature and art, which has variously attempted to express it. In the second and most problematic of these registers, the sphere of literary and cultural theory, the terms "postmodern" or "postmodernism" have been applied to the works of numerous writers, such as Jacques Derrida, Julia Kristeva, and Michel Foucault, who have also been labeled "poststructuralist." Indeed, in this last register, there seems to be no clear demarcation between the two terms, largely because they are not two distinct phenomena which can somehow be related to each other. Rather, postmodernism is a broader phenomenon, one of whose manifestations is poststructuralism. Alternatively, the two terms might be viewed as two perspectives, rather than two phenomena, from which to view the history of modern literary and cultural criticism. The perspective of postmodernism situates modern theory within the context of larger economic and cultural tendencies, whereas that of poststructuralism sees such theory as both emerging from and reacting against the structuralist modes of analysis that predominated in many fields, including literature and political theory, during the 1950s. The major theorists of postmodernism have included Jean-François Lyotard and Jean Baudrillard. The work of Georges Bataille belongs in an earlier, phenomenological, tradition, but was revived in the usage of postmodernists and poststructuralists. The opponents of postmodernism (who have also theorized about it) have included notably left-wing intellectuals such as Jürgen Habermas, Fredric Jameson, and Terry Eagleton. Finally, in the register of literature and art, the term "postmodernism" has been used by a number of critics, such as Ihab Hassan, to distinguish the experimental literature produced after the Second World War from the high modernism of the period roughly between 1910 and 1930. We can now briefly look at each of these three senses of the postmodern.

In the register of historical development, postmodernity designates a society and culture that has evolved beyond the phases of industrial and finance capitalism. This society is often called consumer capitalism, a phase characterized by the global extension of capitalist markets, mass migration of labor, the predominating role of mass media and images, unprecedented economic and cultural interaction between various parts of the world, and an unparalleled pluralism and diversity at all levels of culture. According to many of the theorists of postmodernism, this contemporary social order is no longer based on, or even attempts to pursue, the Enlightenment ideals of progress and justice based on universal reason, a notion of human subjectivity as autonomous, and of the world as knowable (and conquerable) by scientific and technological advance. Rather, the external world is viewed as an ideological construction, refracted through an endlessly circulating world of signs, through media images and the various technologies and institutional codes (of school, workplace, religious centers) that hold us in their sway. Even subjectivity itself is regarded as a product of power structures; power is no longer viewed as an isolable and centralized agency that dominates or coerces subjects that are already there: rather, it is intimately involved in the very production of subjectivities which are then conditioned to regulate themselves. Just as the worlds of objective reality and unified autonomous subjectivity have been dissolved, dissipated through the linguistic and social structures and semiotic codes that ultimately form and define them, so too the conventional worlds of morality and culture in general are viewed as without absolute foundations and grounded in human desire, material need, a libidinal economy and self-projection. Reason itself is viewed as integral to capitalism, as coercive and exclusive, a faculty used to label alternative visions as mad or irrational; even the category of "experience" as used by the bourgeois philosophers has become suspect, as well as their understanding of fundamental notions such as space and time. Many radical critics entering the debates over postmodernism – following a long series of developments since the emergence of the New Left in the 1960s – no longer hold the conventional Marxist view of the economic infrastructure and class struggle as the ultimate determinants of social development: instead, language, images, and the entire cultural sphere are all viewed as crucial to the social and political order, with economics reduced to one of several determinative elements acting as a complex of causes. In this scenario, literature and art are given a high role in impugning the existing orders of capitalism. As in much cultural theory, culture itself becomes viewed as a site of ideological struggle. Some Marxists, however, would still argue that Marxism itself comprehends the interaction of cultural and economic elements, and that the subsumption of economics into the cultural sphere or superstructure – a kind of "superstructuralism" which collapses the terms of conventional Marxist analysis – is itself an ideological strategy of late capitalism.

In general, the postmodern and postmodernism denote a contemporary economic and cultural situation, and a series of perspectives, where the major grand narratives of the recent past – the progress and liberation of humanity (from a liberal or socialist perspective) and the unity or totality of the system of knowledge – no longer command credibility, and lie in ruins. The universal (power, struggle, agency) has given way to the local, identity has yielded to difference, depth (the notion of an underlying reality) has given way to a world of surfaces or mere appearances, and reality is submerged in, and indeed defined by, a world of signs. What has been called the "crisis of representation" – the inability of language to represent reality – reverberates through all of these positions. And all of these positions are shared by postmodernism and poststructuralism. We might add that this so-called crisis – like most of the "crises" identified by poststructuralism – is hardly new; it was recognized by Locke and the bourgeois philosophers, including Hegel and the neo-Hegelian philosophers such as Bradley and Bosanquet. The reaffirmation of such crises – already well recognized as such – highlights the roots (*radices*) of these "radical" modes of thought in the liberal humanist tradition, in the very mode of their reaction against which they reveal themselves as variants, at once gesturally subversive and substantively complicit.

The third register of postmodernism, that of literature and the arts, can be dealt with briefly here. The work of the high modernists, such as Proust, Joyce, T. S. Eliot, Pound, Virginia Woolf, Kafka, and Brecht, was characterized by a number of underlying assumptions: a recognition of the complex nature of reality and experience, of the role of time and memory in human perception, of the self and world as historical constructions, and, underlying all of these, the problematic nature of language. In terms of style, the modernists engaged in a breakdown of narrative structures and conventional poetic forms, the use of allusion, parody, hyperbole, collage, and pastiche. Postmodernism, as expressed in the writings of Beckett, Robbe-Grillet, Borges, Marquez, Naguib Mahfouz, and Angela Carter, also rests on the same assumptions and exhibits the same characteristics.

This raises the vexed question: what, then, is the difference between modernism and postmodernism? The epistemological assumptions are the same: a recognition of the limitations of reason and experience as formulated by the bourgeois philosophers, the mutual construction of the subject and object of knowing as mediated and enabled by language, and a relativistic view of truth as dependent on context and perspective. We can perhaps identify three salient features which differentiate postmodernism from modernism. Firstly, postmodernism – in both subject matter and style – is marked by a recognition of ethnic, sexual, and cultural diversity. Whereas modernist texts like Conrad's *Heart of Darkness* could only describe the other (in this case, Africans) from the outside, postmodernist works tend to give the other a voice, to analyze cultural difference from within (as in the work of Mahfouz). Secondly, whereas high modernism (with exceptions such as Brecht) prided itself on its highbrow status and learned allusions, postmodernism – with equal self-consciousness – deliberately extends into the domain of popular culture, abrogating distinctions between high and low art, and indeed often attempting to lay bare structures of cultural coercion and domination. T. S. Eliot's "The Love Song of J. Alfred Prufrock" may subvert the form and content of a love song and exhibit the painful, unidealized nature of love in the modern world; but some later writers such as the Pakistani poets N. M. Rashed and Kishwar Naheed express a colonial condition where the very possibility of love is withered.

Finally, and most importantly, there is a difference of motive between modernism and postmodernism, even where the same technical devices of fragmentation and allusion are used: postmodernist writing unabashedly exhibits difference, diversity, incoherence, and a world of surfaces, with no attempt to subsume these under identity, a framework of coherence or depth, or any vision of implied unity. Heterogeneity is presented as irreducible, recalcitrant to any form of redintegration. With modernism, difference is still rooted in identity, experimentation in tradition, and relativism in the memory of various absolutes. Even stylistic innovations such as free verse or disruptions of narrative were haunted by the ghosts of the forms that lurked behind them. T. S. Eliot's *The Waste Land*, supposedly an expression of a fragmented world marooned from the past, relies heavily on allusions which point to a retrospective unity in traditional forms of life; Joyce's *Ulysses* insinuates a coherence in its use of the *Odyssey* as an implied background. But a postmodernist work such as Beckett's *Waiting for Godot* exhibits no structure in its allusions, which are random, repetitive, and where the "action" of the play defies the very category of action (and of the dramatic unities), and its location is entirely abstract and unnameable. The only possible modes of coherence are those that the reader or audience might impose, bringing to bear their own assumptions and effectively writing or rewriting the play themselves. Where modernism is nostalgic and retrospective toward vanished schemes of unity and order, postmodernism insists on the heterogeneity of the present, and on the irony of its own retrospections into traditional notions of coherence. We can now look briefly at some of the major theorists of postmodernism, beginning with a thinker whose opposition to postmodernism inspired much debate.

Jürgen Habermas (b. 1929)

The work of the German philosopher and sociologist Jürgen Habermas has spanned social theory, the genesis of capitalism, and the meanings of democracy, rationality, and the functioning of law. He is perhaps best known for his account of the public sphere and the creation of modern civil society, the elements of the public world not directly under state control but open to the exchange of private opinion, as in the various levels of media, religious organizations, and social gatherings. Habermas describes how the public sphere was transformed in the growth of capitalism in his first book, *The Structural Transformation of the Public Sphere* (1962). Though he was for some time associated with the Frankfurt School of Marxist social and cultural theory, the main thrust of Habermas' work has been a defense of modern liberal democracy and its theorization in the Enlightenment ideals of reason, justice, progress, and freedom. Against poststructuralist opponents who claim that reason is relative, coercive, and exclusive, he formulates a notion of communicative reason, of a rationality grounded in the very process of communication, on the basis of which "communicative action" will be possible.

In a lecture of 1980 entitled "Modernity – An Incomplete Project" (later published as "Modernity Versus Postmodernity"),[1] Habermas observes that, from the twelfth to the seventeenth centuries, the word "modern" was used during those periods whose consciousness of themselves as new was based on a renewed relationship to some ancient era; as, for example, in the Renaissance (*MP*, 126). But this defining of the modern with reference to the past dissolved with the French Enlightenment in the eighteenth century. In the nineteenth century, the Romantic spirit had a radical consciousness of modernity as freed from the past, from all historical ties. This is the "aesthetic modernity" which we have inherited (*MP*, 127).

What characterizes aesthetic modernity is an altered conception of time, crystallized in the exaltation of the present, and expressed in exploring unknown territory, engaging in new forms of experience, and in general anticipating an undefined future. This new time consciousness is of course embodied in the philosophy of Bergson, and expresses the experience of mobility in society, of historical acceleration, and discontinuity in everyday life. There is a new value placed on the ephemeral and a celebration of dynamism and flux. This kind of modernity revolts against the normalizing functions of tradition, neutralizing the standards of both morality and utility (*MP*, 128). Part of Habermas' purpose in this lecture is to reject the thesis of neoconservatives such as Daniel Bell that the current crises and contradictions of capitalism are in large part caused by modernist culture, whose values – unlimited self-realization and the experiential demands of a hyperstimulated sensitivity – have permeated everyday life. According to Bell, modernist culture is incompatible with professional life, with "the moral basis of a purposive, rational conduct of life," and underlies the dissolution of the Protestant ethic (*MP*, 129). Habermas points out that Bell effectively blames modernist culture for what has actually been caused by capitalist economic and social modernization. The role of culture in this transformation is actually "very indirect and mediated" (*MP*, 130).

Habermas urges that continued cultural traditions and social integration require a "communicative rationality" (*MP*, 131). The project of Enlightenment was a project of modernity: this project aimed to "develop objective science, universal morality and law, and autonomous art according to their inner logic" (in other words, they were to be treated as autonomous spheres requiring specialized expertise, and not merely falling under various branches of religion or metaphysics). Moreover, the Enlightenment philosophers wanted to use this specialized culture for the enrichment and "rational organization of everyday social life." The arts and sciences would promote not only control of nature but also understanding of the world, the self, moral progress, and justice (*MP*, 132). But the twentieth century has shattered this optimism, differentiating these various spheres into such specialized autonomy that they are isolated from everyday life. Since the mid-nineteenth century, art has become regarded as increasingly autonomous and devoid of reference to any real world, immersed rather in self-reference (*MP*, 133). This situation can be cured only by reintegrating the aesthetic with the cognitive and the moral-practical (*MP*, 134). We should not be led by the threat of domination of any one of these spheres over the others to denounce the surviving Enlightenment tradition as rooted in a "terroristic reason." We should reject the exclusive focus on aesthetic concerns which excludes aspects of truth and justice, an isolation which dissolves as soon as aesthetic experience is absorbed into ordinary life (*MP*, 135).

Habermas classifies the poststructuralists Derrida and Foucault and their precursors such as Bataille under the aegis of aesthetic modernity: their emphasis on decentered subjectivity, freed from the imperatives of work and utility, forces them to "step outside the modern world." He calls them "young conservatives." The "old conservatives," on the other hand, reject cultural modernism altogether and withdraw to a stance anterior to modernity, often a neo-Aristotelianism. Finally, the neoconservatives effectively depoliticize the content of cultural modernity, and assert the pure immanence of art, viewing the aesthetic experience as merely private (*MP*, 137).

Jean Baudrillard (1929–2007)

The sociologist Jean Baudrillard has sometimes been called the high priest or prophet of postmodernism, though some have questioned this affiliation, given his evident aversion to many of the forms and elements of postmodernity. Baudrillard was teaching at the University of Paris at Nanterre in 1968, and so was at the heart of the student unrest and revolt of that era, a phenomenon which (largely through its failure) deeply influenced his outlook. His early work, such as *The System of Objects* (1968) and *The Consumer Society* (1970), was broadly Marxist in orientation. But a further study, *The Mirror of Production* (1973), was highly critical of Marx, viewing his analysis of capital as insufficiently radical and trapped within the very categories of capitalism (such as production itself). This criticism was continued in Baudrillard's own assessment of capitalist economics in *Symbolic Exchange and Death* (1976), and subsequent collections such as *Simulations* (1983).

The underlying theme running through Baudrillard's analyses of modern culture and society is that "reality" has in the late capitalist era been replaced by codes of signification. This theme is perhaps most clearly laid out in *Simulations* where Baudrillard argues that today, reality has been replaced by simulacra, by images which purport or pretend to be the real thing. At one time, images would claim to represent a reality that was already there. In contrast, what we are witnessing now is a "precession of simulacra," a series of images which do not even claim to represent reality but offer themselves in its place: "Simulation . . . is the generation by models of a real without origin or reality: a hyperreal." What we have inherited is the "desert of the real itself."[2] Present-day simulators try to make reality coincide with their simulation models. What has disappeared is the notion of the "representational imaginary, the difference between reality and simulation. And with this has also gone the entire subject matter of metaphysics, its quest to define reality" (S, 3). In this age of simulation which liquidates all referents, there is no longer a question of imitating or even parodying reality: "it is rather a question of substituting signs of the real for the real itself" (S, 4). According to Baudrillard, one of the motivations of religious iconoclasts who objected to the representation of the divine in images was their fear that simulacra might evoke in people the "destructive truth . . . that ultimately there has never been any God, that only the simulacrum exists, indeed that God himself has only ever been his own simulacrum" (S, 8). And if God himself can be simulated, then the whole system is merely "a gigantic simulacrum . . . never again exchanging for what is real, but exchanging in itself, in an uninterrupted circuit without reference or circumference" (S, 11).

A perfect model of all the orders of simulation is Disneyland: in this can be traced the profile of America, whose values "are exalted here, in miniature and comic strip form" (S, 23–24). Disney exists to conceal the fact that it is the real America which is Disneyland: it "is presented as imaginary in order to make us believe that the rest is real," when in fact America itself is "no longer real, but of the order of the hyperreal and of simulation. It is no longer a question of a false representation of reality (ideology), but of concealing the fact that the real is no longer real, and thus of saving the reality principle" (*S*, 25). The infantile world of Disneyland elicits our belief that the adults are elsewhere, in the real world, and to conceal the fact that real childishness is everywhere. There are many sites with the same function as Disneyland (Enchanted Village, Magic Mountain) surrounding Los Angeles – which itself is a "network of endless, unreal circulation . . . an immense script and a perpetual motion picture" (*S*, 26). The tendencies Baudrillard describes are even more pronounced today: the infantilism has deepened its grip to all kinds of game shows, where prizes are awarded on the basis of answering (with many prompts and lifelines) the most banal questions; cartoon movies whose audience is just as much adults as children; and indeed, the manufacture of entire political and social visions through the news media, in their coverage of war, other nations, education, and a host of social and ethical issues.

In a section entitled "The Order of Simulacra," first published in *Symbolic Exchange and Death*, Baudrillard traces the emergence of three orders of simulacra since the Renaissance: the counterfeit in the early modern period; production in the industrial era; and simulation in the current code-governed society. These forms of simulacra are based respectively on a natural law of value, then a market law of value followed by a structural law of value. The modern sign, as first manifested in the counterfeit, arose when the feudal order was undermined by the bourgeois order. In the former, signs were clear and prohibitive, their circulation restricted in a brutal hierarchy; in the early modern era, the arbitrariness of the sign was inaugurated, with the sign being emancipated, and every class able to participate in a competitive democracy. The sign exists as a simulacrum of a "natural" value.[3] By the time we reach our own era, reality has collapsed into hyperrealism or the "meticulous reduplication of the real," exercised by an objective gaze or perspective which has attained "an objectivity finally free of the object" (*SED*, 71–72). In this situation, reality is defined by its very reproducibility: "we are now living entirely within the 'aesthetic' hallucination of reality . . . Reality has passed completely into the game of reality . . . This is the end of metaphysics and the beginning of the era of hyperreality" (*SED*, 74). Art can no longer imitate or parody or distance itself from reality: "art is everywhere, since artifice lies at the heart of reality" (*SED*, 75). Reality, then, is manufactured, and passed off as itself.

In *The System of Objects* Baudrillard attempts to analyze how, in the contemporary world, objects are experienced, their function, their relation to mental structures, their cultural underpinnings, and, in general, the system of meanings that objects institute. He considers objects from what he calls the "technological plane," which reveals the rationality of objects, whereby they can be understood in relation to production, consumption, possession, and personalization. He argues that it is no longer material needs that generate the circuits of production; rather, those circuits are driven by a semiotic code of equivalences between the identity of consumers and the commodities they acquire; it is the latter that determines the former. Baudrillard argues that the ideology of competition has shifted from the sphere of production to the sphere of consumption. It has created, through the psychological manipulation of needs, a class of "normal" consumers who, paradoxically, wish to feel unique while resembling everyone else in their possessions.[4] In fact, the ideology of competition is giving way to a philosophy of self-fulfillment whereby individuals actualize themselves, their identities, and personality, in consumption. The "philosophers of consumption," such as Dichter and Martineau, claim that this "new humanism" of consumption offers individuals an opportunity for fulfillment and liberation; the underlying premise is to offer consumers the ability to feel moral even as they indulge in a hedonistic morality "founded purely on satisfaction," even as they regress to childlike and irrational behavior. Being free to be oneself effectively means being free to project one's desires into produced goods (SO, 185), thereby releasing drives that were blocked by guilt, superego, or taboo. But this freedom does not extend into any substantive or critical function. This consumerist philosophy substitutes personalized relations to objects for lived human relations, based on a "forced integration of the system of needs into the system of products" (SO, 188). In industrial society, it is the system of objects (not needs, as in earlier societies) that imposes its own coherence on and structures an entire society.

The object/advertising system comprises not a language but a code, a code of "status" or social standing which is universal inasmuch as advertising converts us all to it: other forms of recognition or valuation are giving way to this. The code is totalitarian: notwithstanding our individual revolts, we participate daily in "its collective development" (SO, 193–194). But on the positive side, the code emancipates social relations in that it renders obsolete the rituals of class and caste and preceding social discriminations. For the first time in history, the code establishes a universal system of signs. But this is obtained at the price of regression to the language of value whereby all individuals are defined in terms of their objects. Moreover, rather than being an impulse toward democratization, this reduction to one plane of valuation exacerbates the desire for discrimination and hierarchy. Finally, the code offers the image of a false transparency of social relations which masks the real structures of production (SO, 195–196). Consumption is not defined by the particular objects we acquire but in their signification: to be consumed, the object must become a sign (SO, 200).

These insights concerning the semiotic code reach into the nature of capitalist production itself: in *Symbolic Exchange and Death* Baudrillard displaces the Marxist terminology of use-value and exchange-value with his own terminology of symbolic exchange and commodity exchange; capitalism, he argues, is not a mode of production but a system of codes premised on the "law of value" (which in Marx broadly signifies the equivalence between the value of a commodity and the amount of labor power necessary to produce it). In this substitution lies Baudrillard's insight that, as capitalism proceeds, it undermines the very oppositions between economic base and superstructure, as well as between capital and labor: the law of value extends beyond the economic sphere into all realms of culture. And it is the realm of signification which apportions their place to the economic and ideological spheres: as Mike Gain points out, in Baudrillard's assessment, the symbolic order in the capitalist system (the order of language and signs) "almost appears as a replacement for the notion of a social infrastructure."[5] For Baudrillard, emphasis on the notion of symbolic exchange effectively displaces a Marxist emphasis on the economic sphere as the ultimately determining force of social and political change; the notion of symbolic exchange opposes cultural and human values to the bourgeois values of utilitarianism and profit; it is taken from Bataille's view that capitalism's values of production and accumulation are contrary to our basic human impulses of expenditure, sacrifice, and destruction. In the notion of symbolic exchange Baudrillard sees a richness of human activity beyond the reductive ethic of capitalism.

In formulating his notion of symbolic exchange, Baudrillard draws on the notion of the "gift" articulated in relation to primitive societies by the French sociologist Marcel Mauss (1872–1950). When a gift is given, it bears something of the identity and status of the giver, imposing an obligation to reciprocate on the part of the receiver. Baudrillard also draws on Saussure's posthumously published research on anagrams (in Latin poetry), which he saw as a foundation for a theory of poetry. This research, found over fifty years after Saussure's death, goes against the grain of Saussure's linguistics as it has been commonly received. This research found anagrams (of gods or patrons) encoded into poems, and led Saussure to see the poetic as a further dimension to language, whose elements and operations contradict grammatical rules and produce unexpected correspondences and effects.

The basic principle that Baudrillard sees in these notions of Mauss and Saussure, as well as in Freud's death drive, is the principle of reversibility: the reversibility of the gift via a counter-gift, of the terms in an anagram, of life in death (*SED*, 2). Death is the form in which determinacy is lost, through the demand for reversibility: reversibility is fatal to any system, any coherence, any identity: this, Baudrillard says, is what is meant by "symbolic exchange" (*SED*, 5, n. 2). What, then, is the broader significance of this principle of reversibility? In a chapter entitled "The End of Production," Baudrillard describes the structural revolution of value. Saussure saw a signifier as related to a specific signified and as possessing a *structural* value in relation to all other signifiers in a system. Baudrillard claims that this situation is analogous to Marx's analysis of the value of a commodity in terms of use and exchange, as expressed by the commodity law of value. A commodity has its own specific use or reference; but it can be exchanged for any number of other items or for money. But, says Baudrillard, a revolution has put an end to this classical economics of value: now, the referential value of the sign or commodity is annihilated, and its structural value – its position in the system of signs or other commodities – is autonomous. In other words, the value of the commodity is not based on its use, as the value of the sign is not based on the signified to which it refers but merely its place in the sign system (*SED*, 6). In this new phase, value is a product of simulation: signs are exchanged against each other, not against the real: signs become free of any "determinant equivalence" with reality. A similar change occurs at the level of labor power and production: the annihilation of any goal of production (as, for example, meeting certain human needs) allows production to function as a code. In this new stage, money, signs, needs, labor, all float in an endless mutual commutability or exchangeability (*SED*, 7). We have moved from the commodity law of value to the structural law of value, where reality is "absorbed by the hyperreality of the code and simulation" (*SED*, 2). The age of simulation of reality is announced by this absolute mutual commutability: "All the great humanist criteria of value, the whole civilisation of moral, aesthetic and practical judgment are effaced in our system of images and signs. Everything becomes undecidable, the characteristic effect of the domination of the code." This indeterminacy extends even to the realm of the economic infrastructure, which can no longer be regarded as determining all other realms, such as culture, art, and politics (*SED*, 9). In this new regime, capitalism is no longer a mode of production but a mode of domination: the structural law of value is the purest form of domination, no longer locatable within a class or a relation of forces, but "entirely reabsorbed . . . into the signs which surround us, operative everywhere in the code in which capital finally holds its purest discourses" (*SED*, 10). The fundamental law of this society is not the law of exploitation but the code of normality (*SED*, 29).

Jean-François Lyotard (1924–1998)

Like Baudrillard, Jean-François Lyotard was at the University of Nanterre during the student revolt of 1968, and he was also an activist against French imperialism in Algeria. He was deeply embroiled in the debates concerning postmodernism in the last decades of the twentieth century, especially opposing Jürgen Habermas' sanction of the project of Enlightenment, universal reason, and modernity. Lyotard's reaction against Marxism in *Starting from Marx and Freud* (1973) expressed the grave misgivings of much poststructuralist thought toward Marxist categories of analysis. For example, Lyotard saw the function of social class as displaced by modern technocratic and bureaucratic regimes. He saw capitalism and totalitarianism as suppressing what he called the "libidinal economy" of desire, and saw the task of experimental art as revolutionary in releasing desire. Lyotard is perhaps best known for his work *The Postmodern Condition* (1979). But this work is primarily concerned with assessing the status of contemporary scientific knowledge. It is in the famous preface to the book and other articles that he defines most clearly his understanding of the postmodern. In that preface, he suggests that the term "postmodern" designates the state of our culture subsequent to the transformation of the sciences, literature, and the arts since the end of the nineteenth century.[6] Science is now in a state of crisis, since narratives are in crisis. In a sense, scientific knowledge, proceeding as it does through logical inquiry, is of a different order from narrative, which it usually regards as nothing more than fable. But modern science needs to legitimate its own rules by a discourse of legitimation, a metadiscourse which appeals to some "grand narrative," such as the emancipation of the human subject in terms of reason or economics, or the creation of wealth (he sees the two modern grand narratives as liberal humanism and Marxism). This is part of the Enlightenment narrative, which also has as its aim the realization of such ideals as justice and peace. Lyotard defines postmodern as "incredulity toward metanarratives." The obsolescence of the metanarrative apparatus of legitimation, he observes, is evident in the crisis of metaphysics and of the university institutions which have embodied them. The narrative, divested of its great purpose, is dispersed through heterogeneous language games. Political attempts at homogenization – judging everything, for example, by criteria of operability and efficiency – represent a form of terror (*PC*, xxiv). We cannot seek legitimacy, as Habermas does, in rational consensus, since this is coercive: postmodern knowledge, Lyotard suggests, "is not simply a tool of the authorities; it refines our sensitivity to differences and reinforces our ability to tolerate the incommensurable" (*PC*, xxv).

In an appendix to the book entitled "Answering the Question: What is Postmodernism?" Lyotard suggests that realism is outmoded because today's reality is so destabilized, and capitalism constantly derealizes familiar objects and institutions. Much of the market caters to this "endemic desire for reality"and simplicity, attempting to stabilize the referent and to ensure quick communication that will also reassure consumers of their own identity; mass communication, refusing to re-examine its own artistic rules, is an exercise in mass conformism. Such realism is defined by its very avoidance of the question of reality (*PC*, 74–75). Equally, we should recall that science and industry have the same problematic relation to reality as art: they can hardly be said to describe or represent reality. This relation is displaced by the "technological criterion," a consensus between political or industrial partners as to what comprises reality. But no matter what criteria are currently deployed, it is undeniable that capitalism and science emerged as a result of the decline of metaphysical, religious, and political certainties concerning the nature of reality. This is where Lyotard defines an important circumstance for the emergence of modernity, which, "in whatever age it appears, cannot exist without a shattering of belief and without discovery of the 'lack of reality' of reality, together with the invention of other realities" (*PC*, 77).

In order to understand the distinction that Lyotard now makes, we need to have some sense of Kant's notion of the sublime. Kant says that when we make an aesthetic judgment about the beauty of an object, our imagination (our ability to reproduce images) and our understanding (our conceptualizing power) are in harmony, and appear to be adapted to nature or the external world. It is this harmony which gives us pleasure. But in a judgment of the sublime, we are confronted by something in nature which our imagination cannot comprehend or present in images; but we have a power of reason – a higher faculty which unifies the various concepts of the understanding – which we realize is superior to anything that the sensible world of nature can present to us, no matter how boundless or awesome. This feeling, of "negative pleasure," is what Kant calls sublimity. So the sublime involves, not a harmony of imagination and understanding, whereby the imagination presents images which cohere with our intellectual faculty, but rather, a conflict, a struggle between them: imagination is incapable of presenting certain aspects of nature (such as infinitude) to our understanding. There is a gap between presentation and conception, between what is presentable (in images) and conceivable (in concepts).

Lyotard claims that both modern and postmodern art (which are indissolubly related) practice an aesthetic of the sublime: they both withdraw from the real and attempt to present, to make visible, the fact that the unpresentable exists. But they offer the connection between the presentable and the conceivable (in Kant's terms, between imagination and understanding) in two different ways, one stressing the incapacity of imagination to present, the other stressing its capacity to create new rules and forms (*PC*, 79–80). Modern aesthetics is nostalgic, presenting the unpresentable only as something absent (for example, lost religious faith), but its form possesses a recognizable consistency. The postmodern "puts forward the unpresentable in presentation itself," searching for new rules and forms. An example of the modern is Proust, whose expression of the unpresentable by altered syntax and treatment of time consciousness nonetheless leaves intact the unity of the narrative. Joyce, on the other hand, allows the unpresentable to appear in his writing itself, which challenges the very notions of grammar, syntax, and unity. The postmodern artist is like a philosopher, seeking new foundations. In fact, postmodernism, as understood by Lyotard, is intrinsically part of the modern: a work can become modern only by first being postmodern: it must break the rules and seek a new grounding; but, as soon as its new form is founded, it has already given way to the need for a new search (*PC*, 77–81). Lyotard ends by urging that those who are calling for a return to order and stability, a return to the referent, are effectively calling for a "return of terror," which must be resisted, given its coercive, consumerist, art-killing nature (*PC*, 82).

In another article called "Defining the Postmodern," Lyotard characterizes modernity in general as a principle of breaking with the past and beginning "a new way of living and thinking." He cites three attributes of postmodernity. Firstly, the difference between modern and postmodern lies in the latter's no longer appealing to a "horizon of general emancipation," and as marked by a "disappearance of the idea of progress within intentionality and freedom."[7] Postmodern style entails bricolage or collections of quotations from previous styles and periods. A second, related, connotation of postmodernism is loss of belief in the idea that the arts, technology, and liberty would be profitable to humankind as a whole, and the shared belief that all enterprises are legitimate "only insofar as they contribute to the emancipation of mankind" ("DP," 2). These beliefs have of course been shattered: neither economic or political liberalism nor Marxism is free of suspicion of crimes against humankind. Lyotard suggests that no kind of thought can sublate Auschwitz, no kind of project of universal progress and emancipation can account for this. Another failure of the modern project is manifested in the fact that humankind is now divided into two parts, the one confronted with the challenge of complexity, and the other with the "terrible ancient task of survival" ("DP," 2). Finally, postmodernity – as Lyotard seems to suggest in his final statements – is expressed in literature and art by an investigation of the foundations and presuppositions of modernity itself ("DP," 3).

Though Lyotard's works are often cited as offering the definitive assessments of postmodernism, he appears to use Kant's notion of the sublime as a vague metaphor for inexpressibility. And his definitions are somewhat problematic, as in the examples he offers: if Joyce's text is postmodern, using as it does an allusive ancient narrative framework, how can we distinguish between Joyce and Beckett, where even the process of allusion is divested of any regulatory function? Finally, it is arguable that the loss of certainty regarding language, the stability of the human subject, and even of the grand narratives of progress and knowledge, occurred even at the end of the nineteenth century, and that this loss informs much of what we call high modernism.

bell hooks (Gloria Jean Watkins; b. 1952)

Another important critique of postmodern theory has issued from African American critics such as Cornel West and bell hooks, who have observed that, for all its emphasis on difference, postmodern theory has ignored the work of black writers and intellectuals. hooks (who writes her name in lower case to direct emphasis to the substance of her books rather than her self) is a feminist scholar and activist who has produced much work on the intersections of gender, race, and class. In her essay "Postmodern Blackness," hooks argues that postmodernist discourses have been exclusionary and are dominated by white male voices.[8] A radical postmodernist practice should incorporate the voices of oppressed blacks, and the politics of difference should be integrated with the politics of racism (hooks, 25). Postmodernism's critique of identity politics comes at a time when black people are just coming to consciousness of their identity, and are in the process of forming a radical black subjectivity (hooks, 28).

hooks stresses that postmodernity is a social and economic condition. She observes that even in the era of postmodernity the collective African American condition is one of "continued displacement, profound alienation, and despair" (hooks, 26). This hopelessness creates a "yearning" which, at its profoundest, is a "longing for critical voice," intensified by postmodern deconstruction of master narratives (hooks, 27). Hence, postmodernism's critique of essentialism can be useful to black studies in a number of ways: by promoting the notion of multiple black identities and experiences, by resisting colonial paradigms of a monolithic black identity, and by seeing the connections of race with issues such as class mobility. In general, the critique of essentialism needs to be harmonized with an emphasis on the "authority of experience" (hooks, 29).

Modern Feminism

Like most other critical tendencies since the 1960s, modern feminism is distinguished from its precursors by having been forged in the same fire as much poststructuralist thought, questioning fixed and stable notions of gender, sexuality, and even the category of "woman." It has, moreover, moved into further areas of inquiry such as the connections of gender with class and race, power structures, the semiotic codes through which ideology operates, and the construction of subjectivity itself. The rich flowering of feminist thinking in France, America, and Britain, each with its specific areas of emphasis, can be considered in the following sections.

French Feminism

The impetus for much modern French feminism was drawn from the revolutionary atmosphere of May 1968, which saw massive unrest on the part of students and workers. In that atmosphere, an integral component of political revolution was seen as the transformation of signifying practices and conceptions of subjectivity, based on a radical understanding of the power of language. Drawing heavily on the ideas of Jacques Lacan and Jacques Derrida (which they often modified against the grain of these thinkers), feminists such as Annie Leclerc, Marguerite Duras, Julia Kisteva, Luce Irigaray, and Hélène Cixous variously participated in advancing a notion of *l'écriture féminine*, a feminine writing that would issue from the unconscious, the body, from a radically reconceived subjectivity, in an endeavor to circumvent what they held to be phallocentric discourse. For

Kristeva, such language came from a pre-Oedipal state, from the realm of the "semiotic," prior to the process of cultural gender formation. She was aware, however, that reliance solely on this "maternal" language would entail the risk of political marginalization. Indeed, Luce Irigaray advocates undermining patriarchal discourse from within, a strategy she pursues in her readings of several discourses from Plato through Freud and Marx to Lacan. She does, however, indicate that a feminine language would be more diffuse, like female sexuality, and less rigidly categorizing than male discourse. Hélène Cixous also sees a "solidarity" between logocentrism and phallocentrism (where the phallus is a signifier, a metaphor of male power and dominance), an alliance that must be questioned and undermined. Women, she urged, must write their bodies, to unfold the resources of the unconscious. All of these writers revaluate the significance of the maternal, viewing this as empowering rather than as oppressed. Other feminists, however, such as Christine Fauré, Catherine Clément, and Monique Wittig, have challenged this emphasis on the body as biologically reductive, fetishistic, and politically impotent. Monique Wittig wishes to do away with the linguistic categories of sex and gender.

American Feminism

Feminist criticism in America received a major stimulus from the Civil Rights Movement of the 1960s, and has differed somewhat in its concerns from its counterparts in France and Britain, notwithstanding the undoubted impact of earlier figures such as Virginia Woolf and Simone de Beauvoir. A seminal work, *The Feminine Mystique* (1963), was authored by Betty Friedan (1921–2006), who subsequently founded the National Organization of Women in 1966. This widely received book expressed the fundamental grievance of middle-class American women, their entrapment within private, domestic life, and their inability to pursue public careers. A number of other important feminist texts were produced around this time: Mary Ellman's *Thinking About Women* (1968), Kate Millett's *Sexual Politics* (1969), Germaine Greer's *The Female Eunuch* (1970), and Shulamith Firestone's *The Dialectic of Sex* (1970), which used gender rather than class as the prime category of historical analysis. Millett's influential book concerned female sexuality and the representation of women in literature. It argued that patriarchy was a political institution which relied on subordinated roles for women. It also distinguished between the concept of "sex," which was rooted in biology, and that of "gender," which was culturally acquired. Other critics in this tradition of examining masculine portayals of women included Carolyn Heilbrun and Judith Fetterly.

A number of feminist texts have attempted to identify alternative and neglected traditions of female writing. These have included Patricia Meyer Spacks' *The Female Imagination* (1975), Ellen Moers' *Literary Women* (1976), and Sandra Gilbert and Susan Gubar's *The Madwoman in the Attic*

(1979). The most influential work of this kind was Elaine Showalter's *A Literature of their Own* (1977), which traced three phases of women's writing, a "feminine" phase (1840–1880) where women writers imitated male models, a "feminist" phase (1880–1920) during which women challenged those models and their values, and a "female" phase (from 1920) which saw women advocating their own perspectives. Recent debates within American feminism, conducted by figures such as Showalter, Lillian Robinson, Annette Kolodny, and Jane Marcus, have concerned the relationship of female writers to male theories, the need for feminist theory and a female language, the relation of feminism to poststructuralist perspectives, as well as continuing problems of political and educational activism.

Also hotly debated has been the possible connection of feminism and Marxism. In her seminal text *Women's Oppression Today: Problems in Marxist Feminist Analysis* (1980), Michèle Barrett outlines some of the central problems facing any attempt to forge a coalition of Marxist and feminist perspectives. How can a Marxist analysis, conceived on the basis of "a primary contradiction between labour and capital," be reconciled with a feminist approach, which must begin with the relations of gender?[9] Barrett focuses on three concepts that have been central to the Marxist feminist dialogue: patriarchy, reproduction, and ideology. According to Barrett, the most significant elements of the oppression of women under capitalism are "the economic organization of households and its accompanying familial ideology, the division of labor and relations of production, the educational system and the operations of the state," as well as the processes of creation and recreation of gendered subjects (*WT*, 40–41). Other works in this vein include Judith Newton and Deborah Rosenfelt's *Feminist Criticism and Social Change* (1985), which also argues for feminist analysis that takes account of social and economic contexts. A notable recent development has been the attempt to think through feminism from black and minority perspectives, as in Alice Walker's *In Search of Our Mothers' Gardens* (1983) and Barbara Smith's *Toward a Black Feminist Criticism* (1977).

British Feminism

Twentieth-century British feminist criticism might be said to begin with Virginia Woolf, whose work is considered in detail in chapter 2. Much British feminist criticism has had a political orientation, insisting on situating both feminist concerns and literary texts within a material and ideological context. In her landmark work "Women: The Longest Revolution," later expanded and produced as *Women's Estate* (1971), Juliet Mitchell examined patriarchy in terms of Marxist categories of production and private property as well as psychoanalytic theories of gender. Her later works such as *Psychoanalysis and Feminism* (1974) continue to refine her attempt to integrate the insights of Marxism and psychoanalysis. Other important critics have included Jacqueline Rose and Rosalind Coward, who have integrated certain insights of Jacques Lacan into a materialist feminism; Catherine Belsey, who also has drawn upon Lacan in assessing Renaissance drama from a materialist feminist perspective; and the Norwegian-born Toril Moi, who has developed insights from Woolf and engaged in a critique of the humanism and implicit essentialism of some American feminists. Also critical of the tendency of American feminists to combat male stereotypes and to recover female traditions are Judith Newton and Deborah Rosenfelt. Finally, a number of critics such as Cora Kaplan, Mary Jacobus, and Penny Boumelha have comprised the UK Marxist-Feminist Collective, formed in 1976. Like Barrett, they attempted to formulate a materialist aesthetics and insisted on integrating Marxist class analysis with feminism in analyzing and influencing gender representation.

The final two sections in this discussion of modern feminism will consider briefly the work of two of the more difficult but influential French feminist thinkers, Julia Kristeva and Hélène Cixous.

Julia Kristeva (b. 1941)

Aptly characterizing herself as a "female intellectual," Julia Kristeva has been a powerful influence on literary theory. She integrates insights from linguistics, psychoanalysis, and philosophy into her theories, the most important of which concern the development of subjectivity in relation to both language and the play of drives and impulses anterior to language. Born in Bulgaria, Kristeva studied in France from 1965; her teachers in Paris included Roland Barthes, Lucien Goldmann, and Claude Lévi-Strauss. In the late 1960s, she was appointed to the editorial board of *Tel Quel*, an outlet for structuralist and poststructuralist perspectives. Her work exhibits the profound impact of Hegel and Freud, as well as the influences of Mikhail Bakhtin, Jacques Lacan, and the psychologist Melanie Klein. Kristeva's first book, *Semeiotike: Recherches pour une Semanalyse* (1969), advances a theory of the sign. Her later publications are psychoanalytic in their approach and emphasis. Her best-known and most influential work is *Revolution in Poetic Language* (1974), some of the central ideas of which will be examined here.

Kristeva observes that modern linguistic theories treat language as a formal object which is marked by arbitrary relations between signifiers and signifieds, the substitution of the sign for the extra-linguistic (or reality outside of language), the discreteness of its elements, and finitude.[10] However, language considered as such a formal object lacks a *subject* of enunciation; and this merely passes over the question of "externality"or the possible existence of the subject beyond language. Two recent trends have addressed this issue of externality: the first attempts to examine signifying systems in which the arbitrary connection of signifier and signified is seen as "motivated" by unconscious processes: the externality to which linguistic relations are here connected is the psychosomatic realm, the "body divided into erogenous zones." These theories rehabilitate the notion of the pre-Oedipal fragmented body, but fail to explain this body's link to the post-Oedipal subject and his symbolic language (*RPL*, 22). The other trend begins from the subject of enunciation or transcendental ego and, purveying the necessary connections that linguistics bears with semantics and logic, views signification as an ideological and historical process (*RPL*, 23). Kristeva calls the first trend "the semiotic," and the second "the symbolic." These two modes, she says, "are inseparable within the *signifying process* that constitutes language, and the dialectic between them determines the type of discourse (narrative, metalanguage, theory, poetry, etc.) involved." And this necessary dialectic between the two modes of the signifying process, she says, is also "constitutive of the subject," a subject which is thus both semiotic and symbolic (*RPL*, 24). Kristeva sees her notion of the semiotic as positing a post-Freudian subject which decenters the transcendental ego of conventional Western thought (*RPL*, 30). The semiotic process includes "drives, their disposition, and their division of the body, plus the ecological and social system surrounding the body, such as objects and pre-Oedipal relations with parents." The realm of the symbolic encompasses the emergence of subject and object as well as the constitution of meaning structured according to categories tied to the social order (*RPL*, 86).

Kristeva sees the realm of the arts as engaging a *jouissance* that threatens to disrupt the symbolic order. She sees this potential especially in poetry and literature. This revolutionary poetic language has a subversive potential inasmuch as it threatens to reach back into the semiotic realm, to release energies and drives that have been thwarted by the conventional structure of the symbolic, disrupting the symbolic from within and reconceiving its notions of subject, object, and their connections. In the signifying practices of late capitalism, according to Kristeva, only certain *avant-garde* literary texts, such as those of Mallarmé and Joyce, have the ability to transgress the boundaries between semiotic and symbolic; such texts can open up new possibilities of meaning, new modes of signification. The text, therefore, is instrumental in social and political change: it is the site where the explosive force of the semiotic realm expresses itself (*RPL*, 103). Reading such a text is to subject one's subjectivity to "impossible dangers" and risks, such as leaving behind one's identity, family, state, and religion, as well as the very notions of continuity and constancy (*RPL*, 104). This "infinite" process can occur through various modalities, through art or revolutionary processes of labor and political practice. The radical transformation of linguistic and signifying practices is "logically (if not chronologically) contemporaneous" with transformations in the social, political, and economic order (*RPL*, 104). Quoting Marx's comment that freedom can arise only when the notion of labor is transformed, Kristeva urges that the signifying process as practiced by "free" texts "transforms the opaque and impenetrable subject of social relations and struggles into a subject in process/on trial." She thus draws attention to the "social function of texts: the production of a different kind of subject, one capable of bringing about new social relations, and thus joining in the process of capitalism's subversion" (*RPL*, 105).

Hélène Cixous (b. 1937)

The radical nature and impact of Hélène Cixous' work is also rooted in the political and social protests and upheavals of the 1960s, a period when leading French intellectuals such as Roland Barthes, Jacques Derrida, Jacques Lacan, and Julia Kristeva were re-examining some of the basic categories and assumptions of Western thought, especially as these were embodied in the structure of language. All of these thinkers challenged conventional representational or idealist views of language; they variously explored the implications of Saussure's observation of the discrepancy and distance between signifier and signified; and they variously promoted conceptions of writing or *écriture* which emphasized the relational, sensuous, material, and cultural-historical dimensions of language, and the "textuality" of discourse. Cixous' peculiar contribution to this radical project was to promote *écriture féminine* or feminine writing, as expressed in her powerful and outspoken manifesto "Le Rire de la Méduse" (1975), translated as "The Laugh of the Medusa" (1976).

"The Laugh of the Medusa" might be seen as structured like a poem in its implicit refusal to engage with the conventional rhetorical formats of argumentation and expository prose. While its themes – the need for a female writing, the nature of such writing, and its momentous implications at both personal and societal levels – are clear, these themes surface into prominence in Cixous' text through an almost poetic refrain, through patterns of recurrence and reiteration in altering contexts. What is more, the "argument" of this text relies heavily on the materiality of language, the texture of words, the effect of word combinations and wordplay, as well as on an overtness of metaphor that peripheralizes the possibility of attributing literal meaning – grounded as this spurious notion is on centuries-old traditions of masculine categorizations of concepts – to any portion of the text. The text attempts to move beyond even poetic stratagems inasmuch as its "parts" resist assimilation into unity or into any preceding literary critical tradition or into any reductive hierarchy that might assign a status of centrality to any of its claims.

Given its deliberated fluidity, it would be difficult to claim that Cixous' text revolves around any central metaphor: the very notion of centrality is treated as tentative and transitory, one set of concerns sliding into centrality, then receding as they are continually displaced by other notions. It may be worth, however, beginning by looking at the metaphor that issues from the text's title: the laugh of the medusa. This metaphor is not taken up until the middle of Cixous' text, where, addressing women (as she does through-out the text), she charges that men have "riveted us between two horrifying myths: between the Medusa and the abyss."[11] The "abyss" refers to the connotations and implications of Freud's designation of woman as a "dark continent," pregnant with a mystery recalcitrant to analysis and under-standing, and signifying lack, castration, negativity, and dependence (on the positive identity of the male). Cixous of course resists this view, this myth, of woman as unexplorable. And, countering the other myth, that of woman as Medusa, she affirms: "You only have to look at the Medusa straight on to see her. And she's not deadly. She's beautiful and she's laugh-ing" ("LM," 289). Why beautiful? And why laughing? For Cixous, as for symbolist poets like Laforgue and heterological thinkers such as Schopen-hauer and Bergson, laughter is a symbolic mode of refusing the history of (male) conceptuality, of truth as defined by masculine traditions of thought. It is not that laughter *opposes* truth with some other truth in the same conceptual mold. Rather, laughter is a way of *exceeding* the very notion of truth, of refusing to engage in the thought processes and categorizations of the world that have generated this notion. Another way of putting this would be to say that laughter exceeds or transcends "theory," which by its very (historically determined) nature is "male." Cixous states that a "femi-nine text" is "more than subversive," designed to "smash everything, to shatter the framework of institutions, to blow up the law, to break up the 'truth' with laughter" ("LM," 292). And it is the Medusa, in her newly envisaged beauty, who wears this laughing countenance, beyond the assaulting reach of her own reflectedness in the male shield of self-protective truth. In her demythified and remythified status, she cannot be destroyed like the Medusa of myth.

The myth of Medusa: in classical mythology, the Medusa was one of three sisters known as Gorgons, daughters of Phorcys and Ceto. The first two sisters, Stheno and Euryale, were immortal, but Medusa was mortal. Serpents were entwined in their hair, their bodies were covered with armor-like scales, and their hands were made of brass. Their gaze turned any onlooker to stone. Perseus, the son of Zeus and Danae, armed by Athene with a shield of brilliant bronze that would serve as a mirror, cut off the Medusa's head. In his *Metamorphoses*, Ovid has Perseus explain to his in-laws why the Medusa had snakes twining in her hair. The Medusa, he says, "was once renowned for her loveliness, and roused jealous hopes in the hearts of many suitors. Of all the beauties she possessed, none was more striking than her lovely hair." But Poseidon, he continues, "robbed her of her virginity" in the temple of Athene, who punished her "immodesty" by changing her hair into revolting snakes: "To this day, in order to terrify her enemies and numb them with fear, the goddess wears as a breastplate the snakes that were her own creation."[12]

If the Medusa represents one of the archetypal myths into which men have molded the image of woman, this myth expresses the repression of female sexuality and beauty: the very symbol of this sexuality, the Medusa's hair, becomes a symbol of terror in its draconian transformation. And although the agent of this repression and punishment was a female goddess, Athene, this happens to be a goddess with very "masculine" attributes, as expressed in her conventionally represented fierce countenance, and her powerful frame, robed in the attire of war. What Cixous effectively does is to redeem that part of the Medusa myth which has been repressed: the Medusa as she was prior to the repression of her sexuality, prior to the disfigurement of her beauty, and prior to her metamorphosis into a monster. To focus on the "laugh" of the Medusa, then, is to redeem woman, to liberate her from her degraded status in the history of male mythology. It is also to undermine the entire conceptual apparatus that has perpetuated the myths of woman. The Medusa's laugh returns woman to a pre-mythical state, to the state of actuality behind the myth, to the reality that has been repressed: it does not oppose theory but laughs in its face, creating through its laughter a mode of engagement with theory that cannot be reduced to simple opposition but gestures toward a reformulation of the very grounds of communication between the system of language on which conventional notions of truth are grounded, and an alternative, female language. This new language will subsist in the relation of laughter (not opposition) to conventional male language.

Indeed, what recurs throughout this text is a poetic exhortation to women to bring into being a female language: "Woman must write her self . . . Woman must put herself into the text – as into the world and into history – by her own movement" ("LM," 279). These broad categories – text, world, history – underlie the movement of Cixous' account of the significance and implications of female writing. First and foremost, feminine writing acknowledges its rootedness in the body: "Write your self. Your body must be heard" ("LM," 284). The significance of "body" in this context, as in many of the texts of feminism, is complex and far-reaching, since it is the body, the female body, that has been repressed historically by the apparatus of male theology and philosophy, social systems, and even psychoanalysis. Male visions of the world have achieved the status of "theory" precisely by abstracting from the data of actual experience, by withdrawing from the world of the senses and the unconscious into an ideal world, whether of pure forms, substance, the absolute idea, the transcendental ego, or the soul. The most blatant cases of such repression of the body occur in theologies which advocate negation or denial of one's body and its drives and desires, and in particular the female body, which is regarded as a source of temptation and often as unclean; the most explicit examples in philosophy occur in Plato, who denies the status of reality to the world of the body, the physical world of sensation, and also in Descartes' dualism between mind and matter, between the human self identified as a disembodied thinking substance and its body which occupies the world of matter and extension, and is external to the human self as such. Historically, then, to write *without* the body, to refuse to accommodate the claims of the body in a given view of the world, has been the norm, from Plato to the movements in modern philosophy commencing with Descartes. To write *with* the body implies facilitating a return of the repressed, a resurrection of that which has been subordinated and treated as secondary, as dirty, as weighing us down and preventing us from rising to the perception of higher truths. It is to reinstate the claims of the body as legitimate in the overall constitution of humanity, a restitution that is initially most visible in the constitution of femininity and its expression in feminine writing. Cixous suggests that, more "than men who are coaxed toward social success, toward sublimation, women are body" ("LM," 290). Whereas Simone de Beauvoir had viewed the rootedness of woman's experience in bodily functions as a kind of imprisonment within immanence, Cixous regards woman's greater attunement to bodily needs and drives as potentially liberating.

For it is indeed, in a sense, the body that resists pure theory: the latter, if not constrained, can ascend through infinite orbits of speculation and can envelop us, as Kant showed, in a spiraling regression of contradiction. We can use pure theory to prove almost anything: that God exists and that he doesn't exist: in either case, our conclusion is not rooted in the world of actual experience. The body is a name, a metaphor for many things: the uniqueness of experience which refuses to be subsumed under a general category or to be reduced to exemplifying status; and, as Cixous reminds us, it can express the individuality of the self, inhabiting a determinate position in place, time, class, color, race, and religion. To write with the body is to refuse to annul these differences. If I am a black woman, born into a certain economic class and raised in a specific ideological and cultural climate, all of these factors will of course influence my reading of any given situation. I cannot, as the male tradition would have me do, simply dismiss these factors to arrive at some neutral perspective, which is somehow based on "pure" reason or pure thought and which thereby pretends to objectivity. One of the great achievements of feminism as a whole has been to remind us on many levels that we *all* – not just women – speak from a perspective that is overdetermined, that is highly conditioned by numerous factors beyond our control. For me to be aware of my body when I write, then, is to recognize the profundity of its contribution to, and determination of, my thought processes; we do not think in some Cartesian vacuum, in some pure mind abstracted from all of the concrete circumstances in which it is embodied. It has become conventional for us, in the process of understanding anything, to see how a number of particular entities or events can be brought under universals or general concepts: this attempt to see patterns of unity or similarity in the vast diversity of phenomena is one of the fundamental ways in which we have tried to make sense of the world. But feminism has shown that individuality cannot be wholly abrogated, its richness and uniqueness cannot be wholly left behind, in the process of thinking through general concepts. As Cixous insists, "there is . . . no general woman." One can talk of what women have in common, but the "infinite richness of their individual constitutions" prevents us from talking about "*a* female sexuality" that might be "uniform, homogeneous, classifiable into codes" ("LM," 280).

If the body represents resistant particularity, particularity that is recalcitrant to the generalization of its nature, this is because it harbors an irreducible and unique richness. This new writing, expressing the "new woman," and based on the "empire" of the body, will resist the "analytic empire" built up in the language and categories of men ("LM," 296). Cixous equates the history of writing with the history of reason; and this history "has been one with the phallocentric tradition," an "enormous machine that has been operating and turning out its 'truth' for centuries" ("LM," 283). Hence the implications of a "new," feminine, writing will be momentous: "writing is precisely *the very possibility of change*, the space that can serve as a springboard for subversive thought, the precursory movement of a transformation of social and cultural structures" ("LM," 283). This new, "insurgent writing" will cause a "rupture" in the history of women, at two levels: it will effect a "return" of woman to her body, whereby she can realize a "decensored" relation to her sexuality; and it will tear her away from the "superegoized structure in which she has always occupied the place reserved for the guilty." Writing will emancipate "the marvelous text of her self that she must urgently learn to speak." Secondly, when woman thus seizes the occasion to speak, this will mark her "shattering entry into history," her use of writing as "the antilogos weapon" ("LM," 284). Woman's writing will confirm a place for her other than that reserved by the symbolic order, the order established by male institutions and history. It is time, says Cixous, to break with male-written history, and to write a new history ("LM," 279, 282). As subject for history, woman "un-thinks [spends] the unifying, regulating history that homogenizes and channels forces, herding contradictions into a single battlefield" ("LM," 286).

The body, then, is an emblem of drives, the resistant particularity of experience, the uniqueness of individuals that cannot be subsumed under coercive classifications, the impossibility of abstracting the historical and the national from the personal. And the writing that writes the body refuses codification and closure, resists obeisance to the throne of reason and insists on its living connections with the materiality of the body, its drives, the unconscious, the libido ("LM," 295).

Cixous suggests that woman's oppressed history gives her a better knowledge "about the relation between the economy of the drives and the management of the ego than any man." Woman is a "giver," who attempts to "unhoard," who thrills in endless change and becoming ("LM," 297), and who "stands up against separation" ("LM," 286). She is "an integral part of all liberations," carrying on the class struggle into "a much vaster movement" ("LM," 286). She will bring about "a mutation in human relations," embodying a new, "*other bisexuality*," that designates "each one's location is self . . . of the presence . . . of both sexes," a bisexuality that will supersede man's "glorious phallic monosexuality" ("LM," 288). If there is a "propriety of woman," urges Cixous, it is her "capacity to depropriate unselfishly: body without end" ("LM," 293). When we write, "everything we will be calls us to the unlagging, intoxicating, unappeasable search for love. In one another we will never be lacking" ("LM," 297).

Gender Studies

In general, gender studies includes feminist studies of gender, gay and lesbian criticism, and queer theory. These fields are by no means distinct from one another and often overlap considerably. Gender studies is interdisciplinary in both its roots and its methods, having arisen in literary and cultural theory, sociology, anthropology, and psychoanalysis. It examines the oppressive history of gays, lesbians, and other erotic groups, the formation and representation of gender, as well as gender as a category of analysis of literature and culture, and the intersection of gender with divisions of race, class, and color. Feminist anthropologists such as Gayle Rubin and thinkers such as Michel Foucault had highlighted the constructed nature of gender: indeed, in his *History of Sexuality* (1978), Foucault had shown that homosexuality was itself an invented category, formulated by the medical establishment in conjunction with ideologies of normative sexuality.

The birth of the Gay Rights Movement in America is often traced to the "Stonewall Riots" of 1969 in New York City, a prolonged conflict over several days in which gays, transvestites, and other oppressed groups (of various color and nationality) offered resistance against police raiding of the Stonewall Inn. Prior to this, especially just after the Second World War (in which young men found the opportunity to experiment sexually), a number of gay and other erotic communities had taken root in the margins of big cities such as New York, San Francisco, and Los Angeles. This led to a series of repressions in the 1950s. But during the 1960s, even before Stonewall, policies toward gays had relaxed somewhat, and as gays assumed a certain solidarity and political identity, further liberalization followed during the early 1970s, after which further backlashes erupted, in terms of both legal enactments and popular feeling. The effect of such repression was partly to solidify the alternative erotic communities, who self-consciously struggled in the political sphere to achieve a voice, and to achieve self-definition in theoretical terms. Even prior to the Stonewall Riots, gay self-consciousness emerged in many aspects of culture: in the history of literature, where figures such as Walt Whitman, Walter Pater, Oscar Wilde and the Bloomsbury Group with its ethic of androgyny, and the 1930s poets W. H. Auden, Christopher Isherwood, and Stephen Spender had variously articulated their sexuality and were revived as figures of interest, in the novels of James Baldwin and Gore Vidal which portrayed homosexual relations and encounters, in leading personalities of pop art such as Andy Warhol and Jasper Johns, and in pornography.

By the early 1970s, gay studies and gay theory were beginning to proliferate and to achieve a theoretical self-consciousness. In 1974 an issue of *College English* was devoted to the questions of gay identity and formulating a gay literary tradition. Just as women's studies established the importance of gender as a fundamental category of analysis, so lesbian/gay studies aims to establish the analytic centrality of sex and sexuality in several fields. The overlap between gay/lesbian studies and women's studies is a matter of continuing debate. As the editors of the *Lesbian and Gay Studies Reader* state, these studies focus on the "cultural production, dissemination, and vicissitudes of sexual meanings." Like women's studies, lesbian/gay studies are informed by the "social struggle for . . . sexual liberation" and personal freedom, as well as by resistance to homophobia and heterosexism or the "ideological and institutional practices of heterosexual privilege." Like feminism, they aim to break down the barriers between scholarship and politics.[13] Some of the important early gay and lesbian scholars include: Guy Hocquenghem, who analyzed the psychological motivations of homophobia; the gay historian Jeffrey Weeks, who has analyzed the history of homosexuality in Britain in relation to nineteenth-century sexual ideologies; the scholar K. J. Dover, who published his celebrated study *Greek Homosexuality* in 1978; Lillian Faderman, who studied lesbianism in the Renaissance; and Terry Castle, who conducted wide-ranging studies of the lesbian presence in Western literary history.

Gender studies has its roots partly in feminist theory, and indeed, was until the 1980s associated with the feminist enterprise, until lesbian critics such as Bonnie Zimmerman attacked the implicit feminist assumption that there was some essential female identity underlying differences of race, class, and sexuality. Some critics, such as those associated with the Radicalesbian collective, whose manifesto was "The Woman-Identified Woman" (1970), urged the need for a field of inquiry distinct from mainstream feminism, which had marginalized lesbianism. They saw lesbianism as the purest feminism since it asserted female autonomy and refused complicity with all forms of masculinist exploitation. Jill Johnston's *Lesbian Nation* (1973) saw lesbianism as the "solution" for feminism. The lesbian feminist poet and theorist Adrienne Rich also affirmed lesbianism as a kind of archetypal image of the broad feminist endeavor, and urged a dissociation of lesbian from male gay allegiances. In an influential and controversial essay entitled "Compulsory Heterosexuality and Lesbian Existence" (1980), she introduced the idea of a "lesbian continuum" to denote a range of experiences between women, including mutual practical and political support, bonding against male tyranny, and sharing a rich inner life. Separatist lesbianism was also advocated by the Chicana lesbian poet and critic Gloria Anzaldúa in *Borderlands – La Frontera: The New Mestiza* (1987), and by Monique Wittig in her essay "The Straight Mind" (1980), as well as by Luce Irigaray's *This Sex Which is Not One* (1977), which urged the autonomous existence of lesbians. During the 1970s the separatist modes of lesbian theory grew, helped by the development of women's studies programs. This era saw the beginnings of an attempt to integrate issues of sexuality, gender, and race. In her powerful essay "Toward a Black Feminist Criticism" (1977), Barbara Smith offered a controversial lesbian interpretation of Toni Morrison's *Sula*. Much of this earlier work aimed to deconstruct stereotypes of lesbians as unnatural or sexless, and to redeem a hitherto neglected tradition of lesbian thought and writing, as well as reinterpreting "conventional" figures such as Emily Dickinson and Virginia Woolf. It was underlain by certain assumptions: that there was a definable lesbian identity, and that there was an analyzable category of lesbian experience.

A more radical kind of approach, known as queer theory (a derisive term subversively adopted as a positive designation), emerged in the 1990s, grounded in a Conference on Queer Theory at the University of California, Santa Cruz. Queer theory was imbrued with many of the anti-essentialist assumptions of poststructuralism, especially the undermining of any fixed sexual identity, viewing identity as a subject position created by cultural and ideological codes. It more clearly emphasized sexuality rather than gender in the formation of identity. Indeed, the lines of allegiance were also shifted from gender to sexual orientation: lesbian theorists now identified with the theorizing of gay men rather than with straight women. But much of this theory, as in work by Diana Fuss, Judith Butler, and Eve Sedgwick, attempts to deconstruct any absolute distinction between hetero- and homo-sexuality. Judith Butler's groundbreaking work *Gender Trouble* (1990) saw all gender as a cultural performance; similarly, Lee Edelman's *Homographesis* (1994) deconstructed the notion of gay identity; while Sedgwick's *Epistemology of the Closet* (1990) exhibited the operation of homophobia in the supposedly normal system of gender. Her earlier, vastly influential work *Between Men* (1985) saw a continuum between male sexual and non-sexual relationships. Much queer theory, such as Simon Watney's *Policing Desire* (1987) and Donna Haraway's "The Biopolitics of Postmodern Bodies" (1989), attempted to analyze the AIDS epidemic in the late 1980s and its presentation in the media. Other queer theorists such as Michael Moon drew attention to the "queer" attributes of what presumed to be sexual normality. The American photographer Robert Mapplethorpe stirred public controversy, related to government funding for art, with his homoerotic, sadistic, and masochistic photographs which aimed to exhibit gay sexuality. Later gay and lesbian theory also attempted to cast attention on writers from other cultural backgrounds such as Garcia Lorca and Yukio Mishima.[14] Gender theory continues to debate issues of sexuality, its relation to power structures, and to a radically democratic agenda. The following section will briefly analyze the work of three of the pioneers in this field, Gayle Rubin, Eve Kosofsky Sedgwick, and Judith Butler.

Gayle Rubin (b. 1949)

A feminist anthropologist, Gayle Rubin has produced influential studies of gender, her work embracing anthropological theory, lesbian literature, sadomasochism, and feminism. In her early essay "The Traffic in Women" (1975), she originated the expression "sex/gender system," which she defined as the arrangements whereby society transforms biological sexuality into products of human activity. In other words, she saw sex – spanning gender identity, fantasy, and notions of childhood – as itself a social product. In a later essay, "Thinking Sex: Notes for a Radical Theory of the Politics of Sexuality" (1984), she made an influential new distinction between gender and sexuality which highlighted the limitations of feminism: she acknowledged that feminism was a potent theory of gender oppression. But this must be incorporated into a radical theory of sex which explains sexual oppression (by way of example, she points out that lesbians are persecuted not just on account of their gender but also because of their sexual orientation).[15] In general, she argues in this essay that, like gender, sexuality is political, and that the modern sexual system has been the object of political struggle. Industrialization and urbanization have led to a reorganization of family relations and gender roles, enabling the formation of new identities and new erotic communities (for example, gays, and subsequently other groups such as transsexuals and transvestites in enclaves of cities such as New York, San Francisco, and Los Angeles) (*LGR*, 16, 34).

The emergence of these erotic communities provoked various periods of sexual panic or repression in the 1880s, 1950s, and again in the 1980s. This persecution from right-wing groups was both psychological, urging the damage resulting from illicit sex (blindness, stunted growth, socialist views), and institutionalized in legislation such as the 1885 Act, which outlawed "indecent acts" between consenting adults, or the Family Protection Act (introduced in 1979 but never actually passed), which was a broad assault on feminism, homosexuals, and non-traditional families (*LGR*, 5–8). It was during the early decades of the twentieth century that new erotic communities were formed, mass-produced erotica became available, and the possibilities for "sexual commerce" expanded (*LGR*, 34). By the 1970s relatively large-scale sexual migrations had occurred, large enough to affect certain political landscapes. Though they were subjected to legal persecution based on the ideology that they were dangerous, inferior, and undesirable, these new communities – gays, for example – enjoyed a new solidarity, possessed a literature and a press, and were engaged in collective political activity. In other words, they had a social and political identity (*LGR*, 17). Rubin urges that a radical theory of sex must explain and denounce erotic injustice and oppression. Some of the obstacles to its formation include: sexual essentialism, the idea – fostered by medicine and psychoanalysis – that sexuality is somehow natural, standing above time, context, and history; sexual negativity, the idea that sexuality is a dangerous and destructive force; and the notion of a sexual hierarchy which distinguishes between acts that are permissible, ranging through questionable acts to those considered with extreme contempt. Underlying this hierarchy is the notion of a single, ideal sexuality. Rubin urges all those who consider themselves progressive to rethink these fundamental issues of sexuality and gender (*LGR*, 35).

Eve Kosofsky Sedgwick (b. 1950)

An American critic and poet, Eve Kosofsky Sedgwick has produced pioneering work in the field of gender studies, especially in queer theory. Her major works include *Between Men: English Literature and Male Homosocial Desire* (1985), *Epistemology of the Closet* (1990), *Tendencies* (1993), *A Dialogue on Love* (1999), and *Touching Feeling* (2003). In general, Sedgwick aims to show that the discourses of gender and sexuality, usually confined to a narrow ghettoized mode of analysis, are not marginal but integral to Western culture, and to the operations of power, race, and class. Indeed, in *Between Men*, she states her view, influenced by Lacan, French feminism, and deconstruction, that all human culture is structured by the "drama of gender difference."[16] This book's focus is on male homosocial desire, as expressed especially in a series of English novels. She defines the term "homosocial" as denoting "social bonds between persons of the same sex" (*BM*, 1). Though this term is meant to be distinguished from "homosexual" and often denotes a kind of male bonding which is indeed homophobic and marked by a hatred of homosexuality, she hypothesizes – through the notion of desire – a continuum between the two terms, which has been disrupted in our society but was intact in certain periods, as for example in ancient Greek culture (*BM*, 2–4). The brutal homophobia of our own society is tightly knit into the structure of our family, gender, age, class, and race relations. This situation contrasts with the relatively continuous connection between female homosocial and homosexual bonds: there is a much more congruent connection between women loving women and women promoting the interests of women (*BM*, 3). Sedgwick's basic purpose is to analyze male homosocial bonds "through the heterosexual European erotic ethos," and to reconcile historicist Marxist approaches, using ideology as an analytic category, with structuralist feminist perspectives in the analysis of sexuality (*BM*, 16). Her focus on male homosocial desire places it in the structural context of triangular heterosexual desire: the rivalry between two men for a woman's love entails a stronger bond between the two men than that of either with the woman; this bond is mediated by what Gayle Rubin calls the "male traffic in women," the use of the woman as an exchangeable "symbolic property" (*BM*, 26). She also shows how homophobia has been a tool for manipulating male bonds and the entire gender system, and how it interacts with divisions of class and race. She insists that the distinction between the sexual and non-sexual is fluid, given that sexual relations affect the distribution of non-sexual forms of power, including "control over the means of production and reproduction of goods, persons, and meanings" (*BM*, 22). She argues that there is a special relationship between male homosocial desire and the structures of patriarchal power; the status of women and gender definitions and relations is deeply inscribed in structures, such as male homosocial relationships, that seem to exclude women (*BM*, 25). Sedgwick sees the erotic triangle not as an ahistorical, Platonic form but as a construct informed by gender, language, and class, as a register of relationships of power and meaning (*BM*, 27). In general, Sedgwick's work shows the sheer fluidity of the distinctions between homosexuality and heterosexuality, as well as the contextual and indeterminate and contingent nature of both gender and sexuality. What counts as "sexual" or "homosexual" can vary.

Judith Butler (b. 1956)

The American philosopher Judith Butler has contributed influentially to the study of gender, feminism, and political and ethical theory. Her *Gender Trouble: Feminism and the Subversion of Identity* (1990) is arguably the most important book produced in the field of gender studies. Her central argument (extending through this and many of her other works) is that what we call gender is not an inherent fact or attribute of human nature but a *performance*, a cultural performance. Her other works include *Bodies that Matter* (1993), *Excitable Speech: A Politics of the Performative* (1997), and *Giving an Account of Oneself* (2005). In *Gender Trouble* she takes the title of her book from the John Waters film *Female Trouble*, which starred the drag queen Divine (Harris Glenn Milstead) acting the part of the heroine. This kind of impersonation of women, says Butler, dramatizes the signifying gestures through which gender is produced.[17] Butler sees herself as conducting what Foucault calls a genealogical inquiry, one that investigates the political motivations behind assigning origins and fixed identities to the categories of gender and sexuality, which are actually the effects of defining institutions, in this case, phallogocentrism (the grounding of masculinist domination in absolute terms beyond debate or discourse) and compulsory heterosexuality (*GT*, xi). Her approach draws upon feminist, lesbian, and gay perspectives as well as on the work of poststructuralist thinkers such as Foucault (*GT*, xiii). But the effect of her work, in decon-structing the category of woman, has been to distinguish lesbian studies from feminism. She argues that the very category of woman, the starting point of much feminist inquiry and activism, is no longer stable; it is a category produced by power structures and intersects intimately with race, class, politics, and culture (*GT*, 1–3, 128).

In the most brilliant section of her book, she argues that the body itself is shaped by political forces. Both the distinction between sex and gender and the category of sex itself presuppose that there exists a somehow neutral body prior to its sexual signification. Indeed, the tradition of Chris-tianity saw the body as a non-entity, as a "profane void," signifying a fallen state. Equally, Cartesian dualism (between mind and matter) saw the body as so much inert matter, attached to the thinking essence of the human. Even the existentialism of Sartre and de Beauvoir viewed the body as "mute facticity." Nietzsche and Foucault, too, saw the body as a surface or blank page on which cultural values were inscribed. In all these cases, materiality and the body are assumed to exist prior to signification: not only is the body indifferent to signification, but signification (as in Descartes' dualism) is the act of a disembodied consciousness. The body is simply regarded as external to the signifying process, which is the province of the thinking mind (*GT*, 129–130).

Drawing on Mary Douglas and Kristeva, Butler argues that it is cultural norms that maintain the boundaries of the body, its permeability sanc-tioned by the hegemonic order. For example, homosexuality violates the kinds of permeability permitted. Part of Butler's argument is that taboos on incest and homosexuality have been generative moments of the forma-tion of gender identity along a grid of compulsory heterosexuality (*GT*, 132–135). Foucault helps us to see that regulation and the law are not somehow externally imposed upon bodies that are already there, but are internal to the bodies they subjectivate, whose subjectivities they form and motivate along given orientations. This disciplinary production effects a false stability and coherence of gender, as a natural and fixed identity. But in fact there is no organizing principle or identity underlying the acts, words, and gestures occurring at the body's surface: these gestures are performative and the identity they express is a fabrication through the discourse of corporeal signs. The "regulatory fiction of heterosexual coher-ence" actually produces the gendered bodies that it purports to describe objectively (*GT*, 136).

This fabrication produces the illusion of an interior core of gender, which conceals its political and discursive origin. In fact, the gendered body is performative, and "has no ontological status apart from the various acts which constitute its reality" (*GT*, 136). Butler observes that the practices of drag artists parody this notion of an original gender identity, revealing the distinctness of anatomical sex, gender identity, and gender perfor-mance, dramatizing the cultural mechanism of their fabricated unity. They do not parody any original identity but the very notion of an original (*GT*, 138).

So the body is not a being but a surface, a signifying practice within a field of gender hierarchy and compulsory heterosexuality (*GT*, 139). There is no essence of gender: it is repeated acts that create the notion of gender, which is a stylized repetition of acts. This performative character of gender opens up performative possibilities for gender configurations "outside the restricting frames of masculinist domination and compulsory heterosexuality" (*GT*, 140–141). In a conclusion entitled "From Parody to Politics," Butler suggests that the instability of the "subject" in the category of women highlights the foundational restrictions of feminist political theory. She argues that it is wrong either to see agency as a prediscursive "I" (prior to the networks of language, discourse, and signs) or to view the determination of the "I" by discourse as somehow foreclosing agency. She reformulates agency as related to how signification and resignification work: if gender is created by signification, by "a regulated process of repetition," we can define agency as a variation on that repetition. It is only within signifying practices that we can subvert the notion of identity, resignifying body surfaces as a site of "dissonant and denaturalized performance" (*GT*, 145–146). Hence the critical task is to engage in local strategies of "subversive repetition" to displace gender norms, recognizing that there is no agency or reality beyond discursive practices (*GT*, 147–148). Then, "a new configuration of politics would surely emerge from the ruins of the old" (*GT*, 149). Butler's powerful critique of the notions of identity and body on which gender is constructed is an important step toward reconfiguring the performative potential of gender. But the connection between performance or parody and politics remains abstract.

Notes

1   This lecture was published in *New German Critique*, 22 (Winter 1981). It is reprinted in *Modernism/Postmodernism*, ed. Peter Brooker (London and New York: Longman, 1992). Hereafter cited as *MP*.

2   Jean Baudrillard, *Simulations*, trans. Paul Foss, Paul Patton, and Philip Beitchman (New York: Semiotext[e], 1983), p. 2. Hereafter cited as *S*.

3   Jean Baudrillard, *Symbolic Exchange and Death*, trans. Iain Hamilton Grant (London: Sage Publications, 1993), pp. 50–51. Hereafter cited as *SED*.

4   Jean Baudrillard, *The System of Objects*, trans. James Benedict (London and New York: Verso, 1996), p. 183. Hereafter cited as *SO*.

5   Mike Gain, introd., *SED*, pp. xi–xii.

6   Jean-François Lyotard, *The Postmodern Condition: A Report on Knowledge*, trans. Geoff Bennington and Brian Massumi (Minneapolis: University of Minnesota Press, 1989), p. xxxiii. Hereafter cited as *PC*.

7　Jean-François Lyotard, "Defining the Postmodern," p. 1. This article can most easily be accessed online at: qcpages.qc.edu/ENGLISH/Staff/richter/Lyotard. htm. Hereafter cited as "DP."

8　This essay is contained in bell hooks, *Yearning: Race, Gender, and Cultural Politics* (Boston: South End Press, 1990), p. 23. Hereafter cited as hooks.

9　Michèle Barrett, *Women's Oppression Today: The Marxist/Feminist Encounter* (London and New York: Verso, 1980), p. 8. Hereafter cited as *WT*.

10　Julia Kristeva, *Revolution in Poetic Language*, trans. Margaret Waller (New York: Columbia University Press, 1984), p. 21. Hereafter cited as *RPL*.

11　Hélène Cixous, "The Laugh of the Medusa," trans. Keith Cohen and Paula Cohen, in *The Signs Reader: Women, Gender, and Scholarship*, ed. Elizabeth Abel and Emily K. Abel (Chicago and London: University of Chicago Press, 1983), p. 289. Hereafter cited as "LM."

12　Ovid, *Metamorphoses*, trans. Mary Innes (Harmondsworth: Penguin, 1977), IV, 774–803.

13　Introd., *The Lesbian and Gay Studies Reader*, ed. Henry Abelove, Michele Aina Barale, and David M. Halperin (London and New York: Routledge, 1993), p. xvi. Hereafter cited as *LGR*.

14　This account is indebted to two excellent articles on "Gay Theory and Criticism" by Richard Dellamora and Bonnie Zimmerman in *The Johns Hopkins Guide to Theory and Criticism*, ed. Michael Groden and Martin Kreiswirth (Baltimore and London: Johns Hopkins University Press, 1994), pp. 324–331.

15　Gayle Rubin, "Thinking Sex," in *LGR*, pp. 32–34. This article was first published in *Pleasure and Danger*, ed. Carole Vance (London and New York: Routledge, 1984).

16　Eve Kosofsky Sedgwick, *Between Men: English Literature and Male Homosocial Desire* (New York: Columbia University Press, 1985), p. 11. Hereafter cited as *BM*.

17　Judith Butler, *Gender Trouble* (New York and London: Routledge, 1990), p. x. Hereafter cited as *GT*.

Chapter 6

The Later Twentieth Century: New Historicism, Reader-Response Theory, and Postcolonial Criticism

In the 1980s, the political mood in both Europe and America swung to the right. The increasingly unchallenged predominance of capitalism in the 1980s and 1990s oversaw the emergence or intensified popularity of New Historicism, which called for the literary text to be situated not, as in Marxist criticism, within the context of an economic infrastructure, but within a superstructural fabric of political and cultural discourses, with the economic dimension itself given no priority and indeed treated as another superstructural discourse. One of the prime influences on New Historicism was Michel Foucault, who saw knowledge as a form of power and analyzed power as highly diffused and as not distinctly assignable to a given set of political or ideological agencies. Another approach that attained prominence during these decades was reader-response or reception theory, whose roots went back to the reception theories of the German writers Hans Robert Jauss and Wolfgang Iser, as well as to Wayne Booth's *The Rhetoric of Fiction* (1961). This perspective engaged in a recognition of the dialogical nature of textual production, redefining the meaning of the text as the product of an interaction between text and an appropriately qualified community of readers. It could be argued that both the New Historicism and reader-response theory represented a return of the literary and cultural critic to political non-commitment, a newer and more fashionable guise – laden with all the trimmings of poststructuralist terminology – in which liberal humanist notions of pluralism, tolerance, and claims to political neutrality could strut once more on the academic stage.

The 1990s saw the concerted growth of two critical tendencies that were inextricably political. One was postcolonial studies, whose roots can be traced back through Edward Said's landmark work *Orientalism* (1978) to writers such as Frantz Fanon and Aimé Césaire who were directly engaged in struggles against colonialism. The other was ethnic studies, inspired largely by critics such as Henry Louis Gates, which also proliferated during this period. In general, both postcolonial and ethnic studies engage in a broad redefinition of terms – such as identity, gender, sexuality, and power – that had already undergone a radical critique in the works of feminist, and more generally, poststructuralist, thinkers. These studies insisted on examining such categories in the altered contexts of colonial and racial oppression. For example, it was held that the insights of white, middle-class feminism did not apply universally over diverse races and cultures. Each of these approaches can now be considered in some detail.

New Historicism

Historicism began toward the end of the eighteenth century with German writers such as Herder, and continued through the nineteenth-century historians Von Ranke and Meinecke to twentieth-century thinkers such as Wilhelm Dilthey, R. G. Collingwood, Hans Georg Gadamer, Ernst Cassirer, and Karl Mannheim. Powerful historical modes of analysis were formulated by Hegel and Marx, who themselves had a profound impact on historicist thinking; and literary historians such as Sainte-Beuve and Hippolyte Taine also insisted on viewing literary texts as integrally informed by their historical milieux. Much of what passes under the rubric of the "New" Historicism is not radically new, but represents a return to certain foci of analysis as developed by previous traditions of historicism.

Historicism has been characterized by a number of concerns and features. Most fundamentally, there is an insistence that all systems of thought, all phenomena, all institutions, all works of art, and all literary texts must be situated within a historical perspective. In other words, texts or phenomena cannot be somehow torn from history and analyzed in isolation, outside of the historical process. They are determined in both their form and content by their specific historical circumstances, their specific situation in time and place. Hence, we cannot bring to our analyses of Shakespeare the same assumptions and methods that we bring to Plato; the fact that they belong to different historical periods and different social, political, and economic circumstances will profoundly shape their notions of truth, of art and polity, and hence whatever meanings we might attribute to their texts. In other words, literature must be read within the broader context of its culture, in the context of other discourses ranging over politics, religion, and aesthetics, as well as its economic context. A second feature of historicism is that the history of a given phenomenon is sometimes held to operate according to certain identifiable laws, yielding a certain predictability and explanatory power; this feature is pronounced in the writings of Hegel and Marx. A third concern arises from the recognition that societies and cultures separated in time have differing values and beliefs: how can the historian "know" the past? The historian operates within the horizon of her own world view, a certain broad set of assumptions and beliefs; how can she overcome these to achieve an empathetic understanding of a distant culture? How, for example, can students fed on the epistemological fat of a New Critical diet begin to appreciate the world of the Homeric epics, the language of which we are not even sure how to pronounce, and the actions of whose characters are, by our moral standards, often bizarre? How can we avoid imposing our own cultural prejudices, not to mention our own interests and motives, on texts historically removed from us? Thinkers such as Dilthey, Gadamer, and E. D. Hirsch have offered various answers to this dilemma. Hirsch's position aspires to be "objectivist," effectively denying the historical and context-bound nature of knowledge, and proposing a distinction between "meaning," which embraces what the author meant or intended by his particular use of language, and "significance," which comprehends the subjective evaluation of the text according to the values and beliefs of the critic. Gadamer proposed a notion of "horizonfusion" whereby we acknowledge both that what we call the "text" is in fact a product of a tradition of interpretation (with no "original" meaning) and that our own perspective is informed by the very past we are seeking to analyze. Recognizing both of these limitations, we can begin to effect an empathetic fusion of our own cultural horizon with that of the text.

Hence, the dilemma of historical interpretation can easily lead to a kind of aesthetic formalism on the one hand, which denies history any constitutive role in the formation of texts, and, on the other hand, a historical view of texts as culturally and socially determined, a view that reduces emphasis on authorial intention and agency. The fundamental principles of historicism, then, are opposed to those of many twentieth-century movements such as Russian Formalism and New Criticism. In general, structuralism also has been ahistorical, focusing on synchronic analyses of language and literature. Yet structuralism differs from rigid formalism in that it does not isolate the literary text but situates it within the broader codes, sign systems, and registers of other discourses. In this sense, its endeavors are compatible with those of historicism. Also, certain adaptations of structuralism, as for example in the work of Mikhail Bakhtin, have a strongly historical dimension in which language itself is seen as an ideological phenomenon. Elements of historicism also inform hermeneutics and reader-response theory, which is obliged to take into account the different meanings that a text might have for readers of various historical periods. Indeed, the influence of Schleiermacher, usually viewed as the founder of hermeneutics, has extended not only to historicists such as Dilthey and Gadamer but also to reception theorists such as Hans Robert Jauss.

The "New" Historicism which arose in the 1980s reacted against both the formalist view of the literary text as somehow autonomous and Marxist views which ultimately related texts to the economic infrastructure. It saw the literary text not as somehow unique but as a kind of discourse situated within a complex of cultural discourses – religious, political, economic, aesthetic – which both shaped it and, in their turn, were shaped by it. If there was anything new about this procedure, it was its insistence, drawn from Foucault and poststructuralism, that "history" itself is a text, an interpretation, and that there is no single history. It also rejected any notion of historical progress or teleology, and broke away from any literary historiography based on the study of genres and figures. In the same way, the "culture" in which New Historicism situated literary texts was itself regarded as a textual construct. Hence, New Historicism refused to accord any kind of unity or homogeneity to history or culture, viewing both as harboring networks of contradictory, competing, and unreconciled forces and interests. Perhaps the most general direction in which Foucault influenced the New Historicism was that his contextualizations were "superstructural" (rather than referring literary and cultural phenomena to an economic base): even the realm of economics, like history itself, was seen as a discourse, as textual. Indeed, the language of economics gave way before Foucault's terminology of power, viewed as operating in diffuse and heterogeneous ways without clear appurtenance to any given agency. The New Historicists tended, then, to view literature as one discourse among many cultural discourses, insisting on engaging with this entire complex in a localized manner, refusing to engage in categorical generalizations or to commit to any definite political stance. Indeed, New Historicists have been criticized for a political quietism that accompanies their alleged principled indefiniteness, as well as for accepting uncritically Foucault's somewhat disembodied and abstract notion of power which floats free of political and economic agency. They are also accused of arbitrariness in the ways in which they relate literary texts to other cultural discourses. Notwithstanding such reservations, New Historicism – perhaps precisely because it appears to open the possibility of accommodating social context from a non-committed perspective – has enjoyed considerable influence since the 1980s and has arguably contributed to a more pervasive concern among formerly liberal humanist and New Critical academics with the larger cultural patterns and forces within which literature operates. Having said all of this, it should be noted that many New Historicists and cultural materialists have been profoundly concerned not only with situating literary texts within power structures, but also with seeing them as crucially participating in conflicts of power between various forms of social and political authority.

The "New" Historicism dates back to Stephen Greenblatt's use of the term in 1982 in an introduction to an issue of the journal *Genre* devoted to the Renaissance. His statements concerning the new movement will be considered here. In general, both Greenblatt and subsequent critics identified with New Historicism rejected the notion that it was a theory or a specific doctrine. Rather, they identified some persistent concerns and approaches, some of which have been indicated above, such as the rejection of the formalist notion of aesthetic autonomy and the situating of literature within a broader cultural network. Louis Montrose stressed that this contextualization of literature involved a re-examination of an author's position within a linguistic system. Montrose also points out that New Historicists variously recognize the ability of literature to challenge social and political authority. It is significant that this subversive potential of literature has been brought out by many New Historicist critics – who in Britain have identified themselves in Raymond Williams' terminology as "cultural materialists" – in relation to Renaissance thought and literature. Greenblatt's own work has focused on this period, and critics such as Jonathan Dollimore have produced groundbreaking studies such as *Radical Tragedy* (1984) which have reassessed the work of Shakespeare and his contemporaries, rejecting critical orthodoxies such as art ordering the chaos of reality, essentialist and providentialist readings of texts, the Bradleyan notion of tragedy as Hegelian reconciliation, the criterion of coherence whereby discontinuity is viewed as artistic failure, and recognizing the increasingly historical and ideological functions of drama.[1] The book *Political Shakespeare*, edited by Jonathan Dollimore and Alan Sinfield, also challenged the liberal humanist notion of Shakespeare as a timeless and universal genius. Instead, the political dimensions of Shakespeare's work are emphasized, embracing a broad range of issues such as the subversion of authority, sexuality, and colonialism, as well as modern receptions and appropriations of Shakespeare in education, film, and theater.[2] Another powerful reinterpretation was formulated in *Alternative Shakespeares* (1985), in which a range of writers, including Catherine Belsey, Terence Hawkes, Jacqueline Rose, John Drakakis, and Francis Barker, challenged the liberal humanist language of character analysis, artistic coherence, and harmony. Drawing on a vast range of theories, ranging from psychoanalysis and structuralism to Marxism and feminism, they drew attention to the manner in which Shakespeare's texts produce meaning, construct the human subject, and engage in larger structural and ideological issues.[3] These studies have not only questioned prevailing images of the Renaissance but have also shown how issues raised in the Renaissance context have implications for theory itself. For example, the complexity of the cultural processes of the Renaissance were seen as undermining any attempt to treat the culture of any period as a homogeneous or coherent entity. Other critics such Jerome McGann have extended New Historical concerns into other historical periods such as Romanticism. Some of the major principles of New Historicism can now be examined as they are practiced by the figure who is perhaps the primary influence on this critical tendency, Michel Foucault.

Michel Foucault (1926–1984)

Along with figures such as Jacques Derrida, Foucault has exerted an enormous influence on many branches of thought in the latter twentieth century, including what is broadly known as "cultural studies." He had a seminal impact on the New Historicism that was initiated by Stephen Greenblatt, as well as on queer theory. Born in France the son of a physician, Foucault criticized the institutions of medical practice in his first two publications, *Madness and Civilization* (1961) and *The Birth of the Clinic* (1963). Indeed, the central theme of most of Foucault's works was the methods with which modern civilization creates and controls human subjects, through institutions such as hospitals, prisons, education, and knowledge; corollary to these investigations was Foucault's examination of power, its execution and distribution. Foucault's next works, *The Order of Things* (1966) and *The Archaeology of Knowledge* (1969), offered a characterization of the growth of knowledge in the modern Western world, as manifested in the emergence of disciplines such as linguistics, economics, and biology. He elaborated a historical scheme of three "epistemes" (outlooks underlying the institutional organization of knowledge) that characterized the Middle Ages, the Enlightenment (called the "Classical" period in this text), and the modern world. Foucault's essay "What is an Author?" (1969) questions and examines the concept of authorship and, in insights that were taken up by the New Historicism, argued that analysis of literary texts could not be restricted to these texts themselves or to their author's psychology and background; rather, the larger contexts and cultural conventions in which texts were produced needed to be considered. Subsequently, Foucault offered extended critiques respectively of the institutions of the prison and of sexuality in *Discipline and Punish: The Birth of the Prison* (1975) and *The History of Sexuality* (1976).

In the first part of *The History of Sexuality*, entitled "We 'Other Victorians,'" Foucault examines the conventional "repressive hypothesis": that, at the beginning of the seventeenth century, a certain frankness was still common in sexual discourse and practice. But this "bright day" was followed by the "monotonous nights of the Victorian bourgeoisie." Sexuality was confined to the home, silence became the rule, and sex was repressed into the heterosexual bedroom for procreative purposes.[4] Modern puritanism, the argument goes, "imposed its triple edict of taboo, nonexistence, and silence" (*HS*, 5). This theory of modern sexual repression, says Foucault, appears on the surface to hold up well: repression is made "to coincide with the development of capitalism: it becomes an integral part of the bourgeois order" (*HS*, 5). The principle of explanation behind this is that sex, the dissipation of oneself in pleasure, is "incompatible with a general and intensive work imperative" (*HS*, 6). But this definition of the connection between sex and power in terms of repression, rejoins Foucault, is sustained by the opportunity it gives us to speak out against the prevailing powers, and to enter into a (professional) discourse about sex (*HS*, 7). Hence, this alleged repression has been "coupled with the grandiloquence of a discourse purporting to reveal the truth about sex, modify its economy within reality, subvert the law that governs it, and change its future." Foucault's point is that the two phenomena, the repression and the discourse, are "mutually reinforcing" (*HS*, 8).

As against this repressive hypothesis, Foucault intends to "define the regime of power-knowledge-pleasure that sustains the discourse on human sexuality" (*HS*, 11). His own thesis is that since the end of the sixteenth century, the discourse on sexuality, "far from undergoing a process of restriction, on the contrary has been subjected to a mechanism of increasing incitement; that the techniques of power exercised over sex have not obeyed a principle of rigorous selection, but rather one of dissemination and implantation of polymorphous sexualities; and that the will to knowledge . . . has persisted in constituting . . . a science of sexuality" (*HS*, 12–13). It is clear that Foucault's investigation of the discourse on sexuality is equally an investigation into the workings of power, which will be seen as far more complex and subtle than a procedure of mere repression.

Foucault's general hypothesis, then, is that bourgeois society did not refuse to recognize sex but rather "put into operation an entire machinery for producing true discourses concerning it . . . it also set out to formulate the uniform truth of sex" (*HS*, 69). The aim was to inscribe sex within an economy of pleasure and an "ordered system of knowledge." In speaking the truth about itself, sex also tells us the deeply buried truth about ourselves, its part in the constitution of the subject. Indeed, the science of the subject has "gravitated . . . around the question of sex" (*HS*, 70). The proliferation of discourses about sex has been "carefully tailored to the requirements of power" (*HS*, 72). Within a few centuries, says Foucault, the inquiry into what we are has led us to sex, to "sex as history, as signification and discourse." After being immersed in binary oppositions (body/soul, flesh/spirit, instinct/reason) that relegated sex to irrationality, the West has effectively annexed "sex to a field of rationality" and brought us "almost entirely – our bodies, our minds, our individuality, our history – under the sway of a logic of concupiscence and desire." This logic provides the "master key" to what we are: sex, as grounding our psychology and reproduction, the very mechanisms of life, is seen as "the explanation for everything" (*HS*, 78).

Foucault offers an explicit statement of his conception of power, a conception that has underlain his arguments on sexuality. He rejects the conventional notion of power that is based on a "juridico-discursive" model, and is seen as straightforwardly restrictive and repressive. Such a conception of power, deriving from the development of monarchic power and the concept of right, says Foucault, overlooks precisely what makes power so effective and accepted (*HS*, 85–86). New methods of power, he maintains, operate not "by right but by technique, not by law but by normalization, not by punishment but by control." And, in order to operate effectively, power must mask at least a part of itself (*HS*, 87, 89). Foucault states that power is not "a group of institutions and mechanisms that ensure the subservience of the citizens of a given state." Nor is it a "mode of subjugation" or a "general system of domination exerted by one group over another . . . these are only the terminal forms that power takes" (*HS*, 92). Nor must power be sought "in the primary existence of a central point, in a unique source of sovereignty from which secondary and descendent forms would emanate" (*HS*, 93). Nor is power something that is "acquired, seized, or shared." Moreover, "there is no binary and all-encompassing opposition between rulers and ruled at the root of power relations" (*HS*, 94).

What *is* it, then? According to Foucault, power "must be understood in the first instance as the multiplicity of force relations immanent in the sphere in which they operate and which constitute their own organisation . . . as the support which these force relations find in one another, thus forming a chain or system . . . and lastly, as the strategies in which they take effect" (*HS*, 92). Foucault insists that power "is everywhere; not because it embraces everything, but because it comes from everywhere." It is "simply the over-all effect that emerges from all these mobilities" (*HS*, 93). A conventional Marxist critique of Foucault would impugn his apparent removal of political agency from the operations of power. Yet he characterizes power relations as "both intentional and nonsubjective." He acknowledges that "there is no power that is exercised without a series of aims and objectives. But this does not mean that it results from the choice or decision of an individual subject" (*HS*, 94–95). He also concedes that where "there is power, there is resistance, and yet . . . this resistance is never in a position of exteriority in relation to power." Foucault stresses that there is "no single locus of great Refusal, no soul of revolt, source of all rebellions, or pure law of the revolutionary. Instead there is a plurality of resistances, each of them a special case" (*HS*, 95–96). What makes revolution possible is a "strategic codification of these points of resistance" (*HS*, 96).

Reader-Response and Reception Theory

Another critical approach that proved widely congenial during and since the 1980s was reader-response theory, with roots in earlier thinkers such as Husserl. The role of the reader or audience of a literary work or performance has been recognized since classical times. Plato was acutely aware of the disturbing power of poetry to affect people at the level of their passions and morality, as well as their basic conceptions of the gods and indeed of reality itself. He saw poetry as appealing to our lower natures, disposing us toward irrational behavior, and distracting us from the rational pursuit of truth. Aristotle, who had a more tolerant conception of poetry, made

the response of the audience an integral component of his famous definition of a properly structured tragedy: such a tragedy must inspire the
purgative emotions of fear and pity in the audience. Many classical and
medieval writers viewed literature as a branch of rhetoric, the art of per-
suasive speaking or writing. As such, literature had to be highly aware of
the composition and expectations of its audience. Subsequently, several
Romantic theories stressed the powerful emotional impact of poetry on the
reader, and various later nineteenth-century theories such as symbolism
and impressionism stressed the reader's subjective response to literature
and art. Several other kinds of theories, such as feminism and Marxism,
have long acknowledged that literature, necessarily operating within
certain social structures of class and gender, is always orientated toward
certain kinds of audiences, in both aesthetic and economic terms. The
hermeneutic theories developed by Friedrich Schleiermacher, Martin
Heidegger, Hans Georg Gadamer, as well as the phenomenological theories
inspired by Edmund Husserl, such as that of Roman Ingarden, examined
the ways in which readers engaged cognitively and historically with literary
texts.

It was partly in reaction to both the subjectivist theories of the nineteenth century and theories that situated literature within larger historical
contexts that various kinds of formalism, including the New Criticism,
emerged. The formalists wanted to carve out the domain of literature as a
scientific, autonomous realm, where the emphasis lay not on mere subjective reactions of the reader nor the connections of the text to its broader
social circumstances but on the literary work itself: they saw the study of
literature as an objective activity, and they saw the literary object itself as
the repository of meaning. What needed to be studied, they argued, was
the "objective" verbal structure of the literary artefact, and what needed to
be identified were its specifically literary qualities, as opposed to any moral,
religious, or other significance it might contain.

At one level, reader-response theory was a reaction against such formalism and objectivism; it was also, however, a renewal of a long and diversi-
fied tradition that had acknowledged the important role of the reader or
audience in the overall structure of any given literary or rhetorical situation. There are elements of a reader-response outlook in the theoretical
writings of Virginia Woolf, Louise Rosenblatt, and Wayne Booth, author
of an influential work, *The Rhetoric of Fiction* (1961), whose distinctions
between real author and the "implied author" who tells the story, between
actual reader and the "postulated reader" created by the text itself, and
whose critical language such as "unreliable narrator" became standard
terms in analyzing fiction. All of these figures recognized that the author
of a literary text uses certain strategies to produce given effects in readers
or to guide their responses. A number of poststructuralist movements such
as deconstruction had challenged the formalist and New Critical assertion

of the objectivity of the text. But it was not until the 1970s that a number of critics at the University of Constance in Germany (the "Constance School") began to formulate a systematic reader-response or "reception" theory. The leading members of this school were Wolfgang Iser and Hans Robert Jauss (b. 1921). The aesthetics of this school had its roots not only in the hermeneutic and phenomenological traditions mentioned above but also in the earlier thought of Alexander Baumgarten, Kant, and Friedrich von Schiller.

The phenomenological method of Husserl and the hermeneutics of Heidegger paved the way for what became known as reception theory. Hans Robert Jauss studied at the University of Heidelberg with the hermeneutic philosopher Hans-Georg Gadamer. In 1966 he became a professor at the University of Constance. One of his most important texts was "Literary History as a Challenge to Literary Theory" (1969, 1970), a refined version of a lecture he had given at the University of Constance as his inaugural address. In this text, Jauss challenged objectivist views of both literary texts and literary history, urging that the history of a work's reception by readers played an integral role in the work's aesthetic status and significance. The following pages will consider the work of two reader-response theorists, Wolfgang Iser and Stanley Fish.

Wolfgang Iser (b. 1926)

Iser's theories of reader-response were initially presented in a lecture of 1970 entitled "The Affective Structure of the Text," and then in two major works, *The Implied Reader* (1972) and *The Act of Reading* (1976). After examining a number of English novels in *The Implied Reader*, Iser outlines his approach in a section of this book entitled "The Reading Process: A Phenomenological Approach."[5] Iser begins by pointing out that, in considering a literary work, one must take into account not only the actual text but "the actions involved in responding to that text." He suggests that we might think of the literary work as having two poles: the "artistic" pole is the text created by the author, and the "aesthetic" pole refers to "the realization accomplished by the reader" (*IR*, 274). We cannot identify the literary work with either the text or the realization of the text; it must lie "half-way between the two," and in fact it comes into being only through the convergence of text and reader (*IR*, 275). His point here is that reading is an active and creative process. It is reading which brings the text to life, which unfolds "its inherently dynamic character" (*IR*, 275). If the author were somehow to present a story completely, the reader's imagination would have nothing to do; it is because the text has unwritten implications or "gaps" that the reader can be active and creative, working things out for himself. This does not mean that *any* reading will be appropriate. The text uses various strategies and devices to limit its own unwritten implications, but the latter are nonetheless worked out by the reader's own imagination (*IR*, 276).

In *The Act of Reading*, Iser further elaborates his important concept of the "implied reader." He points out that when critics talk about literature in terms of its effects, they invoke two broad categories of reader: the "real" reader and the "hypothetical" reader. The former refers to an actual reader whose response is documented, whereas the hypothetical reader is a projection of all possible realizations of the text.[6] Iser sees both of these concepts as deficient. Real readers are difficult to reconstruct and the "hypothetical" or what is sometimes called the "ideal" reader is often nothing more than a creation of the critic's mind (*AR*, 28–29).

Iser evaluates newer models of the reader that have arisen in more recent years, models that have sought to break free of the traditional restrictive models cited above: the "superreader" of Michael Riffaterre, the "informed reader" of Stanley Fish, the "intended reader" of Erwin Wolff, and the "psychological reader" of Norman Holland and Simon Lesser. According to Iser, all of these models are restricted in their general applicability. His concept of the "implied reader" is intended to overcome these restrictions. In analyzing responses to a literary work, he says, "we must allow for the reader's presence without in any way predetermining his character or his historical situation." It is this reader, who is somehow lifted above any particular context, whom Iser designates the implied reader (*AR*, 34). The implied reader is a function not of "an empirical outside reality" but of the text itself. Iser points out that the concept of the implied reader has "his roots firmly planted in the structure of the text; he is a construct and in no way to be identified with any real reader." He defines the implied reader as "a textual structure anticipating the presence of a recipient without necessarily defining him." The implied reader, then, designates "a network of response-inviting structures," which prestructure the role of the reader in the latter's attempt to grasp the text (*AR*, 34). In a novel, there are four main perspectives: those of the narrator, characters, plot, and the fictitious reader. The meaning of the text is generated by the convergence of these perspectives, a convergence that is not itself set out in words but occurs during the reading process (*AR*, 35). Iser also sees the notion of the "implied reader" as explaining the tension that occurs within the reader during the reading process, a tension between the reader's own subjectivity and the author's subjectivity which overtakes the reader's mentality, a tension between two selves that directs the reader's ability to make sense of the text. In historical terms, then, Iser aims to shift critical focus away from the text toward the reader, and while he stresses the experience of the reader during the reading process, his analyses are concerned primarily with individual acts of reading.

Stanley Fish (b. 1938)

The American reader-response theorist Stanley Fish attempts to situate the reading process in a broader, institutional context. Fish's earlier work, focusing on the reader's experience of literary texts, included an important study of Milton, *Surprised by Sin: The Reader in "Paradise Lost"* (1967) and *Self-Consuming Artifacts: The Experience of Seventeenth-Century Literature* (1972). His essay "Interpreting the *Variorum*" (1976) introduced his concept of "interpretive communities," a concept explored more fully in his book *Is There a Text in this Class? The Authority of Interpretive Communities* (1980),[7] where he addresses the important question of the role of institutions, and in particular the literary institution, in the construction of meaning.

According to Fish, a formalist analysis, which locates meaning within the forms and verbal structure of the text itself, will ignore the reader's experience of the text, which is temporal and contains modifications and shifts of viewpoint. The central assumption of formalist analysis to which Fish stands opposed is that "there *is* a sense, that it is embedded or encoded in the text, and that it can be taken in at a single glance." Fish calls these assumptions "positivist, holistic, and spatial." The goal of such analysis is "to settle on a meaning," to step back from the text, and then to put together or calculate "the discrete units of significance it contains." Fish's objection to such an approach is that it takes the text as a self-sufficient entity, and ignores or devalues the reader's activities. What we should be describing, he believes, is "the structure of the reader's experience rather than any structures available on the page." The reader's activities should be "the center of attention, where they are regarded not as leading to meaning but as *having* meaning." These activities, which include the making and revising of many kinds of decisions, are already interpretative; hence a description of them will be an interpretation. Fish points out that his approach differs from the formalist methods primarily through its emphasis on the temporal dimension of the reading process and the creation of meanings.

Fish acknowledges that the intended reader he has in mind is the "reader whose education, opinions, concerns, linguistic competences . . . make him capable of having the experience the author wished to provide." Notwithstanding Fish's insistence that it is the reader's experience of the text that creates meaning (or, his terminology, *has* meaning), he views this meaning as always constrained by the central goal of readers: "the efforts of readers are always efforts to discern and therefore to realize (in the sense of becoming) an author's intention." The difference between Fish's model of reading and traditional intentional models is that whereas those earlier models saw the grasping of an author's purpose as a "single act," Fish sees this as "the succession of acts readers perform in the continuing assumption that they are dealing with intentional beings." Fish equates this understanding of an author's intention with "all the activities which make up . . . the structure of the reader's experience." Hence, according to Fish, if we describe these activities of the reader, or the structure of the reader's experience, we will also be describing the structure of the author's intention. So Fish's overall thesis, in his own words, is: "that the form of the reader's experience, formal units, and the structure of intention are one, that they come into view simultaneously." In his book *Is There a Text in this Class?* (containing Fish's widely anthologized essay of the same title), Fish argues that what constrains interpretation is not fixed meanings in a linguistic system but the practices and assumptions of an institution. It is not the linguistic system that gives determinacy to the meaning of an utterance but rather the context of the utterance (*ITC*, 309–313).

There are some problems with Fish's account: in his model of the reading process, the text disappears. Whereas, for the formalists, the text was a stable object, for Fish there is *nothing* beyond intersubjective agreement, and the text is reduced to merely the area of overlap of subjective responses. The problem here is that the process of *interaction* between text and reader is elided: where Iser saw reading as a dialectical interaction between a "virtual" text and an implied reader, Fish removes even that virtual status, reducing textuality to an effect of intersubjectivity. Fish employs a naive notion of objectivity as somehow entirely independent of subjectivity. But philosophers for more than a century have been arguing that objectivity and subjectivity arise in the same, mutually constructive, process. Fish fails, moreover, to distinguish *degrees* of objectivity; his procedure freezes our analytical power within the abstract insight that all objectivity is the product of collective subjectivity: once we acknowledge this, we still have to make distinctions and evaluations of the vast variety of "objects." Fish's procedure sensibly states what is undeniably true: we bring our assumptions (learned from our community) to bear on what we see "in" a literary text: but if this is true for all literary texts, it remains frozen as a general insight and does not furnish a basis from which to analyze the ways in which a particular work might actively direct our response as readers. Indeed, Fish does not explain how our mere "experience" of a work can *have* meaning (his phrase); how does this experience enter a structure of signification? It might also be objected that Fish invokes a naive, pre-Kantian, empiricism whereby the notion of "experience" is blandly opposed to thought and conceptuality: each element in a reader's experience is somehow "legitimate" simply because it is experience. Fish claims that a formalist analysis is incapable of analyzing an experiential, temporal process. But his own description of this temporal process is couched in terms that are (as Bergson might observe) inescapably spatial: he talks of a "sequence" where the reader "structures" the "field" he "inhabits" and is then asked to "restructure" it (*ITC*, 207–209). Each of the enquoted words is spatial, and Fish's analyses follow the reader's response in a linear, sequential manner. Notwithstanding Fish's claim that "[e]verything depends on the temporal dimension," he offers almost no analysis of this dimension of the reader's response; his model in some ways rehearses the old intentional model of reading within an abstractly conceived temporality.

Postcolonial Criticism

Another, more overtly political, approach to interpretation gathered intensity in the 1980s, concerned with the economic, cultural, and psychological effects of imperialism and emancipation from colonial rule. Indeed, since postcolonial theory is rooted in the history of imperialism, it is worth briefly looking at this history. In modern times, there have been at least three major phases of imperialism. Between 1492 and the mid-eighteenth century, Spain and Portugal, England, France, and the Netherlands established colonies and empires in the Americas, the East Indies, and India. Then, between the mid-nineteenth century and the First World War, there was an immense scramble for imperialistic power between Britain, France, Germany, Italy, and other nations. By the end of the nineteenth century, more than one-fifth the land area of the world and a quarter of its population had been brought under the British Empire: India, Canada, Australia, New Zealand, South Africa, Burma, and the Sudan. The next largest colonial power was France, whose possessions included Algeria, French West Africa, Equatorial Africa, and Indochina. Germany, Italy, and Japan also entered the race for colonies. In 1855 Belgium established the Belgian Congo in the heart of Africa, a colonization whose horrors were expressed in Conrad's *Heart of Darkness* (1899). Finally, the periods during and after the Second World War saw a struggle involving both the countries just mentioned as well as a conflict between America and the Communist Soviet Union for extended control, power, and influence. Needless to say, these imperialistic endeavors have survived into the present day in altered forms and with new antagonists.

The motives behind imperialism have usually been economic (though liberal economists such as Adam Smith and David Ricardo were skeptical of imperialism's economic benefits, arguing that it only benefited a small group but never the nation as a whole). Marxists, especially Lenin and Bukharin, saw imperialism as a late stage of capitalism, in which monopolistic home markets were forced to subjugate foreign markets to accommodate their overproduction and surplus capital. A second and related motive has been (and still is) the security of the home state. A third motive is related to various versions of Social Darwinism. Figures such as Machiavelli, Bacon, Hitler, and Mussolini saw imperialism as part of the natural struggle for survival. Like individuals, nations are in competition, and those endowed with superior strength and gifts are able and fit to subjugate the weaker nations. Karl Pearson's "arguments" belong to this category.

The final motive, propounded by figures such as Rudyard Kipling (in poems such as "The White Man's Burden") and questioned by writers such as Conrad, rests on moral grounds: imperialism is a means of bringing to a subject people the blessings of a superior civilization, and liberating them from their benighted ignorance. Clearly, much of this rationale rests on Western Enlightenment notions of civilization and progress.

After the end of the Second World War in 1945 there occurred a large-scale process of decolonization of the territories subjugated by most of the imperial powers (Britain, France, Netherlands, Belgium), with the significant exception of the Soviet Union and the United States, beginning with the independence of India in 1947. The collapse of the Communist regimes in 1991 left America as the only major remaining colonial power (though America itself had of course held the status of a colony). Indeed, colonial struggle is hardly dead: it has continued until very recently in East Timor, and still persists bitterly in Tibet, Taiwan, Kashmir, and the Middle East.[8]

Postcolonial literature and criticism arose both during and after the struggles of many nations in Africa, Asia, Latin America (now referred to as the "tricontinent" rather than the "third world"), and elsewhere for independence from colonial rule. The year 1950 saw the publication of seminal texts of postcolonialism: Aimé Césaire's *Discours sur le colonialisme*, and Frantz Fanon's *Black Skin, White Masks*. And in 1958 Chinua Achebe published his novel *Things Fall Apart*. George Lamming's *The Pleasures of Exile* appeared in 1960 and Frantz Fanon's *The Wretched of the Earth* followed in 1961. Fanon's now classic text analyzed the conditions and requirements for effective anti-colonial revolution from a Marxist perspective, modified somewhat to accommodate conditions specific to colonized nations. It also articulated the connections between class and race. Indeed, Fanon pointed out the utter difference in historical situation between the European bourgeois class, a once revolutionary class which overturned feudalism, and the African bourgeoisie emerging as successor to colonial rule.

According to Robert Young, the "founding moment" of postcolonial theory was the journal the *Tricontinental*, launched by the Havan Tricontinental of 1966, which "initiated the first global alliance of the peoples of the three continents against imperialism" (Young, 5). Edward Said's landmark work *Orientalism* appeared in 1978. More recent work includes *The Empire Writes Back* (1989) by Bill Ashcroft, Gareth Griffiths, and Helen Tiffin, Gayatri Spivak's *The Post-Colonial Critic* (1990), as well as important work by Abdul JanMohamed, Homi Bhabha, Benita Parry, and Kwame Anthony Appiah. Robert Young sees postcolonialism as continuing to derive its inspiration from the anti-colonial struggles of the colonial era. Anti-colonialism had many of the characteristics commonly associated with postcolonialism such as "diaspora, transnational migration and internationalism" (Young, 2). Ashcroft, Griffiths, and Tiffin also use the term postcolonial in a comprehensive sense, "to cover all the culture affected by the imperial process from the moment of colonization to the present day," on account of the "continuity of preoccupations" between the colonial and postcolonial periods.[9]

Postcolonial criticism has embraced a number of aims: most fundamentally, to re-examine the history of colonialism from the perspective of the colonized; to determine the economic, political, and cultural impact of colonialism on both the colonized peoples and the colonizing powers; to analyze the process of decolonization; and above all, to participate in the goals of political liberation, which include equal access to material resources, the contestation of forms of domination, and the articulation of political and cultural identities (Young, 11). Early voices of anti-imperialism stressed the need to develop or return to indigenous literary traditions so as to exorcize their cultural heritage of the specters of imperial domination. Other voices advocated an adaptation of Western ideals toward their own political and cultural ends. The fundamental framework of postcolonial thought has been furnished by the Marxist critique of colonialism and imperialism, which has been adapted to their localized contexts by thinkers from Frantz Fanon to Gayatri Spivak.

This struggle of postcolonial discourse extends over the domains of gender, race, ethnicity, and class. Indeed, we should avoid the danger of treating either the "West" or the "tricontinent" as homogeneous entities which can somehow be mutually opposed. Such a rigid opposition overlooks the fact that class divisions and gender oppression operate in both the West and in colonized nations. Many commentators have observed that exploitation of workers occurred as much in Western countries as in the areas that they subjugated. Equally, colonization benefited primarily a tiny portion of the population of imperial nations. In this sense, colonialism is a phenomenon internal to imperial nations as well as extending beyond their frontiers (Young, 8–9). Hence, postcolonial discourse potentially embraces, and is intimately linked with, a broad range of dialogues within the colonizing powers, addressing various forms of "internal colonization" as treated by minority studies of various kinds such as African American, Native American, Latin American, and Women's Studies. All of these discourses have challenged the main streams of Western philosophy, literature, and ideology. In this sense, the work of African American critics such as Henry Louis Gates, Jr., of African American female novelists and poets, of commentators on Islam, and even of theorists such as Fredric Jameson, is vitally linked to the multifarious projects of postcolonialism.

One of these projects, or rather, one point of convergence of various postcolonial projects, has been the questioning and revaluation of the literary and cultural canon in Western institutions, through what is loosely called "multiculturalism." In explaining the rise of multiculturalism, Paul Berman suggests that a new "postmodern" generation of activists from the

1960s came into power in American universities. The year 1968 saw left-wing uprisings against the elements of liberal humanism: Western democracy, rationalism, objectivity, individual autonomy. These were all considered to be slogans which concealed the society's actual oppression of blacks, working-class people, gays, women, as well as the imperialistic exploitation of "third world" countries. These oppressive ideas, according to radicals, were embodied and reproduced in the conventional canons of literature and philosophy which we offer to our students: the literary tradition from Homer to T. S. Eliot and the philosophical spectrum from Plato to logical positivism. Berman suggests that this reaction against the Western mainstream tradition was fostered largely by the rise of French literary theory, which insisted that the text was an indirect expression and often a justification of the prevailing power structure. This structure was inevitably a hierarchy in which the voices of minorities, women, and the working classes were suppressed. These voices now had to be heard.

The central conservative argument against multiculturalism was advanced by Allan Bloom, Arthur Schlesinger, and others. It assumed, firstly, that in the past there existed a period of consensus with regard to the aims of education, political ideals, and moral values; secondly, that this consensus, which underlies the national identity of America, is threatened by the cacophonic, irreconcilable voices of multiculturalism. Multiculturalists respond that this past consensus is imaginary: the educational curricula adopted at various stages both in the United States and elsewhere have been the products of conflicting political attitudes. In late nineteenth-century America, conservatives, who desired a curriculum that would foster religious conformism and discipline, were opposed by those, like the pragmatist John Dewey, who wished to stress liberal arts, utility, and advanced research. In 1869, President Charles W. Eliot of Harvard initiated a program of curricular reform, amid much controversy. Disciplines such as history, sociology, and English itself struggled to gain admission into various liberal arts curricula. And the 1920s and 1930s saw a struggle to make American literature part of the English program.

A third assumption of conservatives is that great literature somehow conveys "timeless truths"; Schlesinger states that history should be conducted as "disinterested intellectual inquiry," not as therapy; William Bennett, Lynne V. Cheney, and the National Academies have all appealed to the notion of timeless truths. But, to speak in such language is to dismiss the traditions of Hegelianism, Marxism, existentialism, historicism, hermeneutic theory, and psychoanalysis which have attempted to situate the notion of truth in historical, economic, and political contexts. Various theorists have responded that, in fact, the appeal to "timeless truths" has always subserved a political function. The growth of English literature was from the beginning imbued with ideological motives. Arnold and subsequent professors at Oxford saw poetry as the sole salvation for a mechanical civilization. The timeless truths of literature were intended as a bulwark against rationalist and ideological dogma. Literature was to "promote sympathy and fellow feeling among all classes," to educate citizens as to their duties, to inculcate national pride and moral values. And English was a pivotal part of the imperialist effort. In 1834 Macaulay argued the merits of English as the medium of instruction in India, stating: "I have never found one . . . who could deny that a single shelf of a good European library was worth the whole native literature of India and Arabia." We can refrain from commenting on this except to add Macaulay's own subsequent statement that "I have no knowledge of either Sanscrit or Arabic." Such statements reveal the depth to which constructions of Europe's self-image, resting on the Enlightenment project of rationality, progress, civilization, and moral agency, were premised on the positing of various forms of alterity or "otherness," founded on polarized images such as superstitiousness, backwardness, barbarism, moral incapacity, and intellectual impoverishment. In many areas of the globe – including the United States, where the study of English literature often overbalances that of American writers – the English literary tradition continues to act as a foundation and norm of value, with texts from other traditions often being "incorporated" and viewed through analytical perspectives intrinsic to the English heritage. In India, where English replaced Persian (the language of the former rulers, the Mughals) as the official state language in 1835, English continues to exert a pervasive influence on language, literature, and legal and political thought. It is in profound recognition of this integral relationship between the literary canon and cultural values that writers such as the Kenyan Ngugi Wa Thiong'o have written essays with such titles as "On the Abolition of the English Department" (1968), and important texts such as *Decolonizing the Mind* (1986). Many writers, notably Chinua Achebe, have struggled with the dilemma of expressing themselves in their own dialect, to achieve an authentic rendering of their cultural situation and experience, or in English, to reach a far wider audience. It should be noted also that what conventionally passes as "English" is Southern Standard English, spoken by the middle classes in London and the South of England. This model of English has effectively peripheralized the English spoken not only in other parts of England but also in other areas of the world. Today, there are innumerable varieties of English spoken in many countries, and only recently has their expression in literature been institutionally acknowledged. These various debates can now be examined in some of the major figures who have made contributions to postcolonial criticism and theory.

Edward Said (1935–2004)

Known as a literary and cultural theorist, Edward Said was born in Jerusalem, Palestine. Having attended schools in Jerusalem, Cairo, and Massachusetts, he received his BA from Princeton in 1960 and his PhD from

Harvard in 1964. From 1963 until his death he was Parr Professor of English and Comparative Literature at Columbia University. He was also visiting professor at Harvard, Stanford, Johns Hopkins, and Yale.

Said's thinking has embraced three broad imperatives: firstly, to articulate the cultural position and task of the intellectual and literary critic. Said's formulations in this area, influenced by Foucault, provided a crucial impetus to the so-called New Historicism in the 1980s which was in part a reaction against the tendency of American adherents of structuralism, poststructuralism, and deconstruction either to isolate literature from its various contexts or to reduce those contexts to an indiscriminate "textuality." Said's second concern has been to examine the historical production and motivations of Western discourses about the Orient in general and Islam in particular. Said's own origin (or "beginning" as he would prefer) has defined a third, more immediately political commitment: an attempt to bring to light and clarify the Palestinian struggle to regain a homeland. Some regarded him as a model of the politically engaged scholar while others viewed his enterprise as incoherent. This account of Said's work will pursue the lines indicated above.

In *Orientalism* (1978) Said examines the vast tradition of Western "constructions" of the Orient. This tradition of Orientalism has been a "corporate institution" for coming to terms with the Orient, for authorizing views about it and ruling over it. Central to Said's analysis is that the Orient is actually a production of Western discourse, a means of self-definition of Western culture as well as of justifying imperial domination of oriental peoples.[10] Said concentrates on the modern history of British, French, and American engagement with primarily the Islamic world. Given his crucial treatment of Orientalism as a discourse, his aim is to show not that this politically motivated edifice of language somehow distorts a "real" Orient, but rather that it is indeed a language, with an internal consistency, motivation, and capacity for representation resting on a relationship of power and hegemony over the Orient. The book is also an attempt to display Orientalism as but one complex example of the politically and ideologically rooted nature of all discourse, even those forms which have been veiled under the mantle of innocence. Thus, "liberal cultural heroes" such as Mill, Arnold, and Carlyle all had views, usually overlooked, on race and imperialism (Said, 14). Using a vast range of examples, from Aeschylus' play *The Persians* through Macaulay, Renan, and Marx, to Gustave von Grunbaum and the *Cambridge History of Islam*, Said attempts to examine the stereotypes and distortions through which Islam and the East have been consumed. These stereotypes include: Islam as a heretical imitation of Christianity (Said, 65–66), the exotic sexuality of the Oriental woman (Said, 187), and Islam as a uniquely unitary phenomenon and as a culture incapable of innovation (Said, 296–298). Also considering America's twentieth-century relations with the Arab world, Said suggests that the electronic postmodern world reinforces dehumanized portrayals of the Arabs, a tendency both aggravated by the Arab–Israeli conflict and intensely felt by Said himself as a Palestinian.

Gayatri Chakravorty Spivak (b. 1942)

Born in Calcutta, India, Gayatri Spivak was educated at both Indian and American universities; one of her teachers at Cornell was Paul de Man. She is known for her translation of, and lengthy preface to, Derrida's *Of Grammatology*, and her central concern with the structures of colonialism, the postcolonial subject, and the possibility of postcolonial discourse draws on deconstructive practices, the feminist movement, Marxism, and Freud. In her influential and controversial essay "Can the Subaltern Speak?" (1983), later expanded in her book *Critique of Postcolonial Reason* (1999), she addresses precisely this issue of whether peoples in subordinate, colonized positions are able to achieve a voice. A "subaltern" refers to an officer in a subordinate position; the term was used by the Italian Marxist Antonio Gramsci to refer to the working masses that needed to be organized by left-wing intellectuals into a politically self-conscious force. The term as Spivak uses it also insinuates the "Subaltern Studies Group" in India, a radical group which attempted to articulate and give voice to the struggles of the oppressed peasants of the Indian subcontinent.

In broad terms, Spivak sees the project of colonialism as characterized by what Foucault had called "epistemic violence," the imposition of a given set of beliefs over another. Such violence, she says, marked the "remotely orchestrated, far-flung, and heterogeneous project to constitute the colonial subject as Other."[11] Spivak suggests that this epistemic violence, perpetrated in colonized nations, was a corollary of the epistemic overhaul in Europe at the end of the eighteenth century, of which Foucault speaks: she is both extending Foucault's own argument and situating it within a larger, global, context, suggesting that the narrative of political and economic development in Europe was part of a broader narrative that included imperialism and the definition of Europe in relation to the colonial other. Certain knowledges in both Europe and colonized countries were subjugated or "disqualified as inadequate" (*CPCR*, 267).

Spivak also points out that "the colonized subaltern *subject* is irretrievably heterogenous" (*CPCR*, 270). Hence she rejects any possibility of an outright opposition between colonizer and colonized, oppressor and victim. Even radical intellectuals, she explains, who would speak on behalf of the oppressed, effectively romanticize and essentialize the other: possibly, she says, "the intellectual is complicit in the persistent constitution of the Other as the Self's shadow" (*CPCR*, 266). The temptation is great simply to view the other as a projection or shadow of oneself: an example might be a Western feminist imposing her schema for liberation onto women in colonized areas, a procedure that might overlook the culturally specific character of both oppression and liberation. Such a binary opposition overlooks and perpetuates the complicity between radical discourses and the colonial discourses they seek to undermine. Spivak even sees the Subaltern Studies Group in India as tainted by an essentialist agenda in some ways, as for example, in this group's endeavor to characterize "subaltern consciousness" (*CPCR*, 271–272). Spivak astutely remarks that, although many radical discourses, such as those of feminism, are opposed to essentialism and positivism, a "stringent binary opposition between positivism/essentialism . . . may be spurious" since it represses "the ambiguous complicity between essentialism and critiques of positivism." Her statement here is supported by the insight that the notion of essence pervades the work of Hegel, the modern inaugurator of "the work of the negative," and is recognized by Marx as persisting within the dialectic (*CPCR*, 282).

Homi K. Bhabha (b. 1949)

Like Gayatri Spivak, Homi Bhabha extends certain tenets of poststructuralism into discourses about colonialism, nationality, and culture. These tenets include a challenging of the notion of fixed identity, the undermining of binary oppositions, and an emphasis on language and discourse – together with the power relations in which these are imbricated – as underlying our understanding of cultural phenomena. But, as in the case of Spivak, this "extension" is not a simple extrapolation of poststructuralist principles in their purity to colonial subject matter; the process of extension itself is used to display the limits of these principles and the altered nature of their applicability. Bhabha takes some of the foregoing ideas from Derrida; from Mikhail Bakhtin he draws the notion of the "dialogic" (indicating the mutuality of a relationship) in order to characterize the connection between colonizer and colonized; he draws also on Frantz Fanon's revolutionary work on colonialism, as well as on the concept of "nation" as defined in Benedict Anderson's book *Imagined Communities* (1983).

The notion of "hybridity" is central to Bhabha's work in challenging notions of identity, culture, and nation as coherent and unified entities that exhibit a linear historical development. Hybridity expresses a state of "in betweenness," as in a person who stands between two cultures. The concept is embodied in Bhabha's own life (as in the lives of many intellectuals from colonial nations who have been raised in Western institutions): born into a Pharsi community in Bombay, India, he was educated both in his native country and at Oxford University; he subsequently taught at universities in England and America, and now teaches at Harvard.

Bhabha himself is in no doubt about the continued aspirations of imperialism, as it presses into a "neo-imperialist" phase: "there is a sharp growth in a new Anglo-American nationalism which increasingly articulates its economic and military power in political acts that express a neo-imperialist disregard for the independence and autonomy of peoples and places in the Third World." Bhabha cites, as recent examples, Britain's war against Argentina over the Falklands in 1982 and the First Gulf War of 1991. Such economic and political domination, he adds, "has a profound hegemonic influence on the information orders of the Western world, its popular media and its specialized institutions and academics."[12] There is a tacit admission here that Western academic institutions will fall to some extent under the sway of the Western ideology of political dominance. Nonetheless, he raises the question as it concerns the "new" languages of theoretical critique in the West: "Are the interests of 'Western' theory necessarily collusive with the hegemonic role of the West as a power bloc? Is the language of theory merely another power ploy of the culturally privileged Western elite to produce a discourse of the Other that reinforces its own power–knowledge equation?" (*LC*, 20–21). Bhabha reposes these questions within the specific perspective of postcolonial discourse: he asks what the function of "a committed theoretical perspective might be, once the cultural and historical hybridity of the postcolonial world is taken as the paradigmatic place of departure" (*LC*, 21).

One of the valuable insights in Bhabha's work is that political endeavors cannot be fully theorized in advance because they must always be adapted to local conditions and possibilities. But this insight is somewhat marred by its coercion into more generalized and somewhat vague assertions about the way language functions. The notion of hybridity bears within itself the origins of whatever polarization it was intended to transcend; as such, it is inadequate for comprehending the diverse constitution of political commitment, which is often not marked by a mere blending of two factors such as class and gender. Finally, Bhabha sets up many straw targets: who *does* claim that "culture" or "subjectivity" or "truth" is somehow an unproblematic unity? The so-called opposition between ideological error and truth that Bhabha's notions of ambivalence and hybridity are intended to overcome has already been abrogated – in a dialectic deriving from Hegel – in the long tradition of Marxist thought, which has seen truth as institutionally grounded and as itself the formalized projection of various ideologies.

Henry Louis Gates, Jr. (b. 1950)

The most prominent contemporary scholar of African American literature, Henry Louis Gates, Jr. has sought to map out an African American heritage of both literature and criticism, as well as to promote and establish this heritage in academic institutions, the popular press, and the media. Central to this project has been his endeavor to integrate approaches from modern literary theory, such as deconstructive and structuralist notions of signification, with modes of interpretation derived from African literary traditions. Born in West Virginia, Gates was educated at the universities of Yale and

Cambridge; he has taught at Yale, Cornell, Duke, and Harvard, where he is Chair of African American Studies and directs the W. E. B. Du Bois Institute for African American Research. He has edited a number of pioneering anthologies such as *Black Literature and Literary Theory* (1984), *"Race," Writing, and Difference* (1986), and *The Norton Anthology of African American Literature* (1997), as well as helping to found African American journals. The important works authored by Gates include *Figures in Black: Words, Signs, and the "Racial" Self* (1987) and *The Signifying Monkey: A Theory of African-American Literary Criticism* (1988). One of his goals in these texts is to redefine the notions of race and blackness in the terms of poststructuralist theory, as effects of networks of signification and cultural difference rather than as essences. Gates has been criticized for the integrative and assimilative nature of his work: radicals have seen him as overtly compromising toward the white, elitist, mainstream Anglo-American and European traditions. Yet his work has influenced, and displays analogies with, the output of critics such as Houston A. Baker, Jr. and Wahneema Lubiano.

In the Introduction to his *Figures in Black,* which is perhaps the most succinct statement of his overall endeavor as a black critic, Gates offers a more detailed account of his own engagement with contemporary European and American literary theories and his use of these in analyzing black literary traditions, situating his endeavor within the broader historical development of African American literary criticism. Gates openly declares, adopting a term from Lévi-Strauss and Derrida, that he practices "a sort of critical bricolage," a making do with the materials already at hand, materials which may have been constructed originally for other purposes, rather than somehow starting anew. Yet this very necessity (for it is of course impossible to start anew) poses a problem for Gates: can black critics "escape a mockingbird relation to theory, one destined to be derivative," and mechanically imitative?[13] His point here is that a core of racism runs through much of the Western intellectual tradition. Can black critics "escape the supposed racism of so many theorists of criticism, from David Hume and Immanuel Kant through the Southern Agrarians [later known as the New Critics] . . . Aren't we justified in being suspicious of a discourse in which blacks are signs of absence?" (*FB*, xviii). The dilemma is somewhat analogous to that formulated by many feminists and other oppressed groups: can the oppressed escape speaking the language of the oppressor, thereby perpetuating the basic concepts and the broad world view contained in that language? In Derridean terms, can the language of marginal groups even be spoken without drawing on the syntax and vocabulary of the centers of domination and power? Gates uses Derridean terminology in explaining that some black critics (like many feminist critics) resist the very notion of theory, in "healthy reactions against the marriage of logocentrism and ethnocentrism in much of Western aesthetic discourse" (*FB*, xix). Gates notes, however, that in the eyes of other black critics, "the racism of the Western critical tradition was not a sufficient reason for us to fail to theorize about our own endeavor." He also observes a renewed interest in theory inspired by a recognition that close textual reading has been "repressed" in African American literary criticism; hence much theory is driven by a need to address "the very language of the black text" (*FB*, xix).

Gates suggests that the connection between the development of African American criticism and contemporary literary theory can be charted in four stages, corresponding broadly to his own development: the first was the phase of the "Black Aesthetic"; the second was a phase of "Repetition and Imitation"; the third, "Repetition and Difference"; and, finally, "Synthesis" (*FB*, xxv). The Black Aesthetic theorists of the first stage attempted both to resurrect "lost" black texts and to formulate a "genuinely black" aesthetic, and were persistently concerned with the "nature and function of black literature vis-à-vis the larger political struggle for Black Power" (*FB*, xxvi). Gates identifies his own radical innovation as lying in the emphasis he accorded to the "language of the text," a hitherto repressed concern in African American criticism. His engagement with formalism and structuralism led to the second phase of his development, that of "Repetition and Imitation." Realizing that a more critical approach to theory was called for, Gates' work moved into the stage of "Repetition and Difference," using theory to read black texts but thereby also implicitly offering a critique of the theory itself. The final stage of Gates' work, that of "Synthesis," involved a "sustained interest in the black vernacular tradition as a source field in which to ground a theory of Afro-American criticism, a theory at once self-contained and related by analogy to other contemporary theories" (*FB*, xxix).

Gates urges that an analysis of the connection between a black text and its "critical field" consititutes implicitly "a theory of the origins and nature of Afro-American literature" (*FB*, xxxi). This theory, argued in the current book and elsewhere, is basically that, since its origins in the seventeenth century at least through the New Negro Renaissance of the 1920s, black literature has been produced in defiant response to, and counter-exemplification of, assertions that the dearth of a black literary tradition signifies the black's "innate mental inequality with the European" (*FB*, xxxi). Charged with such lack of intellectual capacity and correlative lack of humanity, black authors have literally attempted to write themselves into existence, to achieve an identity through the narratives of their own lives, an identity that subsists primarily in language: the very language in which they had been designated as absences was itself appropriated as the sign of presence.

While Gates' work addresses the genuinely problematic issue of what kind of language is available to black critics, it could be argued that the terms of his inquiry tend somewhat to perpetuate the subordination of black criticism to the languages of modern critical theory. For example, to talk of "the language of black difference" is merely to transpose into black studies a hypostatization of the very concept of difference: why ground an "alternative" language on a trope that is often abstract even on its native soil? Gates speaks of "theory" as if somehow engagement with "it" will automatically replenish black studies. Yet modern theories do not all speak the same language, and indeed often conflict profoundly with one another's claims and insights. The lately privileged concept of "difference" is merely one of the latest reifications propagated by the aesthetics of late capitalism; as used by many modern theorists, it is torn from its history in philosophy and the history of its connection with the notion of identity. Why accept these categories – dating all the way back to Aristotle (himself an owner of slaves) – as overseeing the project of black criticism? Why even refer to them as a starting point? It may be that there is no choice but to use the "master's" language for one's own ends, but surely our starting point could be more substantial than the contentless and clichéd abstraction of pure "difference." In fairness to Gates, he valuably articulates the problems surrounding any black critical use of so-called "theory." And his own project is indeed informed by recourse to native African idioms and traditions.

Notes

1 Jonathan Dollimore, *Radical Tragedy: Religion, Ideology and Power in the Drama of Shakespeare and his Contemporaries* (New York and London: Harvester Wheatsheaf, 1984), pp. 8, 18, 54, 59, 63, 78.

2 *Political Shakespeare: New Essays in Cultural Materialism*, ed. Jonathan Dollimore and Alan Sinfield (New York and London: Cornell University Press, 1985).

3 *Alternative Shakespeares*, ed. John Drakakis (London and New York: Routledge, 1985).

4 Michel Foucault, *The History of Sexuality: An Introduction*, trans. Robert Hurley (Harmondsworth: Penguin, 1978), p. 3. Hereafter cited as *HS*.

5 Wolfgang Iser, *The Implied Reader: Patterns of Communication in Prose from Bunyan to Beckett* (Baltimore and London: Johns Hopkins University Press, 1974). Hereafter cited as *IR*.

6 Wolfgang Iser, *The Act of Reading: A Theory of Aesthetic Response* (Baltimore and London: Johns Hopkins University Press, 1978), p. 27. Hereafter cited as *AR*.

7 Stanley Fish, *Is There a Text in this Class? The Authority of Interpretive Communities* (Cambridge, MA, and London: Harvard University Press, 1980). This book contains the revised version of "Interpreting the *Variorum*" which is cited in the current chapter. Hereafter cited as *ITC*.

8 Several points in this account are taken from the excellent chapter "Colonialism and the Politics of Postcolonial Critique," in Robert Young's *Postcolonialism: An Historical Introduction* (Oxford: Blackwell, 2001). Hereafter cited as Young.

9   Bill Ashcroft, Gareth Griffiths, and Helen Tiffin, *The Empire Writes Back: Theory and Practice in Post-Colonial Literatures* (London and New York: Routledge, 1989), p. 2. Hereafter cited as *EWB*.

10 Edward Said, *Orientalism* (London: Routledge, 1978), p. 3. Hereafter cited as Said.

11 Gayatri Chakravorty Spivak, *A Critique of Postcolonial Reason* (London and Cambridge, MA: Harvard University Press, 1999), p. 266. Hereafter cited as *CPCR*.

12 Homi K. Bhabha, *The Location of Culture* (London and New York: Routledge, 1994), p. 20. Hereafter cited as *LC*.

13 Henry Louis Gates, Jr., *Figures in Black: Words, Signs, and the "Racial" Self* (Oxford and New York: Oxford University Press, 1987), p. xviii. Hereafter cited as *FB*.

Chapter 7

Cultural Studies and Film Theory

Cultural Studies

As with many of the critical traditions discussed in this book, cultural studies is by no means a new phenomenon. It has a long history: many thinkers and critics from Plato, Aristotle, Horace through Aquinas and Dante to Hegel, Marx, Freud, and Derrida have viewed literature in a broad cultural context. In the nineteenth century, Coleridge, Burke, Arnold, Carlyle, Ruskin, and Morris all wrote extensively on the larger cultural issues surrounding the study of literature. Earlier twentieth-century writers on the subject have included D. H. Lawrence, Virginia Woolf, T. S. Eliot, many Marxist thinkers, F. R. Leavis, and Raymond Williams. But it has been in the last twenty years or so that cultural studies has acquired prominence as a distinct network of concerns and approaches.

Perhaps the most conventional definition of the word "culture" refers to the beliefs, rituals, and practices of a given social or ethnic group or nation. More generally, the word has been used to refer to what is produced by human beings, as opposed to "nature," which is something there already, either in the world or in our innate human constitution. The anthropologist Lévi-Strauss challenged any sharp distinction between culture and nature. Freud, in contrast, did see an opposition between culture or civilization and our unconscious and instinctual life. In modern usage, culture has sometimes designated the highest achievements of a civilization as in its literature, science, and art. In his *Culture and Anarchy*, Matthew Arnold defined culture as "the best that has been thought and said" in the world. Indeed, there is a literary tradition from Arnold and Irving Babbitt through T. S. Eliot and F. R. Leavis to John Carey which sees literature and the arts as the repository of culture, of a complex of aesthetic, moral, and spiritual values which are threatened by the continued advance of a mechanistic and materialistic civilization devoted to the pursuit of wealth. Sociologists and anthropologists, however, have entertained a broader view of culture, one which encompasses not only the high arts but also the various beliefs and social practices of all segments of society. It is clear, as many thinkers from Edward Said to Homi Bhabha have pointed out, that the way in which we define culture can be hierarchical and even exclusive, not only of other nations and ethnic groups but even of other social groups – women, workers, ethnic or religious minorities – in our own society.

When we turn to the term "cultural studies," we can see that this too has a very wide designation; it could encompass inquiries in a wide variety of fields such as sociology, anthropology, history, literature, and the arts. As applied to the study of literature, cultural criticism is marked foremost by its broad definition of what counts as "literature": this includes not only the usual highbrow genres of poetry and drama, and the more recent middlebrow genre of fiction – which have formed the conventional "canon" or tradition of literature – but also popular fiction such as thrillers and romances, mass media (including various kinds of television programs such as comedies, soap operas, and advertising), cinema, magazines, and music. Indeed, the conventionally entitled "Department of English" might nowadays more accurately be termed a "Department of Cultural Studies," since it sees literature and literary meaning as integrally situated and shaped by a larger context that includes many other discourses and wider systems of meaning.

As well as broadening the conventional definition of literature, cultural criticism tends to ground the study of literature in a larger framework which can include the economic institutions of literary production, the ideological context of prevailing beliefs, and broad political issues of class, race, and gender, and the operations of power. Hence cultural analysis tends to stress what is specific or unique – in terms of time, place, and ideology – to a given cultural and literary moment. Typically, cultural studies has extended its methodology beyond the conventional strategies of reading and research to encompass field study, empirical observation, interviewing, active participation, and interdisciplinary collaboration.

This kind of study has in earlier decades also come under the rubric "sociology of literature": as early as 1952 in his book *The Common Pursuit*, F. R. Leavis noted that the sociology of literature was "a field that has had much attention in recent years."[1] In his first book *Mass Civilization and Minority Culture* (1930), he had argued that culture is actually in the keeping of "a very small minority" which constitutes "the consciousness of the race . . . at a given time." This minority keeps alive "the subtlest and most perishable parts of tradition." And what is in its keeping "is the language, the changing idiom, upon which fine living depends . . . By 'culture' I mean the use of such a language."[2] Hence Leavis goes so far as effectively to equate culture and language, affiliating both of these with an intellectual elite, a large part of whose function is to preserve the past.

It is evident that much of what falls under cultural studies could easily be classified under various other labels such as Marxism, structuralism, New Historicism, feminism, and postcolonialism. Indeed, the field of cultural studies has been influenced by structuralism's emphasis on examining a text as a set of semiotic codes operating within a wider complex of social codes. It has been even more heavily influenced by Marxist thought, and some Marxists might argue that it borrows much of the methodology of Marxist analysis without the political commitment characteristic of (and necessary to) Marxism. For example, it might show how a particular novel depicts class relations, without this analysis being part of any practical political enterprise. However, there are some cultural critics such as Pepi Leistyna who see their theoretical study as integral to a program of political action.[3]

It is perhaps the tradition of Marxist thinking which has been the most pronounced in giving the term "culture" a political valency, viewing it as a part of the ideological process whereby the ruling class foists its own values on the rest of society. In this tradition, culture has been viewed as an instrument of domination or oppression. In this vein, the Frankfurt School saw modern mass culture as reduced to a bland commercialism. The School (the Institute for Social Research at the University of Frankfurt) was interdisciplinary, with an emphasis on cultural studies and critical theory. Leading figures of the School included Max Horkheimer, Theodor Adorno, Herbert Marcuse, and Walter Benjamin, who all produced analyses of modern culture, drawing on Marxist and sometimes on Freudian theory. In collaboration, Adorno and Horkheimer produced an incisive critique of modern culture that was to prove seminal for cultural studies: *Dialectic of Enlightenment* (1944). In an important chapter called "The Culture Industry: Enlightenment as Mass Deception," they argue that culture under monopoly capitalism imposes a sterile uniformity on everything: "Films, radio and magazines make up a system which is uniform as a whole and in every part."[4] Moreover, the movies, magazines, popular music, and television shows produced by the culture industry no longer even pretend to be art: "The truth that they are just business is made into an ideology in order to justify the rubbish they deliberately produce" (*DE*, 121). Radio and television are democratic in the negative sense that they turn their audiences into passive listeners and "authoritatively subject them to broadcast programs which are all exactly the same" (*DE*, 122). Part of the reason behind this is that the institutions of culture are weak and must appease the real holders of power invested in powerful sectors of industry such as steel, petroleum, and electricity (*DE*, 123). The "ruthless unity" in the culture industry does not allow anyone to escape its hierarchized classifications: everyone must behave in accordance with "his previously determined and indexed level, and choose the category of mass product turned out for his type" (DE, 123). Indeed, the "whole world is made to pass through the filter of the culture industry." The illusion is created that the outside world is a "straightforward continuation" of what is presented on the screen. Real life becomes indistinguishable from the movies which leave no room for imagination or reflection, confronting the spectator with a "rush of facts," precluding any space for sustained thought (DE, 126–127).

Everything, according to Adorno and Horkheimer, is appropriated stereotypically for mass mechanical reproduction, leaving no room for style as anything but imitation; the constant pressure to produce new effects merely increases the power of existing conventions. The true work of art's struggle with style, engaging the risk of failure in its search for identity and meaning, is lost in mass culture whose inferior products rely on its similarity with others, on a surrogate identity. Today, everything is reduced to this barbarized notion of style, as absolutely imitative, and which signifies merely obedience to the social hierarchy (DE, 131). All cultural products alike ultimately serve to remind people of the "triumph of invested capital" and to ensure that the "might of industrial society is lodged in men's minds" (DE, 127). In general, the culture industry serves to control people's consciousness, impressing upon them their own powerlessness, stubbornly refusing to engage their ability to think independently, equating pleasure with complete capitulation to the system of power, reducing individuals to mere expendable copies of the identities manufactured by the media and film, presenting the world as essentially meaningless and governed by blind chance (rather than by such virtues as merit and hard work). The culture industry can offer no meaningful explanation of life, and in fact the ideologies it promotes are deliberately vague and noncommittal (DE, 147). In these ways, mass culture discloses the fictitious character of the individual in the bourgeois era (DE, 155). Of course, in this system, even art is a commodity; what is new is that it admits to this status, and its very alleged purposelessness or lack of utility is subsumed in a wider usefulness or exchange-value defined by market forces: "The work of art, by completely assimilating itself to need, deceitfully deprives men of precisely that liberation from the principle of utility which it should inaugurate" (DE, 158).

In contrast with the views of the Frankfurt School, Marxists such as Antonio Gramsci have also seen culture – in the development of a working-class counter-culture – as an instrument of possible resistance to the prevailing ideologies. In fact, this dual valency of the term "culture" – as a mode of ideological domination and resistance to such domination – has come to characterize many of the cultural critics' analyses of cultural phenomena. Another way of expressing this would be to say that cultural critics tended to view "culture" as a site of ideological struggle.

The view of culture as oppositional or potentially subversive was developed in England by figures such as Raymond Williams, one of the founders of the New Left movement, the historian E. P. Thompson, and the socialist Richard Hoggart, who in 1964 founded the Centre for Contemporary Cultural Studies at Birmingham University. Leading figures in the Centre included Stuart Hall, whose essay "Cultural Studies and Its Theoretical Legacies" will be considered shortly, and Dick Hebdige, known for his book *Subculture: The Meaning of Style*. As well as analyzing the subversive nature of youth cultures, critics at the Centre examined the ideological function of the media and issues in education. In America, the Marxist critic Fredric Jameson saw modern mass culture as essentially postmodernistic in its form; Janice Radway wrote on the popular form of the romance novel in her widely selling *Reading the Romance* (1984), and examined the institutional workings of middlebrow fiction in her subsequent *A Feeling for Books: The Book-of-the-Month Club, Literary Taste, and Middle-Class Desire* (1997). In the first of these, Radway argues that women who read popular romances see this activity as "combative and compensatory," helping them to carve out a "solitary space" in the midst of domestic lives where their attention is always otherwise focused on the demands of others. Romance reading supplies women "vicariously with the attention and nurturance" which they lack; and romance "opposes the female values of love and personal interaction to the male values of competition and public achievement," demonstrating the triumph of the former.[5] Clearly, in projecting such a Utopian state, women are reading romances "not out of contentment but out of dissatisfaction, longing, and protest" (*RR*, 215). And this Utopian imagining creates a kind of female community. But if viewed from a more external perspective which broadens to include social and historical contexts, it emerges that this community is abstract, since individual readers never combine to share their experiences or to challenge their mutual separation or to implement changes in the public world (*RR*, 212–213). The Utopian projection leaves unchallenged "the very system of social relations" which gave rise to the romance. Romance reading gives the reader "a strategy for making her present situation more comfortable without substantive reordering of its structure" (*RR*, 215). A further danger is that the fictional world of romance reinforces conventional categories and oppositions such as that between the private and public worlds, between the values of love and those of status and wealth; that fictional world also perpetuates the idea that women belong in the private, domestic sphere (*RR*, 216). On the positive side, it seems clear that reading romances does change some women, making them more assertive of their rights and possessive of their time.

While Radway acknowledges the enormous power of contemporary forms of mass culture, she insists those who are committed to social change should not ignore such "minimal but nonetheless legitimate" forms of protest as are enshrined in the reading of romances: we must not only understand these Utopian longings but encourage them and bring them to fruition (*RR*, 222). Whereas Radway locates in the reading of popular fiction a space of resistance to patriarchal norms, other critics such as Susan Bordo, in her *Unbearable Weight: Feminism, Western Culture, and the Body* (1993), emphasize the profound and imposing impact of popular culture on women's self-image and cosmetic practices, showing how much of their alleged freedom to form themselves is illusory.

In Russia, the Marxist Volosinov had already seen the linguistic "sign" itself as the site of ideological and cultural struggle. And in France, the (then) structuralist Roland Barthes had analyzed various aspects of popular culture in terms of its use of linguistic codes. Many cultural critics, such as John Fiske, have drawn on semiotics to analyze elements of popular culture. In his *Television Culture* (1987), Fiske argues that the techniques and codes employed by television mold our perceptions but he rejects the idea that audiences are wholly passive consumers of ideological meanings, arguing instead that a text "is the site of struggles for meaning that reproduce the conflicts of interest between the producers and consumers of the cultural commodity. A program is produced by the industry, a text by its readers."[6] The French sociologist Pierre Bourdieu saw his work as politically motivated, opposing globalization and cultural forms of oppression. His work in general attempted to understand how the human subject was positioned in larger social structures, and he saw aesthetic judgment as integrally located within such structures.

In summary, then, cultural studies might be characterized by its broad definition of literature as including all aspects of popular culture, its situation of literature as a set of semiotic codes among broader social codes, its view of culture as an instrument of subordination or subversion, as a site of ideological struggle, its commitment to broadly left-wing political aims, and its generally empirical, interdisciplinary, and collaborative methodology. In what follows, we can examine certain central statements made by some of the major thinkers in this field.

Raymond Williams (1921–1988)

Many of the concerns of modern cultural studies can be traced back to Raymond Williams' groundbreaking work *Culture and Society 1780–1950*, published in 1958. Here, Williams cited five words which, in the last two hundred years or so, had "acquired new and important meanings": *industry, democracy, class, art,* and *culture.*[7] During this period, "art" and "industry" came to denote institutions rather than merely skills or qualities, "class" acquired political significance, and "democracy" lost its negative connotations (of mob rule and disorder). The word "culture" – the most complex of those listed, in Williams' eyes – answered to the changes in all of these terms. Previously, it had meant something like "nurturing" or "training." Its meaning expanded to denote, first, a general state of mind, associated (as in Arnold's use) with the idea of perfection; then the general intellectual condition of society; then the arts taken as a whole; and finally, "a whole way of life, material, intellectual, and spiritual." Williams traces the emergence of culture as a historical formation from the narrower meanings given above to its most comprehensive signification as "a whole way of life," which includes areas of private experience. This broadened notion of culture, says Williams, was essentially a response to the new political and social developments signified by the altered meanings of democracy, class, industry, and art (*CSoc*, 6–17).

Williams traces the significations of culture through figures such as Coleridge, Arnold, I. A. Richards, and F. R. Leavis, arguing that its evolution in the pages of these writers is toward a general antithesis with modern civilization. "Culture," affiliated by all of these figures, with an elite, embodies a last bastion of resistance against an increasingly mechanized and philistine civilization. For both Leavis and Arnold, "culture" becomes synonymous with "criticism," with a generally critical stance toward mainstream social norms and values. While Williams is somewhat sympathetic to this endeavor, he questions the validity of placing upon literature or criticism any truly redemptive power that would alleviate the ills of the modern world, of giving poets and critics "the responsibility of controlling the quality of the whole range of personal and social experience" (*CSoc*, 248–249). And Williams is of course critical of the idea that culture is somehow the preserve of a "cultivated minority," as well as of any simplistic (and historically inaccurate) implication that capitalist society was somehow preceded by "a wholly organic and satisfying past" (*CSoc*, 255). Williams rightly detects in such implications an impulse originated largely by the Romantics; and he sees in socialists such as William Morris a rehashing of this Romantic tendency newly aligned with social and political imperatives (of liberating the working classes) derived from Marxism. He is doubtful that any Marxist theory of culture could assign it such a transformative role, a role which would usurp that assigned by Marx and Engels to the material, economic, productive process.

In his chapter "Marxism and Culture," Williams acknowledges that a Marxist account of culture must account for the complex connection between the economic base and the superstructure (of politics, philosophy, art, religion, etc.), allowing for shifting connections between economic and other factors. But he insists that, given Marx's view of economic conditions as the most fundamental foundation of the rest of our social and intellectual life, a Marxist theory of culture cannot accord art and literature a substantial agency in social change. On the contrary, Marx "denied that it was this kind of work that decided human development." Williams talks of the "shock" of this insight to "thinkers and artists . . . accustomed to think of themselves as the pioneers of humanity" (*CSoc*, 265–266). Williams reminds us of a fact that is all too often forgotten: Marx's emphasis on the economic conditions – his insight that society's "basic economic organization could not be separated and excluded from its moral and intellectual concerns" – has "passed into the general mind" (*CSoc*, 271). This statement is even more true now than when Williams wrote it: many theories have now registered the impact of Marx's emphasis, including feminism, New Historicism, reader-response, cultural studies, and even deconstruction (partly through its common legacy in Hegel). But we cannot simply relate literature to economics, as naive reflectionist theories have done, because what the economic substructure determines is "a whole way of life" – and it is to this that we must relate literature. And a truly Marxist use of the word "culture" would designate not only superstructural elements such as intellectual and artistic products but also a whole way of life, including the economic conditions of artistic and intellectual production (*CSoc*, 272–274).

In the conclusion to his book, Williams points out that the modern idea of culture is a reaction to a general change in the "conditions of our common life," a change in industry, democracy, class, and art. The idea of culture is a concerted attempt to regain control over the seemingly overwhelming forces of change. Williams identifies three periods in which this general reaction developed: the first, from about 1790 to 1870, saw a sustained effort to "compose a general attitude towards the new forces of industrialism and democracy." In the second period, 1870–1914, there grew increasing specialisms in attitudes to art and a preoccupation with politics. After 1914 there was a growing concern with "new problems arising from the development of mass media . . . and . . . large-scale organizations" (*CSoc*, 286–287). Williams goes on to talk about how the immensely powerful media create a new set of problems, molding and directing public opinion "often by questionable means, often for questionable ends" (*CSoc*, 288).

A further, related, development is of course "mass" culture or popular culture, which is effectively a euphemism for "a great deal of bad art, bad entertainment, bad journalism, bad advertisement, bad argument," much of it known to be bad by its own producers, as embodied in the famous phrase "written by morons for morons" (*CSoc*, 294). Williams urges us to remember that the new institutions were not creations of the working classes themselves but produced for them by others for political or commercial advantage (*CSoc*, 295).

Having said all of this, Williams warns against dismissing all of popular culture, much of which is worthwhile and much of which cannot be assessed in terms of conventional literacy: it is tempting for academics to think – wrongly – that reading is important for the whole populace, which actually engages often in "other forms of skilled, intelligent, creative activity . . . from gardening, metalwork, and carpentry to active politics" (*CSoc*, 297). The whole theory of mass communication depends on a minority in some way exploiting a majority. If we reject this ideology, we must seek a new theory of communication which must be "a theory of community" (*CSoc*, 300–302).

Williams affiliates the idea of community primarily with working-class culture; in contrast with bourgeois culture, which is fundamentally individualist and promotes individual development, the essential working-class ethic is communal, regarding society as a vehicle for the controlled advance and improvement of all people. Hence working-class culture consists of "the basic collective idea" and the institutions, manners, and habits which result from this; bourgeois culture is "the basic individualist idea" and the institutions, habits, and beliefs which proceed from this. In our culture as a whole, there is a constant interaction between the two modes of life (*CSoc*, 312–313). Importantly, the culture produced by the working class since the Industrial Revolution has been marked by "the collective democratic institution," whether in the form of the trade union, the cooperative movement, or a political party. In its essence, working-class culture is social rather than individual.

In general, the idea of culture in modern times has been a critique of the bourgeois idea of society (*CSoc*, 314). Williams recognizes that these notions of class culture have been complicated by various factors, such as the Victorian middle-class idea of service (whose commitment to nation or community has modified bourgeois individualism), England's status as an imperial power, and the idea of the "ladder" on which ascent from one class to another is in principle possible. The problem with the idea of service – as applied to the training of upper servants – is that it fosters conformity, respect for authority, and effective preservation of the status quo, and does not entail active mutual responsibility. The ladder of opportunity – on which some working-class people can rise above their original class affiliations – is merely a substitute for real equality of education and wealth (*CSoc*, 314–317). More fruitful might be the working-class notion of communal solidarity, which alone can provide "the real basis of a society," in defining "the common interest as true self-interest" (*CSoc*, 318). But we must realize that culture is essentially unplannable: we cannot simply impose democracy on ourselves or on others; rather, a democratic culture must be tended as a natural growth (returning to the original meanings of "culture"). We need to recognize that the fundamental forces still changing our world are industry and democracy. The struggle for democracy, says Williams, "is a struggle for the recognition of equality of being, or it is nothing." And this struggle must embody an acknowledgment of both human individuality and variation (*CSoc*, 322).

Stuart Hall (b. 1932)

Along with Raymond Williams and Richard Hoggart, Stuart Hall was one of the pioneers of cultural studies in England. Born in Jamaica, Hall entered Britain in 1951 and, like many modern theorists, occupied a position on the margins of two cultures. His influence has extended in a number of directions: he was a leading figure in the New Left movement of the 1960s and a founder of the *New Left Review*; from 1968 until 1979 he served as Director of the Centre for Contemporary Cultural Studies, formed at the University of Birmingham in 1964 by Hoggart; he has collaborated with and influenced many of the major figures in cultural studies, including Dick Hebdige and Hazel Carby. In the 1960s he helped formulate, in the vein of Raymond Williams, a broad socialism that moved beyond any naive understanding of the Marxist base–superstructure model toward a more comprehensive assessment of the role of cultural factors. But most importantly and most consistently, he has insisted on the need for intellectuals to understand and promote the political and practical significance of their work. His essay "Cultural Studies and Its Theoretical Legacies," first presented at a conference at the University of Illinois in 1990, remains a valuable document of the formation and development of cultural studies, and is of enduring relevance in its call for political relevance.[8]

In this essay, Hall recounts that he entered cultural studies from the New Left, which, from the beginning, had a fraught relationship with Marxism. Indeed, it was out of the "original quarrel" between the New Left and Marxism that cultural studies grew (*CS*, 283). Cultural studies was certainly influenced by central questions on the Marxist agenda, but what seemed lacking in Marxism was an adequate treatment of issues that formed the privileged object of cultural studies: culture, Ideology, language, and the operation of the symbolic (*CS*, 279). Hall records how the Birmingham Centre was essentially attempting to nurture what Gramsci had called "organic intellectuals," though he admits that there then was no emerging historical movement to which the intellectual work of the Centre could be organically referred (*CS*, 281).

Hall recounts two other theoretical moments, two "ruptures" or "interruptions" in the development of cultural studies, the first involving feminism and the second, questions of race (*CS*, 283). A more fundamental dislocation occurred in British cultural studies through what has become known as "the linguistic turn," signifying the discovery "of discursivity, of textuality," or, more simply put, of the recognition that theoretical problems are ultimately rooted in the problematic nature and constitutive role of language. Hall cites the crucial encounters with structuralist, semiotic, and poststructuralist work which highlighted the importance of language to any study of culture (*CS*, 283). This entailed an acknowledgment of the heterogeneity and multiplicity of meanings and of the decentered nature of culture, language, and textuality (*CS*, 284). What "defines cultural studies as a project," says Hall, is that "it holds theoretical and political questions in an ever irresolvable but permanent tension" (*CS*, 284). There is a great difference, he concludes, between "understanding the politics of intellectual work and substituting intellectual work for politics" (*CS*, 286).

In his essay "The Rediscovery of Ideology," Hall attempts to reformulate the conventional Marxist account of ideology in the light of structuralist insights into the nature and operation of language and social codes. He raises the question of how social institutions maintain certain discourses in a dominant position and exclude others, and how they manage to limit the range of possible discourses.[9] In answering this question, he enlists certain insights of structuralism which, in his eyes, impel us toward a redefinition of ideology. Structuralists have insisted that individual utterance is enabled by an underlying system of relations; in this sense, a speaker does not give rise to language but is himself "spoken" by a language that is already there, and whose rules are already in place ("RI," 72). Drawing on insights of Volosinov, Hall observes that the power to signify is an ideological power, and public events and terms are sites of struggle between competing definitions ("RI," 69). The outcomes of these struggles – i.e., which definitions are accepted and pass into the inventories of popular thinking – depend "on the balance of forces in a particular historical conjuncture," on what Hall terms the "politics of signification" ("RI," 70). Particular discourses are ideological because they issue from a limited ideological matrix; the individual utterance made by particular broadcasters may not be intended as ideological but they unconsciously draw upon "the ideological inventories" or the ideological grammar – the correct way of saying things or posing certain problems – of their society ("RI," 72). In theories influenced by Freud and Lacan, this question of how the speaker or subject of enunciation is positioned in language became "the principal mechanism of ideology itself" ("RI," 72). In other words, ideology speaks through people by situating them (for example, as broadcasters within a television network) within a network of discourses, such that they appear to be speaking freely, expressing content that they (and their viewers) have already absorbed as something natural and inevitable.

Drawing on the structural study of myth by Lévi-Strauss, Hall points out that ideological propositions about the social world are embedded or entailed in a framework of linked propositions which has achieved the status of natural or self-evident truth. Any statement in a news bulletin, for example, relies on this deep structure of tacit propositions in order to be accepted as unproblematically true. Such statements appear to be "natural and spontaneous affirmations about 'reality'" ("RI," 74). And this indeed is what produces the "reality effect": reality is no longer understood as a correspondence between words and things, between language and world. Rather, reality is the result of how things are signified. The reality effect is produced when these constructed ways of presenting reality offer themselves as descriptive, as sustaining certain closures of meaning, as advancing an implicit equivalence between themselves and reality ("RI," 74). In other words, the reality constructed by discourse is presented as independently or naturally real. Such discourses also establish the viewer as complicit in this view of reality. Such a theory, says Hall, applies most starkly to television, "the dominant medium of social discourse and representation in our society" ("RI," 75–76).

Hall urges that these newer conceptions of language, advanced not only by Saussure, Lévi-Strauss, Jakobson, and Pecheux, integrated with insights from Marx and Gramsci concerning the workings of ideology, inaugurated three lines of development important for understanding how the class struggle operates in language. Firstly, the multiple referentiality or polysemic nature of language had to be explained. Volosinov saw the sign as an ideologically contested area, as "an arena of class struggle." Secondly, meaning was the result of "a social struggle – a struggle for mastery in discourse," a struggle over which kind of meanings will prevail and win credibility ("RI," 77). Victory in this struggle, according to Volosinov, imparted "an eternal character to the ideological sign," suppressing its history of struggle and allowing the sign to appear natural and as reflecting some objective reality. The closure of meaning achieved by this victory established an "*achieved* system of *equivalence* between language and reality" ("RI," 78). Depending on the outcome and circumstances of such struggles, meanings can be coupled and uncoupled from given associations: for example, the words "democracy," "gay," "freedom," "black," and "terror" have occupied a diverse range of significations in altered contexts. The third point concerned the mechanisms within language which made such struggles possible: essentially, meaning is relational and represents a certain position within the system of linguistic differences ("RI," 79). But the struggle over meaning, says Hall, also includes factors such as the struggle over "access to the very means of signification": who has privileged access to the world of public discourse, and whose statements carry authority and the power to be representative ("RI," 81)?

Returning to the example of the media, the primary means of representation in modern societies: these cannot be seen to take their directives and agendas from big business corporations or certain political parties, but they in practice operate within a constraining circle of what is an ideological consensus or inventory of permissible statements and questions and problems. The media themselves in this way become an important part in the production of such consent; ideology functions not at the level of the "conscious intentions and biases of the broadcasters." Rather, ideology "is a function of the discourse and of the logic of social process, rather than an intention of the agent . . . the discourse has spoken itself through him/her. Unwittingly, unconsciously, the broadcaster has served as a support for the reproduction of a dominant ideological discursive field" ("RI," 88).

Dick Hebdige (b. 1951)

Like Stuart Hall, Dick Hebdige was one of the leading figures of British cultural studies and he also studied at the Birmingham Centre for Contemporary Cultural Studies, later moving to the United States. Again like Hall, his work bears the stamp of Marxist thinking inflected with structuralist insights. Perhaps what is most distinctive about Hebdige's work is his focus on subcultures and marginal groups and their implicit challenging of dominant ideologies through their reconfiguring of certain social signs and their peculiar mode of entry into existing sign systems. It was Hebdige, more than any other member of the Birmingham Centre, who elaborated and extrapolated Gramsci's concept of hegemony.

In his book *Subculture: The Meaning of Style* (1979), Hebdige recounts that in *Mythologies* Roland Barthes' "application of a method rooted in linguistics to other systems of discourse outside language (fashion, film food, etc.) opened up completely new possibilities for contemporary cultural studies."[10] This moment has often been called the "linguistic turn" or the "semiotic turn." Barthes added to the concerns of Hoggart and Williams a Marxist awareness of culture as a site of ideological struggle (*SMS*, 10–11). In this process, the word "ideology" came to acquire a much wider signification. Hebdige stresses Althusser's notion of ideology as a lived relation, beneath consciousness, at the level of "normal common sense" (*SMS*, 11). Hence, Hebdige rejects any crude interpretation of Marx's definition which characterizes ideology as "false consciousness." Rather, as Althusser had said, ideology is profoundly unconscious: ideology is indeed a system of representations but these operate as structures – such as family, cultural and political institutions – imposed on the majority of people (*SMS*, 12). And, drawing on Volosinov, Hebdige remarks that there is "an ideological dimension to every signification" (*SMS*, 13). The dominant classes frame "all competing definitions within their range" so that subordinate groups are controlled or contained "within an ideological space" (*SMS*, 16).

These statements form the important foundation for the subsequent arguments in Hebdige's book. The meanings assigned by the dominant group can at various points be contested, and the consensus can be fractured. Hebdige sees the emergence of youth subcultures as signaling a spectacular breakdown of consensus in the post-war period. However, the challenge to hegemony posed by subcultures is not direct but expressed obliquely, in style, at the "profoundly superficial level of appearances," at the level of signs (*SMS*, 17). Hebdige offers a useful summary of his argument: "Style in subculture is . . . pregnant with significance. Its transformations go 'against nature,' interrupting the process of 'normalization.' As such, they are gestures, movements towards a speech which offends the 'silent majority,' which challenges the principle of unity and cohesion, which contradicts the myth of consensus" (*SMS*, 18). Of all subcultures (including the teds in the 1950s and the mods of the 1960s), it is the punk subculture of the 1970s which has detached itself most decisively from normalized forms, making large claims for illiteracy and profanity, challenging thereby the ways in which signs are read (*SMS*, 19).

In exploring the expressive forms and rituals of "subordinate groups" such as the teddy boys, mods, rockers, skinheads, and punks, Hebdige highlights the circumstance that for these groups the most mundane objects, ranging from safety pins, shoes, clothes pegs, fishnet stockings, and the paraphernalia of bondage such as belts, straps, and chains take on "a symbolic dimension, becoming a form of stigmata, tokens of a self-imposed exile" (*SMS*, 2). These objects, part of the trappings of "confrontation dressing," become signs of "forbidden identity, sources of value" (*SMS*, 3). In general, they signify what Hebdige would like to think of as a subversive refusal, and they offer "self-conscious commentaries on the notions of modernity and taste," jettisoning conventional ideas about prettiness and make-up (*SMS*, 107).

Punk upset not only the wardrobe but "every relevant discourse," ranging from dancing through music to the press. In dance, the pogo caricatured dance styles associated with rock music; punk music was "basic and direct" in its appeal, chaotic, unmelodious, qualities reflected in the names of the bands, such as the Rejects, the Sex Pistols, the Clash, the Worst; above all, it was in the act of performance that punk bands posed the clearest threat to law and order, moving closer to their audiences, with audiences often flooding the stage. Punk intervention in the realm of media was equally notable: this predominantly working-class youth culture created "an alternative critical space" by means of a punk press and fanzines, whose language was profane, grammatically unsound, and replete with undecipherable corrections (*SMS*, 111). Even the name "punk" with its connotations of "petty villainy," "rotten," and "worthless" embodied the "ironic self-abasement" which characterized the entire subculture (*SMS*, 112).

Using Paul Willis' notion of "homology," which implies a kind of coherence and order within the internal structure of any subculture, Hebdige suggests that such underlying orderliness or homology between its various levels of signification allowed punk subculture to signify "chaos at every level" (*SMS*, 113). There was a "homological relation between the trashy cut-up clothes and spiky hair, the pogo and amphetamines, the spitting, the vomiting, the format of the fanzines, the insurrectionary poses and the 'soulless,' frantically driven music. The punks wore clothes which were the sartorial equivalent to swear words, and they swore as they dressed – with calculated effect" (*SMS*, 114). Hebdige cautions that it would be tempting to suggest that the punk paraphernalia of objects and clothes stood "for the spiritual paucity of everyday life . . . of bourgeois society." We could argue that "beneath the clownish make-up there lurked the unaccepted and disfigured face of capitalism; that beyond the horror circus antics a divided and unequal society was being eloquently condemned" (*SMS*, 115). But such readings are, he acknowledges, "too literal and too conjectural." Quoting John Mepham's comments on the workings of ideology, Hebdige urges that the "true text" must be reconstructed not by "piecemeal decoding" but by identifying the "generative sets of ideological categories" behind the subculture's exotic displays (*SMS*, 116).

If we look at the connections between experience, expression, and significance in punk subculture, we are struck by the refusal of these to "cohere around a readily identifiable set of values." Instead, the subculture cohered "*elliptically* through a chain of conspicuous absences" (*SMS*, 120). The punks positioned themselves outside the parent culture, and "played up their Otherness," using their clothing, rituals, and various objects "to escape the principle of identity" (*SMS*, 121). Clearly, these punks had been reading too much Hegel. So, suggests Hebdige, although the punks self-consciously mirrored the inequality, powerlessness, and alienation of bourgeois society, this was possible because the punk subculture broke not only with the parent culture but with its own "location in experience." In other words, it represented the very experience of contradiction in bourgeois society, its subcultural unity being at once ruptural and excessive (*SMS*, 122). It is gratifying to know that the punks arrived at conclusions similar to those of Marx in his critique of the Hegelian dialectic. The sensibility embodied by punk style, says Hebdige, was "essentially dislocated, ironic and self-aware" (*SMS*, 123).

John Fiske

John Fiske was the author of a best-selling work *Television Culture* (1987). At the outset, he defines both terms of his title: television is "a bearer/provoker of meanings and pleasures," and culture is the "generation and circulation of this variety of meanings and pleasures within society."[11] Fiske offers a schema of the codes of television (Fiske, 4). The codes of television comprise three levels. The first level is that of reality: what passes for reality is the product of a given culture's codes, hence an event to be televised is already encoded by social codes such as those of appearance, dress, make-up, behavior, and speech. The second level is that of representation, using the devices of camera, lighting, editing, music, and sound. These devices transmit the conventional representational codes of the narrative, character, action, dialogue, setting, and casting. The third level is that of ideology: the representations of character are organized into coherence and made acceptable by the ideological codes of individualism, patriarchy, race, class, materialism, and capitalism (Fiske, 5). In general, these codes produce "a congruent and coherent set of meanings that constitute the *common sense* of society." But sense can only be produced when all of the various levels of the television codes – reality, representations, and ideology – merge into a coherent and "seemingly natural unity." The task of semiotic or cultural criticism is to deconstruct this unity (Fiske, 6).

Fiske cites the commonly held view that while television programs are intrinsically polysemic and replete with a variety of potential meanings, television typically tries to control and focus this potential into "a more singular preferred meaning that performs the work of the dominant ideology" (Fiske, 1). Fiske acknowledges the "constructed" nature of television programs and the ideological role of this. For example, camera distance can be used to ideological effect: villains and those regarded as a threat to our way of life are subjected to more close-up shots which might emphasize tension or certain facial expressions. Lighting, editing, and music can be used to similar effect. The actors who are cast in given roles bring with them not only the residues of other roles they have played but also their ability to embody certain ideological values. Heroes are of course more attractive than villains; they have been predominantly white, male, and middle class, whereas villains and victims are often portrayed as members of some deviant or subordinate subculture; in fact, characters become metaphors for power relationships in society. Beneath the significance of the characters lie the ideological codes of class, race, morality, and attractiveness which serve to naturalize the choice of certain characters for certain roles (Fiske, 8–10). Inasmuch as we, the viewers, make sense of programs in this way, we are indulging in an ideological practice ourselves, "maintaining and legitimating the dominant ideology," which is underlain by certain constants such as the acquisition of wealth, the dominance of men over women both physically and intellectually, and the promotion of the mainstream culture of the white male middle classes (Fiske, 10–12).

Fiske sees news reporting as perhaps the one area of television broadcasting that is liable to fall under the charge of promoting the dominant ideology. Newsrooms still suffer from the "transparency fallacy," whereby they present their material as a window on the world, somehow free of subjective constraints. They still regard objectivity as an achievable goal and as central to the democratic process (Fiske, 288). News broadcasts struggle to control multifarious events, bringing them under the format of their own conventions; in effect, they attempt to control reality, or at least what the viewer sees as reality. They attempt to hide their own constructed nature and present their vision of the world as natural. In fact, their programs are erected on the basis of selection, categorization, combination, and narrative (Fiske, 282). The news offers itself as metonymic – as presenting a small part of a larger objective picture. But in fact, says Fiske, its essential procedure is metaphorical: reality is not out there to be described in some literal language; rather, it is the *product* of the dominant discourse, and metaphor is a conventionalizing agent insofar as it explains the unfamiliar in terms of the familiar, reinforcing its own basic categories for looking at the world and neutralizing the radical potential of any statement, event, or character (Fiske, 291).

Having said all of this, Fiske's main argument challenges this view of television as promoting the dominant ideology in some linear fashion. To begin with, he distinguishes between a program and a text. A program is a "clearly defined and labeled fragment of television's output . . . Programs are produced, distributed, and defined by the industry: texts are the product of their readers. So a program becomes a text at the moment of reading" (Fiske, 14). Fiske sees texts as the "site of conflict between their forces of production and modes of reception . . . A program is produced by the industry, a text by its readers" (Fiske, 14).

In fact, Fiske prefers to speak of consumers of television programs as readers rather than audiences, since a reader is more active and Fiske rejects the idea of a television audience as passive, as "powerless and undiscriminating, at the mercy of the barons of industry." The reader is a producer of texts, a maker of meanings and pleasures, and can engage in resistive interpretations (Fiske, 17, 18). Indeed, television is so popular in part because it enables "an active participation in that sense-making process" which we call "culture" (Fiske, 19). Moreover, the unpredictability of the market for cultural commodities has forced the culture industries to offer a repertoire of products and possible interpretations: to maintain their financial domination, they "necessarily weaken their ideological power in the cultural" sphere (Fiske, 322). Hence the power of audiences is more considerable in the cultural economy: if, as Foucault says, power is a series of reciprocal relations, the cultural capital of the bourgeoisie is constantly opposed by a popular cultural capital whose ideologies produce resistive meanings that are "a form of social power" (Fiske, 314). There is no singular uniform resistance but a "a multiplicity of points and forms of resistance" (Fiske, 316).

Fiske argues that while the resistive readings of television do not translate directly into political action, challenging dominant meanings and asserting subcultural identities and social differences is an important prerequisite for change in the political domain. The role of television is not neutral: far from being the agent of dominant ideology, it is the primary site where those in power must encourage cultural difference: "The financial economy attempts to use television as an agent of homogenization: for *it* television is centered, singular in its functionality . . . In the cultural economy, however, television is entirely different. It is decentred, diverse . . . and provokes a network of resistances to its own power" (Fiske, 324).

Susan Bordo (b. 1947)

A feminist philosopher, Susan Bordo is best known for her book *Unbearable Weight* (1993), whose focus is given in its subtitle: *Feminism, Western Culture, and the Body*. She notes initially that in its long history Western philosophy has characterized the body "as appetite, as deceiver, as prison of the soul."[12] For the tradition of Christian thought, the body is "unequivocally" gross and instinctual. In the seventeenth century it is regarded as a mechanical, biologically programmed system that can be quantified and controlled. Descartes, however, believed that we could transcend the epistemological limitations of the body (Bordo, 4). What remains constant, throughout all of these historical constructions, is "the *construction* of the body apart from the true self"– whether the latter is viewed as soul, mind, spirit, will, creativity, or freedom – and as undermining that true self (Bordo, 5). This dualism – mind/body, soul/body – is often gendered, with woman cast in the role of the body. The body, and therefore woman, is equated with the negative (Bordo, 6). She also points out that women frequently internalize these ideologies, resulting in shame over their bodies, self-loathing, leading to diseases such as anorexia nervosa and other eating disorders, which have psychological and culturally constructed dimensions (Bordo, 8–11). Diseases such as anorexia nervosa, which Bordo analyzes in detail, cannot be viewed as anomalous but are the "logical (if extreme) manifestations of anxieties and fantasies fostered by our culture" (Bordo, 15).

Bordo reiterates the important point made by Marx then Foucault that our bodies are not merely biologically determined but are "cultural forms." But she stresses what she considers to be all too often neglected: it was feminists who first developed a critique of a politics of the body, viewing the "material body as a site of political struggle" (Bordo, 16). She reminds us that it was Charlotte Bunch who in 1968 stated that there "is no private domain of a person's life that is not political." And it was Mary Wollstonecraft, as early as 1792, who highlighted the social construction of the female body as "delicacy and domesticity," pointing out that women were slaves to their bodies, and that woman was trained primarily to adorn the "prison" of her body. In 1914, at the first feminist mass meeting in America, women demanded the "right to ignore fashion," and the first public act of second-wave feminism in 1968 was the "No More Miss America" demonstration (Bordo, 19). Unfortunately, feminists were labeled from this point on as "bra-burners" (even though no bras were burned at this demonstration). In recent decades, the tide has sadly turned the other way, with breast implants, plastic surgery, and the whole range of eating disorders arising from the way that cultural norms – such as the "tyranny of slenderness" – "shape the perceptions and desires of potential lovers and employers" (Bordo, 20). These fads have even been approved of by some feminists who regard them as expressions of individual free choice in constructing one's body and one's life (Bordo, 20). In contrast, Bordo sees these phenomena as extending "the concept of enslavement to include the voluntary behaviors of privileged women" (Bordo, 22).

Bordo acknowledges that feminist discourse does require reconstruction if it is to "theorize the pathways of modern power." Foucault has been crucial in showing that modern power is not authoritarian and not orchestrated but "produces and normalizes bodies to serve prevailing relations of dominance and subordination" (Bordo, 26). Hence, power can operate "from below," inasmuch as prevailing forms of subjectivity and selfhood are maintained through "individual self-surveillance and self-correction to norms" (Bordo, 27). Much feminist criticism, Bordo urges, has failed to admit female responsibility and collusion in sustaining sexist stereotypes (Bordo, 28).

While the old feminism may have neglected the multiplicity of meaning, it did offer "a systemic critique capable of rousing women to collective action – something we do not have today" (Bordo, 31). Indeed, contemporary feminism is "strikingly muted" on the sexualization and objectification of the female body, and much of it is distressingly at one with the culture that celebrates the "creative agency of individuals" (Bordo, 31). Bordo's own focus is on the "institutionalized *system* of values and practices" in which girls and women believe that they must conform to the prevailing images of slenderness and beauty, what Kim Chernin first called the "tyranny of slenderness," resulting in various kinds of eating disorders: "the escalation of eating disorders into a significant social phenomenon arises at the intersection of patriarchal culture and post-industrial capitalism" (Bordo, 32).

Bordo sees Marx as having played a crucial role in re-imagining the body not merely as a natural, biological entity but as a historical and culturally constructed phenomenon: Marx talked of class, but gender and race also make a difference to the body one inhabits (Bordo, 33–34). Feminism has developed this relocation of the body from the nature to the culture side of the nature/culture dualism: in fact the body is never known directly or simply, but is always *mediated* by cultural images and representations. Eating disorders such as anorexia and bulimia cannot be wholly explained in biological terms because they have been "culturally produced" (Bordo, 35). Again, Bordo insists that the old masculine ideas of a disembodied discourse (as with Descartes) are reproduced by those who merely seek heterogeneity and difference for its own sake, and by the "taboo on generalization," the related "contemporary panic" over essentialism, and the "insistence on creative self-fashioning that is manifest throughout postmodern culture" (Bordo, 39–40).

Bordo's chapter "Material Girl: The Effacements of Postmodern Culture" is a brilliant *tour de force*. It argues that we have moved from previous images of the body as a watch or machine to a postmodern imagination of the body as wholly determinable. "Cultural plastic" is a new paradigm of plasticity, infused with the prevailing intoxication with freedom, change, and self-determination (Bordo, 245–246). But this paradigm effaces certain important material and social realities. For one thing, this rhetoric of choice, which claims that we can create our own bodies, effaces inequalities of privilege, money, and time, as well as the psychological desperation of those women who take up the options for procedures such as plastic surgery (Bordo, 247–248). The homogenizing and normalizing images that surround us are "suffused with the dominance of gendered, racial, class, and other cultural iconography" (Bordo, 250).

Bordo's points are illustrated by a Phil Donohue show in which black women, for example, saw their decision to have their hair straightened or to wear blue contact lenses merely as free play or creative self-expression, no different from a white woman's resolve to have a given color of hair or lipstick: "It's just fashion," where the content of fashion is seen as arbitrary and without cultural significance (Bordo, 251–253). But in fact, straightening one's hair is inflected with an oppressive cultural history – in the nineteenth century black women were subjected to a "comb test" to determine whether or not they could enter certain churches and clubs (Bordo, 254). The general tyranny of fashion, says Bordo, exerts a pressure to normalize all women, and the Caucasian standards of beauty still predominate on television, magazines, and movies (Bordo, 255).

Importantly, Bordo sees the Donahue show as an example of the "postmodern conversation," where all sense of history and cultural determination has gone, and where all distinctions are erased in the "undifferentiated pastiche of differences," in which no items have any more importance than others. Television, she observes, is "our prime modeler of plastic pluralism": on the Donahue show, week after week, rape, incest, and US foreign policy are all subject to a bland leveling. Even more distressingly, particulars reign, and any kind of generality which attempts to connect, emphasize, or criticize is suspect and subjected to charges of totalizing, of being falsely coherent and morally coercive (Bordo, 258–259). And even more distressingly, all of the elements of this postmodern conversation – the intoxication with individual choice, the focus on *jouissance*, the mistrust of pattern and critical perspective – have become a staple of much academic and intellectual discourse which celebrates supposedly new constructions of the self, multiplicity and the undermining of unified conceptions of the self, and "dreary" generalizations about gender and race (Bordo, 260).

Much postmodern theory, says Bordo, views resistance as a refusal to embody *any* positioned subjectivity. The material girl Madonna, as a postmodern heroine, embodies for some academics a rebellious sexuality which is self-defining. But Bordo points out that over the years Madonna has changed her own body type and has in fact "self-normalized." As such, she no longer provides a model of resistance (Bordo, 270). Despite Madonna's claims that she refuses any given construction of gender or sexuality, Bordo sees Madonna's videos as containing a dominant position, the objectifying gaze (Bordo, 274–275).

Film Theory

Another area of what might very generally be termed cultural criticism is centered around the history, analysis, and theorizing of film, on many levels, ranging from purely technical and formal analysis to consideration of audience, psychology, and the broader cultural, ideological, and economic contexts of film production and consumption.[13] For the first half of the twentieth century, film theory was largely the outgrowth of the actual filmmaking of directors; it was not until the 1960s and 1970s that film study became an academic discipline, subjected to the wave of structuralist, semiotic, and psychoanalytic thinking that overtook literary and cultural criticism in general. In the last decade of the twentieth century the so-called digital revolution has marked the beginning of a new era in filmmaking and film study. The history of film can be traced as far back as the 1860s when various devices were invented for producing moving images. Subsequently, the technology for developing motion pictures – such as celluloid, motion camera, and projector – developed rapidly. The first motion pictures shown to the public were in Paris in 1895 and in New York City in 1896. The French philosopher Henri Bergson was aware of these developments and his examination of the concept of time has been considered by some, such as the philosopher Gilles Deleuze, as the starting point of film theory. Bergson had contrasted what he called real time or *durée*, which is time as we actually experience it – including its psychological, subjective dimensions – with the mechanical "clock time" that we use in our everyday lives, which Bergson thought was a merely spatialized way of treating time.

The first theorists of film included the Italian-born French futurist critic Riccioto Canudo (1879–1923), whose best-known work was his manifesto *The Birth of the Seventh Art* (1911); his writings were collected in a volume entitled *L'Usine aux images* (1926). Two other pioneering works were Vachel Lindsay's *The Art of the Moving Picture* (1915) and Hugo Munsterberg's *The Photoplay: A Psychological Study* (1916). Canudo essentially argued that film integrated the spatial arts architecture, sculpture, and painting with the temporal arts music, dancing, and poetry. He saw film as a vehicle for expressing the psychology and unconscious of character as well as of the producer. Lindsay also placed film in the contexts of other arts such as poetry and sculpture, whereas Munsterberg analyzed the psychology of the audience and the aesthetics of film.

Much of the criticism following Munsterberg for the first half of the twentieth century – known as classical film theory, produced in the era of silent films – was centrally concerned with the formal aesthetic qualities and techniques that distinguished film from other arts: camera work, cinematic codes, the question of authorship, the various genres of film, as well as the fundamental question of how film was related to reality. Classical film theory largely arose from the works of directors such as Louis Delluc, Germaine Dulac, and Jean Epstein in France, and the Russians Lev Kuleshov, V. I. Pudovkin, and Sergei Eisenstein, as well as the film theorists Rudolf Arnheim, Bela Balazs, and Siegfried Kracauer. It was Louis Delluc (1890–1924), a French impressionist film director and pioneer of French film criticism, who along with Canudo formed the first significant film society or *ciné-club*. Delluc's writings were collected in two volumes, *Cinéma et cie* (1919) and *Photogénie* (1920). The latter term designated the ability of film to defamiliarize the world, to present it in a novel understanding. Kracauer's *Theory of Film* (1947) suggested that film alienated our world in the very act of revealing it. In his *Bonjour cinéma* (1921), Jean

Epstein drew attention to film's capacity to bring form to reality. The Russian directors mentioned above, Kuleshov, Pudovkin, and Eisenstein, all produced theories of montage, which is usually understood as a series of shots compactly embodying an action or event or mood, rather than portraying these in real time. They saw montage as producing a wide variety of effects – semantic, psychological, emotional – by juxtaposing and arranging single shots to produce impressions, emotions, and meanings that were not inherent in the original shots. Both Pudovkin and Eisenstein believed that the practice of montage would be destroyed by the advent of sound in film.

The complex question of the connection between film and reality was the focus of subsequent major writers. Walter Benjamin, in his famous essay of 1932, "The Work of Art in the Age of Mechanical Reproduction," asserted that the "aura" – the uniqueness inhering in the living presence of a person or object – could not be replicated on film, which was mechanically and mass-produced. In his pioneering work *Film as Art* (1932), the German-born psychologist and art critic Rudolph Arnheim, who later emigrated to America, argued that film could never simply copy reality and that in fact filmic images help shape reality and produce meaning. Arnheim thus drew attention to film as an artistic form. This formal emphasis was retained in a modified manner in the work of the Hungarian-born critic and poet Bela Balazs (1884–1949). In his *Theory of the Film* (1952), earlier published in Moscow in 1945, Balazs advanced his humanistic theory that film or moving images expressed the language of the human body and face in a way that written culture could not; as such it expressed an underlying reality otherwise ineffable. He believed that the most crucial component of film was the close-up: the language of the face, for example, in a close-up could reveal what no number of words could capture.

Realist cinema was championed by two major figures after the Second World War. One was André Bazin, who was a co-founder of the important journal *Cahiers du cinéma* (1951) and who exerted a considerable influence on other thinkers associated with that journal, such as François Truffaut, Jean-Luc Godard, and Claude Chabrol. His writings were published in four volumes as *Qu'est-ce que le cinéma?* (What is Cinema?) (1958–1965). Based on his view of pioneering directors such as Jean Renoir, Orson Welles, and Roberto Rossellini, Bazin propounded a realistic aesthetic whereby film expresses an objective reality with as little intrusion of the director as possible. The medium of the film, since it records in time, is inherently more realistic than photography and other arts. Instead of montage, he urged the use of deep focus (an equal focus on elements close to and far away from the camera), wide shots, and the long take, producing a continuity which the spectator was left to interpret. He argued that depth of focus brings the spectator into a closer relation with the image than that which he has in real life; this makes him more active in contributing to the progress of the action, and allows for ambiguity, whereas montage ruled out ambiguity and merely required the spectator to follow. Nonetheless, Bazin did not naively believe that total objectivity was possible; his insistence, rather, was that the director not indulge in overt subjective manipulation of reality. He held that film should express the vision of its director; in this, he anticipated the *auteur* theory, originated by Truffaut. The other champion of realism was Siegfried Kracauer (1889–1966), who, in his *Theory of Film: The Redemption of Physical Reality* (1960), argued that film should be realistic though not in conventional ways; its images should orientate audiences away from normalized ways of seeing the world.

Film studies attained a more scholarly and rigorous status in the work of Jean Mitry (1907–1988), whose *Esthétique et psychologie du cinéma*, produced in two volumes in 1963 and 1965, attempted to synthesize the two trends mentioned above in classical film theory, the realist and the aesthetic or formal. Mitry's phenomenological approach recognized that we can know the external world only through our subjective perceptual apparatus, hence film reflects the director's perception of the world, imparting structure and meaning to reality.

In 1954 the French film director and critic François Truffaut initiated the *auteur* theory, which proved to be widely influential. In his essay "A Certain Tendency of French Cinema" (1954), Truffaut does not directly espouse the *auteur* theory; rather, in pursuing his main goal of criticizing a tendency toward "psychological realism" in French films, he insists that the directors of whom he speaks are ultimately responsible for the content of their films; they are *auteurs* who write their dialogues and who often invent the stories they direct.[14] It was the US film critic Andrew Sarris who, some eight years later, coined the term "*auteur* theory" and became its leading proponent and popularizer. The theory also has roots in the writings of André Bazin and Alexandre Astruc in *Cahiers du cinéma*, and became the foundation of the French film movement called the *nouvelle vague* or the New Wave. The theory basically held that a film was an expression of the creative vision of its director who was regarded as its author (French *auteur*). Hence, also, a group of films in diverse modes and on diverse subjects could be seen as unified by certain characteristic authorial traits.

But Truffaut, along with Jean-Luc Godard, also turned his attention to popular Hollywood films and promoted genre studies and the notion that films by different directors could be categorized within the same genre. So, for example, "Westerns" might be seen as containing a basic pattern, certain constant elements (wandering cowboys, Indian wars), and a certain setting (Western United States). Hence the two contrasting modes of analysis, *auteur* theory and genre theory, were born around the same time.

It was in the 1960s and 1970s that film theory became an academic discipline, falling under the tide of so-called cultural and literary theory which swept through the universities. Structuralism and semiotics, which tended to view literary texts as systems of signs within larger signifying patterns and codes, extended their analyses to film, the media, and popular culture in general. As with most structuralist analysis, this involved an analogy with linguistic study: the signs and codes of film were analyzed as part of the language of film, as indicated in the title of Christian Metz's book *Film Language: A Semiotics of Cinema* (1974). But Metz argued that it was poetics, rather than linguistics, to which the study of film should turn, seeking the codes that were specific to film. Integral to this institutionalization of film theory was the proliferation of semiotic, psychoanalytic, and Marxist theory, which took root in the British journal *Screen* as well as in the French *Cahiers du cinéma*. This proliferation is sometimes called the "second semiotics," and it was often politically orientated, analyzing the ideologies and psychologies behind film construction and reception. Important figures here include Metz, Jean-Louis Baudry, Jean-Pierre Oudart, Peter Brunette, and David Wills.

Another important approach to film study has been generated by feminist critics such as Pam Cook and Claire Johnson, who have analyzed the images of women portrayed in film, the patriarchal culture that overlooks the making of films, and the nature of sexuality and desire. Laura Mulvey, Kaja Silverman, Mary Ann Doane, and Gaylin Studlar have all conducted influential studies about the nature of the male gaze directed at the images of women. Other notable writers on film have included the American philosopher Stanley Cavell, who has argued that it has endless potential for constructing a world that we do not ordinarily see. As in the field of literary criticism, some writers, such as Noël Carroll, David Bordwell, and Edward Branigan, have reacted against theory, advocating a return to the formal qualities and technique of film and the audience's response to it. Recent significant works include Susan Sontag's *Styles of Radical Will* (1969); Bordwell's *Narration in the Fiction Film* (1985); a historical study by Bordwell, Janet Staiger, and Kristin Thompson entitled *The Classic Hollywood Cinema* (1985); and Gilles Deleuze's two volumes, *Cinema I: L'Image-mouvement* (1983) and *Cinema 2: L'Image-temps* (1985), which argues – drawing on Bergson's concept of time as *durée* – that the "movement-image" of classical film was displaced by the direct "time-image" of post-war film. Scenes are linked not chronologically (using conventional, spatialized, time) and rationally but irrationally, forcing the passage of time into the foreground. Film study has been conducted from a rich variety of perspectives, including culture, authorship, genre, the study of film stars, Marxism, psychoanalysis, feminism, and ethnicity. The following section will briefly consider the central insights of some of the major contributors to film theory.

Andrew Sarris (b. 1928) and *Auteur* Theory

Andrew Sarris is an American film critic best known for his coining and popularizing of the term *"auteur* theory." His influential works include *The*

American Cinema: Directors and Directions 1929–1968 (1968), and he has been a regular contributor to journals such as the *Village Voice* and the *New York Observer*. He is a professor at Columbia University. In his essay "Notes on the *Auteur* Theory in 1962," Sarris suggests that there are three basic premises of *auteur* theory. The first is the "technical competence of a director as a criterion of value." In other words, we can make interesting remarks about a badly directed film, about the script or acting or photography or music, but none of these features will redeem the film in terms of a final critical assessment (*FSR*, 69). The second premise is the "distinguishable personality of the director as a criterion of value. Over a group of films, a director must exhibit certain recurring characteristics of style which serve as his signature" (*FSR*, 69). The group of films should reveal a stylistic consistency. The third and ultimate premise of *auteur* theory is more difficult for Sarris to explain, but he regards it as important, indeed as underlying "the ultimate glory of the cinema as an art." This premise, he says, is "concerned with interior meaning," which Sarris calls an "élan of the soul," that which marks the director's personality as unique (*FSR*, 69).

Sarris views the three premises of *auteur* theory as three concentric circles: "the outer circle as technique, the middle circle personal style, and the inner circle interior meaning." The corresponding roles of the director, then, are those of a technician, a stylist, and an *auteur*. Sarris warns, however, that this theory is a "pattern theory in constant flux," and that there is no set course by which a director passes through all three circles. Directors often move in emphasis between them, in both directions. Sarris observes that among the advantages of *auteur* theory are the viewing of connections between different films by the same director, connections that would have been missed had we simply considered each film in isolation (*FSR*, 71).

Jim Kitses: The Study of Genre

A professor of cinema at San Francisco State University, Jim Kitses is the author of a classic study of Westerns, *Horizons West* (1969), and of *Gun Crazy* (1996), which analyzes the 1950 film of that title. In an introductory chapter to the former, on authorship and genre, he makes some important distinctions and connections between the *auteur* theory and the need to study genre. He points out that, though it has been the most popular and enduring of Hollywood forms, the Western has yet received scant attention from critics, who have focused their energies on the director rather than the form. Kitses acknowledges the gains that have resulted from *auteur* theory, which inaugurated a systematic critical approach to film analysis, helping to establish this as "a subject with its own body of knowledge."[15] Kitses insists that if we are to build a body of film scholarship, we "must begin to explore the inner workings of genre" (*FSR*, 89).

Kitses' particular interest in this regard is to argue for the idea of an American tradition in film, of which the Western is "an admirable and central model." Some of the constituent elements of this genre are its basis in American frontier life, typically set between 1865 and 1890, the Indian Wars, cattle drives, and the arrival of the farmer (*FSR*, 89–90). This is the "raw material" of the Western, and at its heart is a deeply ambiguous concept: the idea of the West. The West has beckoned to statesmen and poets, as a direction and a place, an imperialist theme and a pastoral Utopia. The great empires of the world have moved ever west: from Greece to Rome to Britain to America. As shown by Henry Nash Smith in his *Virgin Land*, the West has functioned as a symbol in America's history and consciousness. On the one hand, it was viewed as a natural garden of innocence, a refuge from the decadence of civilization. On the other hand, it was seen as treacherous and savage, stubbornly resistant to agrarian progress and community values (*FSR*, 90).

What is at stake in this broad ambivalence is "no less than a national world-view . . . the grave problem of identity that has special meaning for Americans. The isolation of a vast unexplored continent, the slow growth of social forms, the impact of an unremitting New England Puritanism obsessed with the cosmic struggle of good and evil, of the elect and the damned, the clash of allegiances to Mother Country and New World, these factors are the crucible in which American consciousness was formed" (*FSR*, 91). Kitses observes that these contradictions pervade American life and culture, evident in the literary heritage and in film, as in the Western (*FSR*, 92). The genre of the Western celebrates America as a national myth, with its contrasting images of garden and desert. Film theory needs to study the archetypal elements within the genre, doing what Northrop Frye in his *Anatomy of Criticism* did for literature (*FSR*, 93).

Christian Metz (1931–1993): A Psychoanalytic Perspective

Christian Metz is associated with what is known as screen theory (named after the journal *Screen*), which arose in the early 1970s. The journal was known primarily for its use of structuralist Marxism and Lacanian psychoanalysis, both of which drew upon structuralist insights of the linguist Saussure. Screen theorists thus analyzed the ideological dimensions of film and held that what we call reality is not somehow already there but was a world created by signifying systems, themselves generated through the ideologies of the dominant power structures. Nor did they believe in any kind of human subject existing independently of her surroundings. Both self and world were created by their positioning within a system of signs. And film could be a part of this very process of creating both subjectivity and the external world. Hence screen theorists were opposed to the aesthetic of realism and any interpretation of film as somehow simply recording reality (they derided the mainstream films which pretended to such realism, and preferred experimental films whose formal elements were foregrounded). They urged instead that film had the potential not only to reproduce prevailing ideologies through which reality – including the reality of the self – was constructed, but also to demystify those realities and offer alternative visions. Moreover, the self was not viewed as an unchanged, passive spectator: the boundaries between film and self were rendered diffuse, there being an interaction and mutual constitution of subjectivity and cinema. Metz was known for both his semiotic approach to cinema, as expressed in his *Film Language: A Semiotics of the Cinema*, and his Lacanian psychoanalytic perspective, employed in *The Imaginary Signifier: Psychoanalysis and the Cinema* (1982).

In his book *The Imaginary Signifier*, Metz brings Lacanian categories to bear on his psychoanalytic understanding of the connection between film and spectator. He stresses that an important aspect of the cinematic institution is its "mental machinery" whereby it regulates the psychology of the spectators, who have been habituated to its workings.[16] He characterizes the cinema's form of signification as perceptual, engaging both visual and auditory faculties. Indeed, it is more perceptual than other arts which enlist fewer modes of perception, such as music which is auditory, and literature whose appeal to sound and sight is more restricted. But in another sense cinema is the least perceptual, since what it offers to perception (unlike the theater) is absent, a mere replica of the actual object of perception. The cinema is unique because of this "dual character of its signifier: unaccustomed perceptual wealth, but unusually profoundly stamped with unreality." More than the other arts, the cinema "involves us in the imaginary," enlisting perception only to direct it toward an absence (*IS*, 45).

Metz engages in an interesting simile based on Lacan's account of the mirror stage – the stage at which the child recognizes itself in the mirror and sees itself reflected in a satisfying wholeness, a reassuring unity between itself and its surroundings. Metz suggests that "film is like the mirror." But there is an essential difference: the spectator's own body is not reflected in it. Having already been through the mirror stage, the spectator is able to constitute a world of objects without having to recognize himself within it. The cinema "presupposes that the primitive undifferentiation of the ego and the non-ego has been overcome" (*IS*, 46).

But then, with *what* does the spectator identify? He can, of course, identify with the character or even the actor herself; but these are merely secondary forms of identification (only the identification of the mirror can be viewed as primary). The spectator's knowledge, says Metz, is of a twofold nature: I know that I am perceiving something imaginary, and I know that it is I who am perceiving it: it is in me that the imaginary material forms an organized sequence, and I am the place, the very location where the perceived imaginary gives way to the symbolic, where the cinematic signifier is inaugurated. In this way, suggests Metz (and we can guess that he will invoke Kant), the "spectator *identifies with himself*, with himself as a pure act of perception . . . as condition of possibility of the perceived and hence as a kind of transcendental subject" (*IS*, 49). Kant had argued that, in order for my various empirical perceptions to be organized, for me to make sense of them, we must presuppose that behind the empirical ego or subject which has these experiences there must be an underlying ego or self (the transcendental ego) which stands behind these experiences and unites them, viewing them all as experiences of the *same* self.

Along with this kind of *identification*, Metz sees the connection of spectator to film as characterized by two other dispositions, voyeurism and fetishism. What defines the cinematic situation in terms of visual perception is "the absence of the object seen." In the theater, actors and spectators are present at the same time and in the same place. But in the case of cinema, the actor and spectator are "there" at different times: the exhibitionist and the spectator have failed to meet. The voyeurism specific to cinema entails a lack of clear consent on the part of the object (actor) (*IS*, 61–62). In this sense, cinematic voyeurism is an "*unauthorised* scopophilia," a practice reinforced by other features of the institution such as the darkness and anonymity in which the spectator is enveloped, the spectator's effective solitude in the auditorium, and finally, a total segregation of the space of the performance from the space of the audience: the space in which the film unfolds, represented by the screen, is "definitively inaccessible" and the spectator's participation is inconceivable (*IS*, 64).

The third characteristic of the institutionalized cinematic signifier, according to Metz, is fetishism. The fetish here is essentially the equipment of the cinema, or, put in another way, its technique. The fetish, like the apparatus of the cinema, is a prop which both disavows and affirms a lack: in other words, the film offers something as present which is absent; and the cinema fetishist is someone who is "enchanted at what the machine is capable of," in other words, at the technical resources and ingenuity which go into making absent things seem present. For the *jouissance* of full cinematic enjoyment, the fetishist's mind must at every moment register both the "force of presence that the film has and of the absence on which this force is constructed" since his pleasure resides in the gap between the two (*IS*, 74).

Metz's argument could be challenged on many fronts. Its account of mirror-identification seems to depend more on Kant than Lacan; and while this in itself is probably a good thing, it does not adequately explain the transition from imaginal to symbolic perception as formulated by Lacan – or it does not adequately apply Lacan's theory. Secondly, it is surely simplistic to say that the actors as objects on the screen have not given their consent: they have of course given their *prior* consent – and indeed their blessing – to such exhibitionism, from which they profit greatly, and it could be argued that what is on the screen controls and defines the spectator, rather than vice versa.

Laura Mulvey (b. 1941): Feminist Film Theory

Like feminist criticism in other areas, feminist film theory – much of which also emerged as "screen theory" – has analyzed the stereotypical representations of women, gender roles in film, the part played by film in social, historical, and psychological constructions of gender, as well as the workings of the audience, the male gaze, and the female spectator. And, like other psychoanalytic perspectives, feminist psychoanalytic film study has highlighted notions of identification, voyeurism, and fetishism. Since the 1970s feminist film criticism has drawn upon Freudian and Lacanian psychoanalysis – sometimes deploying their concepts in contexts which extricate them from their patriarchal subservience – as well as structuralist Marxism in the vein of Althusser.

Laura Mulvey became known in the 1970s through her writing for publications such as *Spare Rib*. Mulvey's essay of 1975, "Visual Pleasure and Narrative Cinema," has had an enormous impact on film theory, establishing a framework for further feminist film criticism, sometimes provoking modifications and disagreements with her views (she herself modified some of her views, as, for example, on the nature of the audience). In the 1970s and early 1980s, Mulvey and her husband Peter Wollen collaborated in writing and producing a number of experimental films dealing with female experience, male fantasies, and patriarchal myths; the most renowned of these was *Riddles of the Sphinx* (1977). In her seminal essay "Visual Pleasure," she uses psychoanalytic theory as "a political weapon, demonstrating the way the unconscious of patriarchal society has structured film form."[17] Using Freudian and Lacanian terms, Mulvey suggests that the function of woman in forming the patriarchal unconscious is twofold: she both symbolizes the threat of castration and, via that threat, enables her child to enter the symbolic order. The cinema, she says, raises questions about how the unconscious – which is itself formed by the dominant order – structures ways of seeing and the pleasure we experience in looking. No matter how self-conscious and ironic Hollywood has been, it has inevitably reflected the dominant ideological concept of the cinema, and it has skillfully manipulated visual pleasure, coding "the erotic into the language of the dominant patriarchal order," according a central place to the image of woman (*VOP*, 15).

The pleasures offered by cinema include scopophilia (literally, love of looking), which Freud identified as one of the components of sexuality, consisting in "taking other people as objects, subjecting them to a controlling and curious gaze" (*VOP*, 16). The sexual satisfaction here derives from the act of watching "an objectified other." Mainstream film, according to Mulvey, actually reproduces this surreptitious observation since it portrays a "hermetically sealed world" indifferent to the audience's presence; the contrast between the dark auditorium and the brilliant shifting patterns on the screen promotes the "illusion of voyeuristic separation," and of looking into a private world (*VOP*, 17). Hence the cinema satisfies this "primordial wish" for pleasurable looking. But its anthropomorphism – its focus on human form and scale – also develops the narcissistic aspect of such scopophilia: we recognize ourselves in these human forms and faces. Speaking of Lacan's account of the mirror phase, where the child recognizes itself in the mirror, as "crucial for the constitution of the ego," Mulvey points out that the child attributes to the mirror image of itself a greater completeness, viewing it as an "ideal ego," effectively misrecognizing itself. It is an image which marks the first articulation of subjectivity. The cinema, according to Mulvey, replicates this process of both identification and misrecognition: it allows a temporary loss of ego while reinforcing it. This sense of forgetting the world as perceived by the ego is "reminiscent of that pre-subjective moment of image recognition" (*VOP*, 18).

But these two modes of pleasure, says Mulvey, are contradictory: scopophilic pleasure derives from objectifying a person as an object of sexual stimulation. Narcissistic pleasure – developed through constitution of the ego – comes from identifying with the image seen. The first implies a separation from the object on the screen, the second an identification with it. The first is a function of the sexual instincts, the second of ego libido, a dichotomy crucial for Freud who saw a tension between instinctual drives and self-preservation. This contradiction between ego and libido, suggests Mulvey, also finds its complement in the fantasy world created by cinema (*VOP*, 18).

Mulvey further points out that in a world ordered by sexual imbalance, pleasure in viewing has been divided between active male and passive female: the male gaze is "determining" and the female figure is characterized by "*to-be-looked-at-ness*." Though woman is indispensable in narrative film, her visual presence tends to interrupt the progression of the story, and "freeze the flow of action in moments of erotic contemplation" (*VOP*, 19). Traditionally, the woman displayed has been an erotic object for both the characters within the screen story and the spectator: for a moment, the sexual impact of the woman "takes the film into a no-man's-land outside its own time and space," as, for example, in conventional closeups of legs or a face. In contrast with the woman's role, the role of the male protagonist is to forward the action, as a "controlling figure with whom the spectator can identify." The spectator projects his look onto the protagonist, his screen surrogate whose power to control events "coincides with the active power of the erotic look, both giving a satisfying sense of omnipotence" (*VOP*, 20). The male movie star assumes the role of the ideal ego conceived in the original moment of recognition in the mirror. Thus the spectator both subjects the woman in the film to a scopophilic look and recognizes his like in the male star through whom he gains control of the woman within the diegesis ("diegesis" referring to the world of sights and sounds in which an image moves).

But there is a problem: the female also connotes the threat of castration and ultimately sexual difference, which threatens to "evoke the anxiety it originally signified" (*VOP*, 21). There are two avenues of escape from this castration anxiety: a sadistic voyeurism which asserts control over the guilty person; or fetishistic scopophilia which can exist outside linear time since the "erotic instinct is focused on the look alone." Mulvey sees the films of Hitchcock as embodying the former, whereas in the films of Sternberg the look of the male protagonist is broken in favor of the direct look of the spectator at the female image. In this case, the woman's body "is the content of the film" (*VOP*, 22). With Hitchcock, the male hero sees exactly what the spectator sees, and portrays the latter's contradictions and tensions. His heroes are "exemplary of the symbolic order and the law . . . but their erotic drives lead them into compromised situations," and the spectator is drawn into this uneasy gaze (*VOP*, 23).

For Mulvey, it is "the place of the look that defines cinema, the possibility of varying it and exposing it." Cinema builds the mode of looking into the spectacle itself (*VOP*, 25). There are three looks associated with cinema: of the camera recording, of the audience watching the final product, and of the characters at each other in the film. The conventions of narrative film subordinate the first two to the third, to achieve the effect of realistic transparency and obvious truth. But the structure of looking contains a contradiction: the female image as a castration threat "constantly endangers the unity of the diegesis and bursts through the world of illusion as an intrusive, static, one-dimensional fetish." Thus the two looks are subordinated to the needs of the male ego. This complex of interactions which is specific to film can be challenged by attempting to "free the look of the camera into its materiality in time and space and the look of the audience into dialectics, passionate detachment" (*VOP*, 26). Mulvey seems to be arguing essentially that the illusion of realism, produced by repressing or backgrounding the materiality or presence of the camera – an illusion reinforced by the fetishistic focus on the woman's body which prevents the spectator from achieving any distance – must be seen as an illusion and the gaze of the audience rendered analyzable by self-distancing. Her overall argument suggests that the institution of cinema is deeply structured by the unconscious demands of the male ego which have been institutionalized; her proposed remedy regarding the camera's materiality is analogous to the demand by many feminists that the body – as a material object in space and time, with its unique set of characteristics and demands – be restored in its foundational role as constitutive of human thought and emotion.

Notes

1   F. R. Leavis, *The Common Pursuit* (1952; rpt. Harmondsworth: Penguin, 1966), p. 200. Hereafter cited as *CP*.

2   F. R. Leavis, *Mass Civilization and Minority Culture* (Cambridge, 1930), pp. 3–5.

3   See especially the introduction to *Cultural Studies: From Theory to Action*, ed. Pepi Leistyna (Oxford: Blackwell, 2005), pp. 1–14.

4   Max Horkheimer and Theodor W. Adorno, *Dialectic of Enlightenment*, trans. John Cumming (New York: Continuum, 2001), p. 120. Hereafter cited as *DE*.

5   Janice A. Radway, *Reading the Romance: Women, Patriarchy, and Popular Literature* (Chapel Hill and London: University of North Carolina Press, 1984), p. 212. Hereafter cited as *RR*.

6   John Fiske, *Television Culture* (London: Methuen, 1987), p. 14. Hereafter cited as *TC*.

7   Raymond Williams, *Culture and Society 1780–1950* (Harmondsworth: Penguin, 1977), p. 13. Hereafter cited as *CSoc*.

8   This paper is reprinted in *Cultural Studies*, ed. Lawrence Grossberg, Cary Nelson, and Paula A. Treichler (New York and London: Routledge, 1992), pp. 277–286. Hereafter cited as *CS*.

9   Stuart Hall, "The Rediscovery of Ideology: Return of the Repressed in Media Studies," in *Culture, Society and the Media*, ed. Michael Gurevitch, Tony Bennett, James Curran, and Janet Woollacott (London and New York: Routledge, 1982), p. 67. Hereafter cited as "RI."

10 Dick Hebdige, *Subculture: The Meaning of Style* (London: Methuen, 1979), p. 10. Hereafter cited as *SMS*.

11 John Fiske, *Television Culture* (London: Methuen, 1987), p. 1. Hereafter cited as Fiske.

12 Susan Bordo, *Unbearable Weight: Feminism, Western Culture, and the Body* (California and London: University of California Press, 1993), p. 3. Hereafter cited as Bordo.

13 Concise and insightful overviews of film theory, to which the present account is indebted, are offered by Ira Konigsberg in the *Johns Hopkins Guide to Literary Theory and Criticism* (Baltimore and London: Johns Hopkins University Press, 1994), pp. 268–273, and *The Film Studies Reader*, ed. Joanne Hollows, Peter Hutchings, and Mark Jancovich (New York and London: Oxford University Press/Arnold, 2000). Hereafter cited as *FSR*.

14 François Truffaut, "A Certain Tendency of the French Cinema," in *FSR*, p. 61. Originally published in *Cahiers du Cinéma in English*, 1, 30–40 (1966).

15 Jim Kitses, "Authorship and Genre: Notes on the Western," in *FSR*, p. 89. Originally published in *Horizons West* (1969).

16 Christian Metz, *The Imaginary Signifier: Psychoanalysis and the Cinema*, trans. Celia Britton and Annwyl Williams (Indianapolis and Bloomington: Indiana University Press, 1982), p. 7. Hereafter cited as *IS*.

17 "Visual Pleasure and Narrative Cinema," in Laura Mulvey, *Visual and Other Pleasures* (Bloomington and Indianapolis: Indiana University Press, 1989), p. 14. Hereafter cited as *VOP*. Originally published in *Screen* 16:3 (1975), 6–18.

Chapter 8

Contemporary Directions: The Return of the Public Intellectual

A remarkable variety of criticism and theory has been produced over the last few years, falling under discourse theory, political criticism, Marxism, feminism, and a continuation of what has conventionally been thought of as the liberal humanist heritage: empirical, historical, biographical, aesthetic, and formal studies. In one important sense, these studies, as varied as they are in critical approach and political perspective, are all moving in one direction: they all represent excursions from a purely academic sphere into the public sphere, into the larger world of cultural and political debate. Given the oppositional nature of much criticism, some might prefer to call this a counter-public or counter-cultural sphere. All of these approaches, in their most recent and prominent expressions, effect a broadening and extrapolation of "literary" study into the cultural and political "texts" that commonly surround us. And those critics not explicitly moving in this direction – usually opponents of what they call "theory" – represent the last defense of what they see as an appropriately formalist or aesthetic study of literature *as* literature.

One of the consequences of the Iraq War is that it has forced us to rethink the nature of our own democracy, of its workings and the complex levels which constitute it: not only a certain system of political parties and voting, but the nature of the media, the education system, access to reliable information and the possibility of public participation. The knowledge and ability to make informed decisions is a crucial component of the democratic process; and the critical foundations of such knowledge lie in the humanities, in a knowledge of history, of religion, of political systems, and, above all, the ability to think and read critically. The following section offers a brief overview of some of the important critics – from various schools of thought – who have moved into the public and political arena, extending their literary and rhetorical expertise into this broader political and cultural struggle.

The New Liberalism: Martha Nussbaum, Elaine Scarry, John Carey

Martha Nussbaum (b. 1947)

A very immediate example of the kind of strategy just mentioned occurs in the work of the philosopher and critic Martha Nussbaum, currently Professor of Law and Ethics at the University of Chicago Law School. The very public range of Nussbaum's concerns is indicated by the titles of some of her major works: *The Fragility of Goodness* (1986), *Cultivating Humanity: A Classical Defense of Reform in Liberal Education* (1997), *Sex and Social Justice* (1998), *Upheavals of Thought: The Intelligence of Emotions* (2001), and *Frontiers of Justice* (2005). In general, Nussbaum's thought can be characterized as universalist and focused on ethical and political concerns, in particular on issues of social justice, especially regarding women and other disadvantaged groups. Perhaps her work could be viewed as united by a central humanistic endeavor: to ask the Aristotelian questions "What is the good life?" and "How should one live?" Her objective, then, is to contribute to, and articulate the ideals of, universal peace, tolerance, and justice, enlisting the ethical and cognitive power of emotions in their complex connection with reason. In this endeavor, she stresses the importance of a genuinely liberal education and in particular of the potential of literature and philosophy to help us understand and overcome many of the ethical and political dilemmas we commonly face.

In general, Nussbaum has argued for the crucial role of the humanities and social sciences in laying the critical foundations for us to examine our own beliefs, to learn about other cultures, including minority cultures in our own country, and also to cultivate our imagination, being able to empathetically place ourselves in the situation of other people and various perspectives. As she urges in her book *Cultivating Humanity*, these skills need to be fostered in order for us to participate in reasoned public debate and discourse. She blames largely the corporate control of the media for the narrowing of education to pander to mere success in the global market, a strategy which is liable to produce docile specialists who are incapable of examining a political speech or engaging in important ethical debates. We need to return to a conception of education as truly liberal and broad in order to prepare students for the tasks of citizenship and the complex task of living.

Given her view of literature as harboring a vast ethical and empathetic potential, Nussbaum is regretful of what she sees as literary theory's self-isolation from the public sphere. In her essay "Perceptive Equilibrium: Literary Theory and Ethical Theory," she notes that despite literary theory's keen interest in philosophy, this interest has been limited to epistemological issues and displays an alarming absence of ethical issues, of the "central ethical and political questions of human life" – at a time when moral philosophy is rich with discussion of justice, well-being, social distribution, moral realism and relativism, emotions and desires. Indeed, the names of the leading moral and political philosophers of our day, such as John Rawls, Bernard Williams, Thomas Nagel, and Judith Jarvis Thompson, do not appear in theoretical discussions. Somehow, all of these important issues have been subordinated to the imperative of textuality, which has focused on the textual nature of literature, its modes of insertion into language and its connections with other texts, on the assumption that "texts do not refer to human life at all." Not only are these questions absent from literary theory, so too is moral philosophy's sense of urgency about these questions, the "sense that we are social beings puzzling out, in times of great moral difficulty, what might be, for us, the best way to live."[1] This absence is all the more remarkable given that great literature itself *does* raise these questions. Nussbaum attributes this absence to a number of factors, including the influence of Kant's aesthetics and early twentieth-century formalism, as well as Kantian and utilitarian ethics which themselves frowned on any dialogue with imaginative literature. Nussbaum proposes a joining of literary and ethical theory, one which would benefit both disciplines. An awareness of ethical theory would clarify exactly what literature offers, by articulating what a literary work may not explicitly ask itself, issues about social structure, economics, or identity (*LK*, 190–191). More importantly and fundamentally, Nussbaum observes that many intellectual disciplines, such as economic, legal, and psychological theories, "are shaping the private and public life of our culture . . . Literary theory has been too silent too long in these debates . . . yet it has a distinctive speaking role to play – a first part of which might be to confront reigning models of political and economic rationality" with a broader vision of human life (*LK*, 192).

In her book *Poetic Justice: The Literary Imagination and Public Life* (1995), Nussbaum illustrates in more detail how a literary vision might challenge mundane economic norms. She argues here that the literary imagination – as suspected by Mr. Gradgrind in Charles Dickens' novel *Hard Times* – is subversive and offers a vision of the world different from that embodied in political economy or the norms of rationality.[2] Mr. Gradgrind's insight is often lost in our modern compartmentalization of the modern academy. Nussbaum argues that in fact literary texts have the potential to make a "distinctive contribution to our public life . . . not only in our homes and schools, shaping the perception of our children, but also in our schools of public policy and development studies, and in our government offices and courts, and even in our law schools – wherever the public imagination is shaped and nourished – as essential parts of an education for public rationality" (*PJ*, 2). Nussbaum sees the literary imagination as a "public" imagination, which should be operative not only in our understanding of personal life but also in the public sphere, informing our vision of larger issues involving class and nation. Throughout her book, Nussbaum argues against the objections usually levied against literature or the imagination: that it is somehow unscientific, irrational inasmuch as it deploys emotions, and is unable to achieve a legal or scientific impartiality. The emotions, she argues, properly used, furnish a guiding foundation for rational thought, and the ability of literature to imagine alternative conditions is an essential component of democratic thinking (*PJ*, 4).

In general, good literature not only forces us to place ourselves in the situations and perspectives of others, but it disturbs and undermines conventional pieties (*PJ*, 5). Drawing on Wayne Booth's insights in his book *The Company We Keep: An Ethics of Fiction*, she stresses that the act of reading is ethically valuable because it demands critical immersion in one's own developing views and those of others. Reading is thus "an activity well suited to public reasoning in a democratic society" (*PJ*, 9). In contrast to much recent thought that is overtly relativistic or constructivistic, Nussbaum unashamedly invokes certain universal humanistic imperatives: the novel constructs a paradigm of ethical reasoning which generates "potentially universalizable concrete prescriptions by bringing a general idea of human flourishing to bear on a concrete situation." It engenders a "valuable form of public reasoning, both within a single culture and across cultures" (*PJ*, 8). But her point is not that the literary imagination should somehow replace moral or political theory; rather, it should have a role in the construction of these theories, given its capacity to develop moral capacities. It can be a "bridge to a vision of [social] justice and to the social enactment of that vision" (*PJ*, 12).

Elaine Scarry (b. 1946)

A Professor of Aesthetics at Harvard University, Elaine Scarry first achieved prominence through her book *The Body in Pain: The Making and Unmaking of the World* (1985). She exemplifies well the recent and sometimes controversial venturing by academics into public discussion, engaging a wide spectrum of issues ranging from the attacks of September 11, 2001, war, torture, citizenship and the Patriot Act through beauty, the body and aesthetic representation to law and the social contract. Her books include *Literature and the Body* (1988), *Resisting Representation* (1994), *On Beauty and Being Just* (1999), and *Who Defended the Country?* (2003). As Scarry has said in an interview: "There is nothing about being an English professor that exempts you from the normal obligations of citizenship . . . In fact, you have an increased obligation, because you know how to do research."[3] Accordingly, Scarry has controversially discussed the defense of America after 9/11, she has argued (in an article of 2004 entitled "Resolving to Resist") that the Patriot Act actually represents an abuse of the notion of patriotism, and has suggested that what comprises the gravest threat of terror is the American government itself, which has undermined the American constitution and fundamental principles of democracy. She has also urged in various articles that nuclear war and current military arrangements are (like torture), in their refusal to be based on consent, profoundly undemocratic.

In *The Body in Pain*, Scarry argues that pain is inexpressible, and as such points to an "absolute split" between one's own reality and that of others. A person's pain is experienced as "certainty" but, being incommunicable, embodies "doubt" for another person. Pain has a resistance to language, which is part of its very essence: it, in fact, destroys language, and returns a person to a prearticulate state.[4] Nonetheless, various groups – individuals in pain, physicians, human rights groups such as Amnesty International, lawyers in the courtroom, and literary artists – have attempted to give some expression, however fragmentary, to pain, as in terms of "throbbing" and "burning," which in turn have been subsumed under broader categories which are temporal, thermal, and constrictive (*BP*, 6–7). These groups have the ability to communicate the reality of pain (Amnesty in cases of torture, lawyers in suits for injuries), enabling it to enter the realm of shared discourse (*BP*, 9). Literature, perhaps surprisingly since much of it concerns suffering, is almost silent on the subject of pain (*BP*, 10–11).

Scarry urges that the inexpressibility of pain has political consequences: clearly there is a connection between verbal representation and political representation. She specifically takes the cases of torture – which is often misrepresented as "information-gathering" – and war, from the strategic and political descriptions of which pain is usually absent (*BP*, 12). Discourses and practices such as torture and war conflate pain with power. In torture, pain comes to embody a regime's fiction of power, while war uses injured bodies as a material index of its victorious cultural constructs (*BP*, 18–19). Torture and war effectively destroy language, miming the process of unmaking or uncreation; this miming and uncreating comprise their internal structure (*BP*, 20). They are acts of destruction, marking a "suspension of civilization" (*BP*, 21). Scarry asserts that her book is essentially about how others become visible or invisible to us, and how we make ourselves available to others through verbal and material artefacts (*BP*, 22).

If war and torture destroy the artefacts of civilization, it is imagination which creates them. Imagination is profoundly related to pain, whose "objectlessness" or lack of immersion in or attention to specific objects is conducive to a state of imagination. Where pain has no object, imagination is also unique among states of mind in that it is wholly consumed by reference to objects (*BP*, 161–162). Scarry observes the centrality of imagination in our everyday perceptual and emotional life, and indeed in creating the fundamental structures of our civilization (*BP*, 179). Like some of the Romantic poets, notably Shelley, she associates the imagination with compassion, self-effacement, and sees it as a force which distributes and projects the facts and responsibilities of human sentience, the human body, into the external world (*BP*, 326). Whereas practices and discourses of torture and war push pain and sentience further into isolation and invisibility in the service of their political and cultural agendas, the truly creative work of civilization consists in externalizing that sentience, and in empathetically sharing it.

In other works, Scarry offers a different assessment of imagination. Her essay "The Difficulty of Imagining Other Persons" suggests that violence toward foreigners, whether those residing in America or those beyond our borders, results from a failure of empathetic imagination, a failure to see and recognize them as human beings, "precisely because we have trouble believing in the reality of other persons."[5] We must foster a fuller imagination of others as human beings, but this must be reinforced by constitutional policies which eliminate the status of "foreigner" by extending citizenship (*HIC*, 58). Again, where Nussbaum sets considerable store by the ethical and imaginative potential of literature, Scarry sees literature's role as minimal. Literary characters, for one thing, have little connection to the actual economic or political world, and much literature has a nationalistic strain. She does acknowledge, however, that literature can "keep us in touch with the beauty of the world . . . to bring us into contact with our best selves and . . . to make us opposed to injury."[6]

Indeed, in her book *On Beauty and Being Just* (1999), Scarry argues that beauty, far from distracting us from injustice and making us turn a blind eye to it, actually leads us toward social justice. Violence, for example, can be thought of as an aesthetic diminution, not merely as morally deficient. She says that the discourse of beauty over the last two decades has all but vanished from the humanities, but the arguments against it are incoherent. Our response to beauty is also profoundly connected with our desire for compassion and justice. We attempt to bring new beauty into the world, to become more beautiful within ourselves, to credit the "aliveness" of the things and persons we deem beautiful, and to follow the "distributive" pressure of beauty toward equality and symmetry in affirming a general responsibility for the continuity of existence.[7] Moreover, in the presence of a beautiful object, we undergo – as Simone Weil, Iris Murdoch, and others have recognized – a radical decentering, whereby we are no longer at the center of our own world. We become "unselved," giving up our imaginary position at the center of things, attuning us perhaps not only to a heightened ethical disposition but even to a greater objectivity, whereby we look with a more disinterested vision, one less clouded by our own personal imperatives and demands (*BBJ*, 109–117). Hence, beauty is intimately connected not merely with goodness but with truth. Following Plato and others, she regards beauty as a call to create something better. One can notice in nearly all of these neo-humanist scholars a return to Platonic and Aristotelian questions and categories.

John Carey (b. 1934)

Former Merton Professor of English at Oxford, John Carey is known for his anti-elitism and sometimes unorthodox views on literature and the arts, as expressed in his acerbic wit and his Orwellian commitment to plain language. As such, he has been one of the few to broaden the function of scholar to public intellectual, combining academic duties with decades of discussion in newspapers, on the radio and on television, and serving as member, then chair, of the Booker Prize committee. Carey co-edited with Alastair Fowler the complete poetry of John Milton (1968), still regarded as the most scholarly single-volume edition of Milton's complete poems. His monographs include a study of Dickens, *The Violent Effigy* (1973), the highly praised *Thackeray: Prodigal Genius* (1977), and *John Donne: Life, Mind, and Art* (1981), a historical and psychological analysis which, through its investigation of the traumatic influence of Catholicism on Donne's literary imagination, has effectively transformed critical perception of Donne both as poet and preacher.

In a recent book *What Good Are the Arts?* (2006), Carey attempts to dethrone extravagant claims about the spiritual or moral benefits of the arts or claims that they can somehow be substituted (as Arnold suggested) for religion.[8] Writing in a populist vein, he suggests that art should not be the province of a privileged elite; that there is no absolute standard or value of art; that anything can be art; and that funding for artistic enterprises should be spread through the community. He observes that though critics have "spun theories" for centuries, few have examined how art has actually changed people's lives (*WG*, 167). Consulting research on excluded social groups such as prisoners and depressives, Carey points out how art and reading have been observed to break the cycle of violence and fear, to give a voice to anguish and pain, and in general to promote self-esteem and a "redemptive self-respect." This success is partly because the standards of achievement in art are "internal and self-judged" (*WG*, 159–166, 255). Carey also makes a case that literature is superior to the other arts on two accounts: it is uniquely critical, and self-critical; and it can moralize, often in diverse and contradictory ways. Literature is the only art capable of reasoning (*WG*, 173–181).

Carey's immense erudition shines even in his advocacy of a more widespread distribution and enjoyment of the arts, as it does in his insights into particular literary passages and texts. But his excursions into more general reflections are sometimes precarious. He insists that all literary preferences are irremediably subjective, makes a spurious distinction between artistic and scientific truth, and offers a bland and unhelpful definition that art can be anything. In arriving at such judgments, he over-hastily dismisses much previous thought on literature and aesthetics. For example, he dismisses Kant's *Critique of Judgment* – perhaps the most carefully argued aesthetic inquiry ever conducted – as a "farrago of superstition" (*WG*, 11).

He mistakenly sees Kant's "supersensible substrate of nature" as a Platonic realm of essences, a "mysterious realm of truth." He thinks that for Kant there is a "fundamental bond" between goodness and beauty in that supersensible realm, and that for Kant, "beauty was . . . essentially connected with moral goodness" (WG, 11). But these notions are not to be found in Kant's Critique, which argues that the aesthetic judgment of beauty is utterly independent of moral or utilitarian considerations. Only after beauty is acknowledged on independent grounds, says Kant, can it serve social, moral, and educational purposes. To see beauty as morally significant is to engage ideals that are both non-aesthetic and culturally constrained.[9] Part of the problem with dismissing the history of literary criticism is that one often ends up repeating what has often been said before – in this case by Horace, Sidney, Hume, Hegel, Arnold, Leavis, and many others – that literature contains neither truth nor falsehood, that it is self-aware, that it offers moral and intellectual edification, and that literary judgments are subjective. But Carey's book nonetheless performs a valuable assessment of the concrete potential of the arts in our world. To read literature, he says, is to be forced to assess alternative personalities and world views: "Literature does not make you a better person, though it may help you to criticize what you are. But it enlarges your mind, and it gives you thoughts, words and rhythms that will last you for life." Carey poignantly suggests that literature's "function as a mind-developing agency gives it especial relevance in our present culture" (WG, 209, 260).

The New Aestheticism

"Something is wrong, terribly wrong, in the department of English. Full professors and graduate students alike are failing – in some cases refusing – to read literature as literature. The integrity of the discipline of literary study, perhaps the integrity of literature itself, is being undermined by the very people who are supposed to guard the flame of literacy and watch over our cultural treasures. Ideologues swarm the halls." This is how Michael Berube (accurately) characterizes the perspective of conservatives such as Lynne Cheney (Head of the National Endowment for the Humanities in the Reagan era), Roger Kimball, author of Tenured Radicals: How Politics has Corrupted Higher Education (1990), and Jonathan Yardley, an art critic for the Washington Post. In recent years, numerous critics have committed themselves to restoring what they see as the neglected aesthetic dimension of literature, as well as its neglected ethical implications, and its potential to impinge upon larger debates concerning morality, classical questions regarding the good life, and more pressing political and even economic issues. Critic Geoffrey Galt Harpham talks of "the project of theory" (my emphasis) as a recent phenomenon and how its vitriolic anti-humanism proclaimed the death of the author, effectively killing the interest of literature as the product of an expressive subject. What survived in departments of literature, according to Harpham, was a climate of "professional occultation" in which literature lost its "aesthetic specificity" and "became enfolded within a generalized textuality."[10] But these claims are reductive: two of the things that the history of literature and criticism teaches us are that theory – which is at least as old as Plato – was never some unified project, and that literature, until very recently, was never accorded any aesthetic specificity, a notion which achieved systematic expression first in the pages of a philosopher (Kant), not a literary critic. Harpham himself appears to return to Aristotelian notions of subjectivity, character (as expressed in criticism), and criticism "as a mimetic practice whose primary purpose is to produce an accurate representation of its object," whereby the critic realizes "his own true and essential nature" (Harpham, 9, 11). This gesture is symptomatic of a common desire – perhaps a desperation – among certain critics to ignore or repress the memory of not only the so-called "theory" of the last fifty years but also the entire history of literary criticism and philosophy. It is a kind of aesthetic fundamentalism, repressing the entire history of critical interpretation. And like other forms of fundamentalism, it posits as its starting point a primordial or mythical condition or time: a time when literature was viewed simply *as* literature. But of course, if we isolate the "purely" literary, leaving out all of the human interest – psychological, social, moral, political – we end up with little more than a series of empty techniques and exercises. Moreover, there is nothing in Aristotle's philosophy or literary criticism or rhetoric which sanctions such a narrow aestheticism or such a narrow vision of literary critical practice. Ironically, Harpham makes these assertions in the very book where his focus – often a highly intelligent one – is on writers such as Žižek, Said, Nussbaum, and Scarry. The conclusion to Harpham's book, entitled "Criticism in a State of Terror," argues that criticism has been in this state – in an atmosphere of constraint, unable to operate freely – for at least the last one hundred and fifty years.

In fairness to Harpham, it could be argued that his project is one of reaffirmation rather than origination of ideas of critical practice, viewing itself as a reclamation of the aesthetic. This project of reinstating the primacy of the aesthetic is advanced by several conservative scholars such as Helen Vendler, who urge that our love of literature – rooted in a response to it which suspends scholarship, criticism, and theory – should focus on its unique uses of language. The editors of a recent book, *The New Aestheticism* (2003), charge that much recent theory has reduced the aesthetic to a static category, though they acknowledge that it cannot be isolated from social and political contexts.[11] Indeed, the call for a more aesthetic focus has also surfaced in the work of critics such as George Levine, who have long been sympathetic with cultural and ideological perspectives toward literature. Levine, somewhat cautiously, urges an endeavor to reclaim the aesthetic, as a province relatively free of the infringements of ideology and politics, as one of the few remaining spaces of free play. In his editorial introduction to *Aesthetics and Ideology* (1994), Levine notes a "radical transformation of literary study" over the last decade, one that fundamentally changes the very conception of literature and challenges the very existence of departments of literature. He suggests that the real subject of literary study has become ideology, and its purpose is political transformation. While he is not averse to current endeavors of cultural studies to place literature within broader schemes of value, he holds that literature has a power of suspension which can hold up the political and the ethical to scrutiny. The aesthetic is a realm which enables the exercise of disinterest and impersonality, allowing a sympathy for and understanding of people and events, furnishing us with a "vital sense of the other." Levine holds that this protection of aesthetic space has neither right-wing nor left-wing political implications, freeing up a space that is necessary to the left as much as it is to the right. Finally, as against much theory which sees literature as co-opted into the exercise of state power, especially at the level of formation of subjectivity, Levine suggests that much literature, even that of a canonical status, is genuinely subversive and resists such absorption into the prevailing exercises of ideological formation. Again, while there may be some merit to Levine's project, its vision of the aesthetic somewhat rehearses what was already articulated by Kant, and its notion of a "Utopian" aesthetic space rehearses Arnold's conception of the critic as operating in a pre-political arena, adopting a longer-term perspective unmolested by such trifles as partisanship. More interestingly, Levine assigns the aesthetic a function in the exercise of academic freedom.

In fact, Michael Berube – who is generally sympathetic to Levine's lately inspired project – offers just this kind of critique of Levine, namely, that he leaves his own view of the aesthetic unformulated.[12] Berube also acknowledges that the "relative autonomy" of literature from political use is an urgent question; he wonders whether there is a deep connection between the categories of civil society and the aesthetic as it has been understood since Kant, and whether their autonomies are mutually defining. Most theorists have answered this question in the negative, viewing even the institutions of civil society as molded internally by prevailing ideologies.

The New Theorists of Revolution:
Žižek, Hardt, Negri

Slavoj Žižek (b. 1949)

In the words of Sarah Kay, Slavoj Žižek is "the most vital interdisciplinary thinker to emerge in recent years." She characterizes the core of his work as "a vigorous reactivation of Lacanian psychoanalysis in the service of a project at once political and philosophical." He contends essentially that

Lacan is heir of the Enlightenment but he radicalizes the quest of European metaphysics from Plato to Kant and Hegel to understand "the nature of being."[13]

Žižek was born in the former Communist state of Yugoslavia, a part now called Slovenia. He worked with other Lacanians at the Institute of Philosophy in Ljubljana. The interests of this group included European philosophy and popular culture, as well as the operations of ideology. Those who have engaged with Žižek's work include the film theorist Michel Chion, the Marxist thinkers Terry Eagleton and Fredric Jameson, the political theorist Ernesto Laclau, gender theorist Judith Butler, and the French philosopher Alain Badiou. Žižek's major works include *The Sublime Object of Ideology* (1989), *Tarrying with the Negative* (1993), and *The Ticklish Subject* (1999). He published a self-interview entitled *The Metastases of Enjoyment* in 1994. According to Kay, what holds Žižek's various concerns together is "sustained interrogation" of what Lacan calls the real. The real is elusive; it is the "disgusting, hidden underside of reality which we cannot fail but step on," it is "the limit of language," it is "what shapes our sense of reality, even though it is excluded from it"; the real is also identified with sexual difference, and with the "unshakeable monolith of capital." Indeed, one of Žižek's primary projects is an anti-totalitarian critique of ideology and an "impassioned attack on capitalism," a plea for a return to universality, and promotion of what he calls "the act," which is "a violent disruption of the *status quo*" so as to "puncture the prevailing ideology and effect political change" (Kay, 3–6). Kay admits that Žižek's writing can seem "utterly chaotic." She claims that Žižek "teases at the limits of our understanding" and that his texts typically have a "loose-knit and disorienting structure" (Kay, 6–7). In general, his writing is characterized by an oblique approach to a topic, his excessive use of exemplification and the highly inconsistent persona behind his personal style of writing (Kay, 7–14). A closer look at one of Žižek's most important works, *The Sublime Object of Ideology*, may provide some insight into his style as well as his essential arguments concerning ideology.

Characteristically of the Slovenian Lacanian school, Žižek's use of Lacanian categories is directed toward the ideological and political spheres and has a broadly Hegelian disposition. In his introduction to the book, Žižek points out that traditional Marxism sees a basic social antagonism – premised on economics and class – which underlies other antagonisms of race, gender, and political systems. And that a revolution in the economic sphere would resolve all of these antagonisms.[14] The basic feature of so-called post-Marxism, he says, is a break with this logic: for example, feminists who argue that gender is more fundamental than class and that inequalities in this sphere must be addressed first. But it is Lacanian psychoanalysis, insists Žižek, that advances decisively beyond the usual post-Marxist anti-essentialism in "affirming the irreducible particularity of particular struggles" (*SOI*, 4). And Žižek sees the first post-Marxist in this respect as none other than Hegel, whose dialectic comprehends the inherent contradictions of capitalism, such as the fact that a radical or pure democracy is impossible. For Žižek, Hegelian dialectics embody an acknowledgment of antagonism: far from being a "story of its progressive overcoming," Hegel's dialectic expresses the failure of all radical attempts at revolution, and his notion of absolute knowledge accepts contradiction "as an internal condition of every identity" (SOI, 5–6).

Žižek realizes that this reading of Hegel runs counter to the "accepted notion" of absolute knowledge "as a monster of totality devouring every contingency" (SOI, 6). As such, his aim in this book is threefold: to introduce the basic concepts of Lacan free of the distortions that interpret him as a poststructuralist. Indeed, Lacanian theory is "perhaps the most radical contemporary version of the Enlightenment" (SOI, 7). The second aim is to effect a return to Hegel, by reading Hegelian dialectics on the basis of Lacanian psychoanalysis: what we find in Hegel is "the strongest affirmation yet of difference and contingency." Finally, Žižek wishes to contribute to the theory of ideology via a new reading of classical motifs such as commodity fetishism and of Lacanian concepts such as le point de capiton and sublime object. This Hegelian heritage, as "salvaged" by Lacan, will allow a new approach to ideology, one that resists postmodernist traps such as the illusion that we live in a "post-ideological" age (SOI, 7). Clearly, Lacan's salvaging powers – encompassing not only Freud, but also Hegel and Marx – have hitherto been overlooked.

Žižek begins by offering Lacan's insight that it was Marx, rather than Freud, who invented the notion of "symptom" (SOI, 11). Readers of Freud are familiar with his use of the word "symptom": in a pathological condition of repression, for example, whatever is severely repressed (usually some early childhood sexual encounter of which the subject is ashamed) produces one or more physical symptoms, which are surface manifestations of the neurosis. Another example occurs in dreams, where the "manifest" content, which is remembered, is a kind of surface expression or "symptom" of the "latent" or hidden or repressed content. Hence the notion of "symptom"conventionally understood, as in Louis Althusser's idea that texts can be read "symptomatically," implies a surface expression of something hidden or repressed or overlooked.

Žižek claims that there is a basic similarity "between the interpretative procedure of Marx and Freud – more precisely, between their analysis of commodity and of dreams" (SOI, 11). Žižek extends the conventional meaning of "symptom" as defined above: for these two thinkers, he says, it is not a question of unearthing a hidden content behind a manifest form, but rather of probing into the secret of this form itself, questioning why this particular form was chosen. In other words, we must ask, not what are the latent thoughts behind the manifest content of a dream, but why the latent content assumed the form of a dream in the first place. We must ask not what underlies the idea of a commodity – the amount of work required to produce it – but why "work" as a social phenomenon can be understood only in terms of its product, the commodity (*SOI*, 11). Hence, in the case of dreams, we must account for a triple structure: not only the latent thought and the manifest dream text, but the *unconscious desire* which mediates their connection. Indeed, it is the unconscious desire that is "the real subject matter of the dream" (*SOI*, 13). Hence, even after "explaining" the meaning of a dream, we still have not explained how or why the meaning disguised itself in this form. We need to explain the unconscious desire.

In the case of the commodity, Žižek notes that, prior to Marx, classical bourgeois economy successfully perceived that the hidden meaning of the commodity, of its value, was the amount of labor time it embodied, and that labor – the labor of the worker – was the true source of wealth. But we must ask, insists Žižek, what is the "secret" or hidden meaning behind the commodity form itself? What was the genesis of the commodity form? We must examine the *process* which generated it. Žižek quotes Marx as stating that bourgeois economy has never asked why "labor is expressed in value" (i.e., the value of the commodity) (*SOI*, 16).

Žižek points out that the Marxian analysis of the commodity-form has exerted a broad impact and fascination over a number of fields because, as Alfred Sohn-Rethel (associated with the Frankfurt School of Marxist thinkers) noted, this analysis of the commodity holds a central place not only in the field of political economy but also in the very process of abstract thinking itself, of the fundamental ways in which we think about the world through concepts and ideas (*SOI*, 16). This is how Žižek articulates Sohn-Rethel's insight: "In other words, in the structure of the commodity-form it is possible to find the transcendental subject: the commodity-form articulates in advance the anatomy, the skeleton of the Kantian transcendental subject – that is, the network of transcendental categories which constitute the *a priori* frame of 'objective' scientific knowledge." Žižek goes on to claim that the "phenomenon" of the "commodity" offers a "key" to solving the fundamental question posed by Kant: how is "objective knowledge with universal validity" possible? (*SOI*, 11). According to Žižek, Sohn-Rethel saw that the "network of notions," the apparatus of mental categories by which we understand the external world, is "already at work in the act of commodity exchange" (*SOI*, 17). Before thought could arrive at "pure *abstraction*," such abstraction was already at work in commodity-exchange, in a dual form.

Žižek explains this "abstraction" as follows: when we give something the status of a commodity, we are ignoring its peculiar qualities and reducing it to an abstract entity, measured solely in terms of "use-value." It is now abstract because, regardless of its actual qualities, it has the same value as any other commodity for which it is exchanged. A second "abstraction" has to do with quantity: before thought could arrive at the abstract idea of quantity, "pure quantity was already at work in money," the commodity which allows other commodities to be measured against one another, regardless of their individual qualities. Similarly with the other "categories" of Kant's subject – which are categories of what Kant calls the understanding (not of pure reason, as Žižek mistakenly suggests) – such as motion, causality, and substance: according to Kant, these categories are imposed by our mental apparatus on the contents of the world, as their form. The "scandal" that Žižek claims to find here as revealed by Sohn-Rethel is that in fact these categories are "already realized" in the marketplace – before they are articulated by thought – in the "transference of property" (*SOI*, 17). This, claims Žižek, corresponds "perfectly" to the "scandalous" nature of the Freudian unconscious, which also is "unbearable" (perhaps meaning unsupportable) from a transcendental perspective. Kantian terminology is being used somewhat loosely here. After all, for Kant, it is the empirical ego, not the transcendental ego, which employs the categories of the understanding. And it hardly makes sense to suggest that somehow *all* twelve Kantian categories are indiscriminately enlisted in bourgeois economic transactions. But, undeterred, Žižek claims that the "homology" between the process of abstraction described above and the unconscious is "striking." And this, it seems, is sufficient warrant for him to conclude that the "real abstraction" is the "*unconscious of the transcendental subject,* the support of objective-universal scientific knowledge" (*SOI*, 18). In other words, the ability of the external world to be known with scientific certainty depends upon our unconscious assumption of a transcendental ego: again, this appears to be a radical misreading of Kant.

Everyday "practical" consciousness is similarly blind: participants in the act of exchange (of commodities) fail to see that it is the abstraction outlined above which is the crucial universal element enabling this act. If they did see it, "the act of exchange would no longer be possible" (*SOI*, 20). In Sohn-Rethel's formulation: "this non-knowledge of the reality is part of its very essence" (*SOI*, 20). This repressed universal and social dimension, says Žižek, "emerges . . . as universal Reason turned towards the observation of nature . . . as the conceptual frame of the natural sciences" (*SOI*, 20). Hence we experience a fissure of consciousness into "practical" and "theoretical": as far as practical action in social reality goes, if we knew too much, if we pierced "the true functioning of social reality, this reality would dissolve itself" (*SOI*, 21).

What these meditations lead to is Žižek's understanding of ideology: he rejects the conventional Marxist notion of ideology as a false consciousness or illusory representation of reality. Rather, reality *itself* is already conceived of in ideological terms: ideology "*is a social reality whose very existence implies the non-knowledge of its participants as to its essence*" (*SOI*, 21). And this, says Žižek, brings us back to the notion of "symptom," which could be defined as "a formation whose very consistency implies a certain non-knowledge on the part of the subject . . . the measure of the success of its interpretation is precisely its dissolution" (*SOI*, 21).

In the section "Cynicism as a Form of Ideology," Žižek quotes the "most elementary definition of ideology," Marx's statement that *they do not know it, but they are doing it*" (*SOI*, 28). He urges that we need to move beyond the classic concept of ideology as a distortion of social reality, a distortion that can somehow be unmasked. He notes that the Frankfurt School offered a more sophisticated definition which held that reality itself could not be produced without the ideological distortion being written into its very nature (*SOI*, 28). He also draws upon Peter Sloterdijk's book *Critique of Cynical Reason* (1983), which argues that ideology operates essentially in a "cynical" way. As Žižek articulates this thesis: "The cynical subject is quite aware of the distance between the ideological mask and the social reality, but he none the less still insists upon the mask." Marx's formula might be modified to read: "they know very well what they are doing, but still, they are doing it" (*SOI*, 29). This cynical position is distinguished from what Sloterdijk calls "kynicism," a popular rejection of the official culture and exposure of its self-interest. In fact cynicism is precisely the ruling culture's answer to this popular subversion: cynicism sees "the particular interest hidden behind an ideological universality . . . the distance between the ideological mask and reality, but it still finds reasons to retain the mask." Such cynicism sees "integrity, as a supreme form of dishonesty, and morals as a supreme form of profligacy, the truth as the most effective form of a lie." This cynicism is a perverted "negation of the negation" of official ideology.

Clearly, thinks Žižek, in the face of such cynicism, we can no longer enlist the traditional critique of ideology which subjects an ideological text to a "symptomatic reading," revealing its blindnesses, since the cynical text is already aware of these. Are we then in a "post-ideological world"? Not quite, answers Žižek, because there is a distinction between symptom and fantasy; indeed, it is on the level of fantasy that ideology structures social reality – a level that even cynical reason, for all its ironic detachment, cannot account for.

Žižek returns to the Marxian formula: "they do not know it, but they are doing it." As far as ideological fantasy goes, it would seem that ideological illusion takes place in the sphere of "knowing" rather than "doing." For example, in the case of what Marx calls "commodity fetishism," money – which merely embodies a network of social relations – is treated as an immediate embodiment of wealth. We forget that behind it lies a network of relations between human beings. As against this, Žižek argues that illusion takes place in the sphere of "doing": people *know* very well that certain social relations lie behind money; but they *act* as if money were the immediate embodiment of wealth. In Žižek's language, they "are fetishists in practice, not in theory" (*SOI*, 31). His point is that such a mystificatory attitude marks the actual practice of people: they *act* as if money were an embodiment of a universal value (in this case, wealth). Hence their "social reality itself, their activity, is guided by an illusion, by a fetishistic inversion . . . They know very well how things really are, but still they are doing it." So there is a double illusion at work here: *overlooking* the illusion that structures our reality (*SOI*, 33). And it is this overlooked, unconscious illusion that Žižek terms the ideological fantasy. Hence the most basic level of ideology for Žižek is not that of an illusion masking the true nature of social reality, but that of "an (unconscious) fantasy structuring our social reality itself" (*SOI*, 33).

This rethinking of the notion of ideology on Žižek's part evolves ultimately from Lacan's insight – contrary to the Freudian notion that dreams somehow reconstruct reality in the light of wish fulfillment – that it is precisely in the form of the dream that we encounter our deepest reality, the "Real of our desire," and that this is more terrifying than external reality. In fact, we escape into so-called (waking) reality in order to continue to sleep, to maintain our blindness. It is the same, insists Žižek, with ideology: this too is a fantasy construction which structures our social reality. The function of ideology is not to offer an escape from reality but "to offer us the social reality itself as an escape from some traumatic, real kernel" (*SOI*, 45). The vagueness of Žižek's final phrase here seems to compound what is already vague – the "Real of our desire" – in Lacan.

The only way to break the power of ideology is "to confront the Real of our desire which announces itself in this dream" (*SOI*, 48). Žižek attempts to offer an example, that of "anti-Semitism." We cannot simply remove our prejudices and see the Jew as he really is. Rather, we "must confront ourselves with how the ideological figure of the 'Jew' is invested with our unconscious desire" (*SOI*, 48). In other words, we must delve deeper than such alleged superficial reasons relating to the Jew as financially exploitative etc. The point is that the anti-Semitic idea of the Jew has nothing to do with Jews, but rather with the need "to stitch up the inconsistency of our own ideological system" (*SOI*, 48). Ideology determines the mode of our everyday experience of reality itself (*SOI*, 49). Žižek's argument rephrases what has long been recognized by philosophers since Hegel: that no reality is independent of construction by concepts and that there is no purely "immediate" experience which is not somehow premolded and mediated by various forms of thought and practice. Žižek's achievement here is to label one of these forms "ideology."

Michael Hardt and Antonio Negri: The Concept of Empire

In the year 2000, the left-wing American philosopher Michael Hardt and the Italian Marxist dissident and philosopher Antonio Negri provoked something of a controversy with their collaborative book *Empire*. This was hailed by Slavoj Žižek and others as a pioneering study and a new Communist manifesto for our age, and somewhat derided by others as fashionable, vague, and merely speculative. Their argument in this book is that, following the collapse of various colonial regimes throughout the world, and then of Communism with its barriers to the expansion of capitalism, a new phenomenon – which they call Empire – is materializing in our postmodern world. Along with the globalization of economic and cultural markets and production, there "has emerged a global order, a new logic and structure of rule – in short, a new form of sovereignty. Empire is the political subject that effectively regulates these global exchanges, the sovereign power that governs the world." The power of the nation-state, they observe, while still effective, has progressively declined, having less and less power to regulate the flow of money, technology, people, and goods across national boundaries.[15] Sovereignty, in fact, has taken a new form, composed "of a series of national and supranational organisms united under a single logic of rule." Empire is the name for this new global form of sovereignty.

Empire, however, is distinct from imperialism, which was in effect "an extension of the sovereignty of the European nation-states beyond their own boundaries." These states policed the purity of their own identities and excluded all that was other. In contrast, Empire has no center of power and does not rely on fixed boundaries: it is a decentered and deterritorializing "apparatus of rule that progressively incorporates the entire global realm . . . The distinct national colors of the imperialist map of the world have merged and blended in the imperial global rainbow" (E, xii–xiii). The old divisions of the globe into first world (the capitalist West), the second world (Communism), and third world have dissolved into a "smooth" world. The dominant productive processes have been transformed: industrial factory labor has largely given way to communicative, cooperative, and affective labor. In this postmodern global economy, the creation of wealth comprehends "biopolitical" production, the production of the entire realm of social life, in which the economic, political, and cultural spheres increasingly overlap (E, xiii).

It would be tempting but wrong, say Hardt and Negri, to identify this new sovereignty with the United States: imperialism is over and no nation-state can today form the core of any imperialist project. But they acknowledge that the United States has a "privileged position" in Empire: the American constitution itself was premised on the ancient imperial model, envisioning a new empire with expanding frontiers. The concept of Empire has a number of distinctive features: it has no boundaries or limits and rules the entire "civilized" world; it presents itself not as a conquering historical regime but as an eternal order that "effectively suspends history" (E, xiv). It operates on all levels of the social order, regulating not only territory and population but also human interaction and even human nature itself: it "creates the very world it inhabits," and is "the paradigmatic form of biopower." Finally, despite the bloodshed it occasions, it pretends that it is dedicated to a perpetual and universal peace (E, xv).

But, even from their communistic perspective, Hardt and Negri do not see this globalization of sovereignty and control over all domains of life as drowning all hope, all possibility of resistance. On the contrary, the passage to Empire and globalization offers "new possibilities to the forces of liberation . . . Our political task . . . is not simply to resist these processes but to reorganize them and redirect them toward new ends," constructing "a counter-Empire, an alternative political organization of global flows and exchanges." This struggle will occur on the imperial terrain itself and will involve "new democratic forms and a new constituent power" that will take us beyond Empire (*E*, xv).

Empire is formed on the capacity to present force as being in the service of right and peace. The various symptoms of Empire include a policy of "permanent exceptionalism," conferring the right to intervene, to engage in "just war" as a police action in the name of emergency situations and superior ethical principles such as justice, peace, and equilibrium (*E*, 14–18). The operation of power in Empire is clarified by appeal to Foucault's analysis of the transition from a disciplinary society to a society of control. In the former, discipline was effected through institutions such as school, family, hospital, and factory (i.e., the institutions that comprise civil society); in the latter, which is the world of Empire, the mechanisms of control operate democratically, through colonizing the very sphere of subjectivity itself. People are trained effectively to discipline themselves. Hence control is exerted not just through consciousness or ideology but through the body itself. Foucault thus brought the domain of social reproduction and the superstructure back within the realm of the material: the new power is biopolitical, regulating social life internally, and itself being the producer of life (*E*, 23–27). In other words, instead of acting on or imposing controls on a person or subject, it produces the kind of subject it desires, constituting subjectivity from within.

Transnational corporations construct the connective fabric of the biopolitical world: they directly structure territories, populations, producing not only commodities but subjectivities, needs, social relations, bodies, and minds. In this biopolitical production of order, it is the communication industries that develop language and communication, and integrate the imaginary and symbolic. It is these industries that legitimate the world order. Empire's strategy of intervention is conducted on military, moral, and judicial levels, using news media, religious organizations, and even non-government organizations such as charities. Enemies of Empire are branded terrorists, in a reductive police mentality (*E*, 31–37). There is no imperial center or margin: power is virtual (but nonetheless real for that). Empire is a high-tech machine, a new economic, industrial, communicative machine which continues to reproduce master narratives (for all the talk that these are dead), presiding over the linguistic production of reality (*E*, 34, 37–40). There is no external standpoint to Empire, no standpoint beyond the field permeated by money (*E*, 32).

Hardt and Negri argue that modern sovereignty is a transcendental concept, positing a "single transcendent power" which controls the members of a society. This applies equally to notions of monarchy (as in Hobbes) or democracy (as in Rousseau), which both entail the population relinquishing power in a "general will" which has authority above them. This tendency, they claim, reaches its climax in Hegel's notion of the state as the transcendent power. In fact, Hegel's philosophy, they say, synthesizes the modern theory of sovereignty with a capitalist (as formulated by Adam Smith) theory of value (*E*, 81–85). But this transcendent notion of modern sovereignty conflicts with the immanence of capital, its operation not from above but in and through networks of domination, with no transcendent center of power. Capital's immanence is visible in its deterritorializing, its separating populations from territories and destroying traditional culture, its linking of all forms of value through money (*E*, 325–326). Imperial control is exerted by the bomb, by money, and by ether (the networks of communication). These new forms of control mark the withering not only of civil society but also of the nation-state, in the dominance of a global regime (*E*, 329, 332, 347).

But if there can be no outside, no external standpoint, how can resistance arise? It is labor power, the authors argue, that comprises the outside of capital. The perspective of the proletarian struggle, as Marx stated, is dual, both inside and outside capitalism. Indeed, it is the cycle of internationalist proletarian struggles in recent history that has been the real motor of capitalist development, through its various phases of manufacture, industry, finance, and globalization (*E*, 208–209). In this sense, it is the multitude of the oppressers and exploited which has called Empire into being (*E*, 43). Just as capitalism, according to Marx, represented an advance over previous forms of society, so Empire is a step forward, increasing the potential for liberation. But the usual modern leftist strategy of localized resistance will not work, since it misidentifies the enemy, and since the local is in any case an ideological and economic *product*. The enemy is Empire, the regime of global relations. And the power of the multitude is configured *within* Empire, a power which must subvert the hegemonic languages, social structures, production, and subjectivity toward a political alternative (*E*, 44–48). Proletarian solidarity lies not in the linking of various acts of resistance as a global chain but in the fact that each act is conducted directly against the global order of Empire, for example against the neoliberal mechanisms of privatization (*E*, 52–55). This notion of the exploited multitude recalls Spinoza's philosophy of immanence which affirmed "democracy of the multitude as the absolute form of politics" (*E*, 77).

The humanistic movement toward immanence is now visible in the democratic principle, exercised in desertion, exodus, and nomadism. "A specter is haunting the world and it is the specter of migration": this global movement of populations in search of better conditions of life comprises a "powerful form of class struggle" (*E*, 212–213). Such movements played a decisive role in the collapse of the Berlin Wall and the Soviet bloc. These subversive developments are today most clearly visible in reconfigurations of gender and sexuality, forging a new body incapable of submitting to command and conventional ideological roles (*E*, 215–216). Tellingly taking their terms from St. Augustine, the authors urge that we should work toward an "earthly city of the multitude," toward "directing technologies and production towards its own joy" and freedom (*E*, 395–396). Empire continues to divide, segregate, and isolate, reinforcing divisions of race, language, and religion. But mass migration and deterritorialization (a notion taken in part from Deleuze and Guattari) represent autonomous movements which overflow the boundaries of capital. Indeed, mass migration (even that branded as illegal) is necessary for production. The authors suggest a number of demands that need to be lodged against Empire: first, the demand of global citizenship, which would give judicial recognition to an existent fact of capitalist production (migration); second, a social wage and guaranteed income for all, which would abolish, among other things, dependence on the male in the family; and third, the right to reappropriate the means of production (*E*, 400–406). The power of labor can be expressed as "self-valorization of the human (the equal right of citizenship for all over the entire sphere of the world market); as cooperation (the right to communicate, construct languages, and control communication networks); and as political power, or really as the constitution of a society in which the basis of power is defined by the expression of the needs of all ... absolute democracy in action" (*E*, 410).

There is not space here to offer a full critique of the thesis advanced by Hardt and Negri. While their ideas concerning globalization, the new nature of capital, of the changed composition of the proletariat and the power of population movement have much resonance, their analysis of the tradition of philosophical thought – for example, of Kant and Hegel – is sometimes questionable, as is indeed the very concept of Empire, as something abstract, stripped of all agency and historical coordinates, and perhaps too infected with Foucauldian notions of power as residing essentially in diffusion and relation. It is difficult to know what one might actually do to subvert Empire, or how the multitude might be transformed from an indifferent mass into an agent of political unity and will.

Notes

1   Martha Nussbaum, "Perceptive Equilibrium: Literary Theory and Ethical Theory," in *Love's Knowledge: Essays on Philosophy and Literature* (Oxford and New York: Oxford University Press, 1990), pp. 169–170. Hereafter cited as *LK*. This essay originally appeared in *The Future of Literary Theory*, ed. R. Cohen (London: Routledge, Chapman, and Hall, 1989), pp. 58–85.

2   Martha Nussbaum, "The Literary Imagination," in *Poetic Justice: The Literary Imagination and Public Life* (Boston: Beacon Press, 1995), p. 1. Hereafter cited as *PJ*.

3   Interview with Emily Eakin, *New York Times Magazine*, November 19, 2000, online version: partners.nytimes.com/library/magazine/home/20001119mag-scarry.html.
4   Elaine Scarry, *The Body in Pain: The Making and Unmaking of the World* (Oxford and New York: Oxford University Press, 1985), pp. 4–5. Hereafter cited as *BP*.
5   Elaine Scarry, "The Difficulty of Imagining Other Persons," in *The Handbook of Interethnic Coexistence*, ed. Eugene Weiner (New York: Continuum, 1998), p. 43. Hereafter cited as *HIC*.
6   Interview with Elaine Scarry, in *Global Values 101: A Short Course*, ed. Kate Holbrook, Ann S. Kim, Brian Palmer, and Anna Portnoy (Boston: Beacon Press, 2006), p. 30.
7   Elaine Scarry, *On Beauty and Being Just* (Princeton and Oxford: Princeton University Press, 1999), pp. 86–93. Hereafter cited as *BBJ*.
8   John Carey, *What Good Are the Arts?* (Oxford: Oxford University Press, 2006), pp. ix–xii. Hereafter cited as *WG*.
9   Immanuel Kant, *Critique of Judgment*, trans. Werner S. Pluhar (Indianapolis and Cambridge: Hackett, 1987), pp. 82–84.
10 Geoffrey Galt Harpham, *The Character of Criticism* (London and New York: Routledge, 2006), pp. 5–6. Hereafter cited as Harpham.
11 Introd., *The New Aestheticism*, ed. John J. Joughin and Simon Malpass (Manchester: Manchester University Press, 2003), p. 5.
12 Both George Levine's introduction to *Aesthetics and Ideology* (New Brunswick: Rutgers University Press, 1994) and Michael Berube's response, first published in *Clio* (1996), are conveniently reprinted in a splendid collection: *Falling into Theory*, ed. David Richter (Boston and New York: Bedford/St. Martin's, 2000), pp. 378–397.
13 Sarah Kay, *Žižek: A Critical Introduction* (Cambridge: Polity Press, 2003), p. 1. Hereafter cited as Kay.
14 Slavoj Žižek, *The Sublime Object of Ideology* (London and New York: Verso, 1989), p. 3. Hereafter cited as *SOI*.
15 Michael Hardt and Antonio Negri, *Empire* (Cambridge, MA, and London: Harvard University Press, 2000), p. xi. Hereafter cited as *E*.

Epilogue

The Myth of Liberal Humanism

Looking back over the history of literary cultural criticism and theory since the early twentieth century, we can discern a number of broad tendencies. The first was a tendency, enshrined in formalism and then institutionalized in the New Criticism, to discover and define what is specific or unique about literature. The connections of literature with all other domains – though implicitly acknowledged – were analytically suppressed. From one point of view, the critical approaches that came to be known as "theory," each with its own inflections and motives, can be regarded as an implicit if not direct reaction against the New Critical claims as to the autonomy, independence, and objectivity of a literary text. In this sense, modern theory embodies a series of endeavors to resituate literature within other domains and broader contexts: Marxism, within larger economic-material and ideological contexts; structuralism, within linguistic categories and broader cultural sign systems; feminism and gender studies, within the construction and representation of gender and sexuality; deconstruction, within underlying presuppositions and overlooked *aporiai* or difficulties; and ethnic and postcolonial studies, within the contexts of empire.

Nearly all of these theories claim to oppose, in one way or another, the complex of ideologies known as liberal humanism. But what *is* liberal humanism? This is not so easy to answer. In the history of modern thought, liberal humanism has comprised the mainstream philosophies of the bourgeois Enlightenment, such as rationalism, empiricism, and utilitarianism. The economic principles of bourgeois ideology, such as rationality, *laissez-faire*, and free competition, were formulated by the classical economists such as Adam Smith and David Ricardo. The political principles of democracy, individual rights, and constitutional government were expressed by

225

figures such as Rousseau, John Locke, and Thomas Paine. The imperial ideology and mission – not only to conquer other parts of the world for their economic resources but to submit them also to the civilizing effects of Western literature and culture – were expressed by figures such as Thomas Babington Macaulay, and many politicians, philosophers, and scientists. All of these tendencies – as refracted partly through the philosophy of Kant – achieve a kind of synthesis in the philosophy of Hegel, the supreme expression of bourgeois thought, built on the philosophical principles of the Protestant Reformation and the French Revolution, uniting the divergent modes of Enlightenment thought such as rationalism and empiricism, and combining these with a Romantic emphasis on totality and the unity of subject and object, all integrated into a notion of historical progress. It was Hegel who most articulately expressed the notion of the relatedness of all concepts and entities, of human identity as a reciprocal and social phenomenon, of the world as a social and historical human construction, of identity as intrinsically constituted by diversity, of language as a system of human perception, and of the very idea of otherness or alterity as it informs much modern thought.

In this sense, the Hegelian system stands at the center of modern Western intellectual and political history. In the second half of the nineteenth century, Hegel's system, whose elements were held in a precarious unity and totality, disintegrated into a number of streams of thought, most of which opposed it: Hegelianism was continued in modified form in Anglo-American idealism and various strands of Marxism (which, however, substituted a materialist, economic base for Hegel's idealism). The many reactions against Hegel include figures such as Schopenhauer and Nietzsche, the various forms of European existentialism, and Anglo-American tendencies toward analytical philosophy and logical positivism. In their diverse ways, these philosophies rejected the notions of totality, of historical progress, and the idea that things in the world were somehow essentially related. Hegel's philosophy was a "philosophy of the negative," which attempted to challenge the world as merely given (by the history of feudalism) and to refashion both the world and human subjectivity in the (then) revolutionary light of bourgeois rationality. In this sense, the most widespread reaction against Hegel's philosophy was positivism. Though positivism had a few radical proponents such as Frederic Harrison, it was in general a conservative philosophy which held that the world as it is given is the only reality we can know. Positivism came to be defined as any system of thought or inquiry which modeled itself on science, restricting itself to the evidence of the senses and refusing to engage in "abstract" metaphysical issues such as the progress of history, the existence of God, or the subjective contribution of the human mind to the construction of what we call reality. In the latter nineteenth century, certain social sciences such as sociology (in the work of Comte and Durkheim) and psychology (and Freudian psychoanalysis) attempted to assume the status of science.

What is important in our context is that the *same* tendency occurred in literature: the movement toward literary autonomy effectively began with Kant and proceeded apace through the nineteenth century, in the Romantics, the symbolists, aestheticism, and then modernism. The modeling of literature on science was expressed first in bourgeois realism and naturalism (which urged that literature follow the laws of probability and exhibit scientific causality and detail). The ideal of a scientific literary criticism, with roots in nineteenth-century French thinkers, emerged in Russian Formalism and then in the New Criticism, as well as in Northrop Frye's work and structuralism: an attempt to treat literature – considered as an autonomous province – scientifically and systematically, evincing its peculiarly literary qualities. Hence, what was happening in literature cohered broadly with the general tendencies of liberal humanist bourgeois thought: a movement toward the relative autonomy and specialization of each discipline, and an aspiration toward scientific status (even literary modernism expressed the ideals of impersonality and objectivity). The main tendencies of liberal humanism, then, have been toward rationalism, empiricism, scientism (an inordinate aspiration to scientific status), as well as toward democracy, individualism, innovation, progress, and an almost exclusive focus on the present. But when we turn to what has been viewed as liberal humanism in the registers of literature and literary criticism, we find another, almost opposed, set of values, as enshrined saliently in figures such as Matthew Arnold, Irving Babbitt, and F. R. Leavis. Most generally, we find an anti-theoretical and even anti-rationalist impulse, sometimes grounded on a mystical or theological basis. We find an insistence on a loosely empirical method, on "practical" criticism, which shies away from broad conceptual or historical schemes. We often find a belief in human nature as something stable and permanent, as well as a belief in universal and timeless truth. We find a commitment to the past or to "tradition." This commitment often embodies a desire to return – as with Edmund Burke and other opponents of bourgeois reform – to a pre-bourgeois harmony and stability, resting on permanent values. And we find an insistence on the moral and civilizing nature of literature, viewed as a broad education in sensibility and (a redefined) citizenship. Literary liberal humanism might be viewed as an afterthought of liberal bourgeois humanism, a concerted attempt of bourgeois humanism to correct itself, to counteract or at least to temper its own most mechanizing and spiritually debilitating tendencies and excesses.

Hence, liberal humanism has included both formalism and historicism, both scientism and moralism, both rationalism and empiricism, both objectivism and subjectivism. The commonly held view of liberal humanism – as harboring fixed notions of identity, the human subject, an independent external world, and as affirming that language represents reality – is a myth. This myth of liberal humanism sets up a straw target, applicable, if at all, only to its reactive and regressive literary variant. These notions are *not* principles of bourgeois thought: they are medieval conceptions, going back to Plato and Aristotle, and they were already beginning to be challenged in the Renaissance. It was the very task of the bourgeois thinkers themselves to undermine these notions, such as the notion of a stable human self or ego: for Locke, the self was a blank slate, acquiring character only as experience writes on it; for Hume, it is a convention; for Kant, it is a mere presupposition; for Hegel, it is a product of historical forces and reciprocation with other human selves, which are equally constructed. The only stable human subject is that presupposed by bourgeois economics, as an abstract unit of economic value, competition, and consumption. All of these philosophers strongly impugn the Aristotelian notion of "substance" as the underlying reality of identity and the world (Kant even makes substance one of the subjective categories *through* which we view the world); they challenge the notion of essence, which Locke effectively relocates from reality to language. In fact, long before Saussure, Locke recognized the arbitrariness of the sign. The major philosophers of the bourgeois Enlightenment wished to reject any transcendent basis for political sovereignty, morality, or for their formulations of identity, subjectivity, and the external world. They even rejected the notion of "reality" as grounded in any extra-human basis: they saw it as a projection of the human mind, of human categories of understanding, and of human language. It is important to realize, however, that the liberal humanist desire in literary and artistic spheres to reverse or react against or harmonize these bourgeois tendencies is not something haphazard but a process so consistent and continuous that it emerges as a structural phenomenon, this internal contradiction being embodied in the Hegelian dialectic. Indeed, two important features of liberal humanism are worth noting: firstly, that it has always been changing. In fact, it could be argued that its very essence is change: not that of total transformation but of self-enlargement and Hegelian sublation or continual expansion to include and assimilate what is currently external to it. The second feature is its inherently internally contradictory nature; for example, the liberal humanism of each of the Enlightenment philosophers is different from that of the others as well as from that of Matthew Arnold or Irving Babbitt. The very essence of liberal humanist thought is non-identity: Hegel recognized that bourgeois ideals embrace many seemingly contradictory movements.

Hence, the commonly cited accomplishments of much literary theory – the critique of essentialism, the discrediting of correspondence theories of truth and meaning, the deconstruction of identity, the exhibition of the constructed nature of subjectivity and objectivity, the emphasis on the constitutive role of language in that construction – had already been conducted *within* bourgeois thought, in the pages of Locke, Hume, Kant, Hegel, and others. They had also been conducted in the alternative or "heterological" streams of thought, from Schopenhauer through Kierkegaard, Nietzsche, Bergson, and Heidegger, which had explicitly challenged the principles of the bourgeois Enlightenment. Again, there is a continuity and common ground between liberal bourgeois thought and the channels of its own subversion.

This continuity between the liberal humanist heritage and many branches of literary theory is expressed most profoundly in the latter's deepening obsession with language, its retreat from referentiality and its sustained focus on the importance of language in structuring our world. The work of modernists such as Proust, Pound, Eliot, Faulkner, and Woolf was marked by an intense awareness, derived from the French symbolists, of the limitations of language and its inadequacy for expressing the highest truths and the most profound strata of experience. The work of Marx, Freud, Bergson, Nietzsche, Wittgenstein, and Bakhtin was informed by an understanding of language as a system of concepts and signs whose capacity to refer to or represent the real world or the human self is merely conventional and practical. Much modern theory is also characterized by this "retreat" from reality. Russian Formalism and New Criticism held that poetic language was unique, untranslatable into prose, erecting a nonreferential, self-contained verbal structure which had emotive impact. Bakhtin, who combined insights of formalism and Marxism, regarded language as the site of ideological struggle. Structuralism examined literary texts and broader cultural phenomena as patterned after language, as a structure of sign systems. The analysis of language has been central to the work of feminists, who have seen it as embodying male modes of thought and oppression, and as potentially transformable to express female experience. Jacques Lacan effectively rewrote much Freudian theory in linguistic terms, and held that the unconscious was linguistic in its structure and operation. For Derrida, there was no possible externality to language, nothing beyond the textual nature of all phenomena. For much readerresponse theory, the language and meaning of a text were dialogic in their very nature, arising from an interaction of authorial and readerly registers. The New Historicism views the social and historical context of literature as itself composed of a network of discourses, of ways of signifying and understanding the world. This twentieth-century emphasis on language – and its heavily ideological role in the formation of various identities as well as of the realities we inhabit – has until very recently tended to displace discussion of the aesthetic, the moral, and the connections of literature to the worlds of *realpolitik*.

Hence, much literary theory is internally structured by the heritage of liberal humanist philosophy, its pluralistic ability – as embodied in the Hegelian dialectic – to encompass several divergent perspectives under the umbrella of its own expansive non-identity. It was Hegel who articulated the capacity of bourgeois thought to sublate (to both transcend and internalize) opposition or variance from itself. His system inscribes and prefigures the internal structure of capitalism, its ability to absorb everything else – art, literature, religion, love, socialism, other cultures – into its own structures of economic value and significance, into its own expansive and ever-changing identity. This movement is also the inner dialectic of impe-rialism, its drive not only to conquer but to assimilate and integrate the Other; the Other is always necessary to capitalism, as something whose overcoming renews, reassures, reaffirms, redefines, and revitalizes its own identity. Ultimately, the notions of difference, otherness, the challenges to identity, the view of meaning and all objects as relational, are Hegelian insights and represent modifications *within* the parameters of bourgeois thought. Even the undermining of authorship is a refraction through a linguistic focus of the Hegelian notion that historical forces act through individuals. Marxism itself has sometimes been co-opted into this exten-sion of bourgeois humanism, its theory floating free of the historical condi-tions which are necessary to its distinctive Marxist characteristic.

Hence, as Hegel, then Marx, then certain feminists, then Derrida and Edward Said acknowledged, the subversion of liberal humanism arises from within itself. Derrida and feminist thinkers have profoundly recog-nized that the very attempt to criticize the liberal humanist heritage entails a profound complicity with it, an obligation to use the language of one's oppressors. What is distinctive about Hegel and Marx is their realization that subversion does not blandly oppose (this idea of opposition is another straw target) but *sublates*: it preserves what is valuable in what it subverts. Marx was clear about this: the impulse toward democracy, toward freedom, individual liberties, and the promise of peace and prosperity for all – which remain at the level of mere potential in bourgeois society – must be *realized*, along with, we might add, our more recent claims for gender, sexual, and ethnic equality. The myth of liberal humanism must be realized. But we cannot view "opposition" in spatial terms, as a possible externality to an inside. Nor can we conceive it in merely temporal terms, or in logical terms as simple contradiction. Opposition implies a perspective wider than the original one, one which realizes the positive potential of its predecessor, while negating its oppressive features. But such opposition – in order not to be lost in the bland pluralism and textual indeterminacy of our so-called post-political, ideologically administered world – must be grounded in political practice.

If clarity was an early bourgeois virtue, obscurity is a late bourgeois vice: not just a linguistic or terminological obscurity but an epistemological refusal of clarity, as in a panicked and manic refusal of binary oppositions, of identity, of distinction between entities: good, bad, man, woman, gay, straight, center, periphery, religion, secularism: all is permissible in our ultra-pluralist world, all combinations, shades, mixtures, all permutations. The endemic phenomenon of such blurring reaches further and further into the depth of liberal pluralism and particularism, into an indifference whose very premise is its political ineffectiveness. We can surely recognize – as philosophers have long done – the constructed and often ideologically charged and oppressive nature of all these terms without sinking into registers of bland indeterminacy and confusion, often marked by a bland hypostatization of difference. The refusal of distinctions tends to be a politically conservative strategy: it is one thing to say that issues of class have a complex relation to issues of ethnicity, or that they internally structure each other; it is another thing merely to substitute or confuse one for the other. In this kind of confusion of registers, the political implications of any given approach are *intrinsically* unclear, such obscurity being inherent in liberal humanism's ability to envelop critiques of itself into its own expansive identity, just as the Hegelian dialectic greedily integrates its other, just as capitalism devours all alternative traditions and cultures into its own, global, non-identity. Foucault's analysis of power has proven widely influential, and is highly congenial to a political state of affairs where everyone engages in Foucauldian patterns of self-regulation. Sadly, to the extent that literary theory has mired itself in unnecessary obscurity, it has ensured its own political silence.

All of this is to reaffirm that opposition – which, again, cannot be conceived in terms of a simple or spatial externality – to prevailing ideologies *is* possible, and indeed is already widespread, as amply evident in the various progressive movements in the West, Latin America, parts of Southeast Asia, the Middle East, and elsewhere. Equally, such opposition cannot bypass some of the core values of liberal humanism – freedom, tolerance, justice – which must be *realized* within a broader conception of its original goals of both economic opportunity and cultural and intellectual enlightenment. The foregoing pages have argued that the oppositional nature of much literary theory – with the best intentions – is still caught within the negative phase of the Hegelian dialectic, in the phase of *mere* negation, without a positive political agenda beyond various modes of localized internal reformation. Again, this is not to deny the value of such opposition: it *does* rest on a moral and ethical agenda, and concrete values of economic opportunity and justice, racial, religious, and sexual tolerance, and the striving after genuine democracy. Recently, overarching political circumstances have precipitated a welcome development in literary and cultural theory: the values cited above – of democracy, freedom, as well as the integrally related values of close critical reading and liberal education – are beginning to be asserted by literary and cultural critics moving into a greater conception of their own public roles. Many of these critics are engaged in a revival of much-needed discussions, somewhat neglected in recent theory but nonetheless enhanced by the frameworks of theoretical inquiry: discussions of beauty, of aesthetics, of literature's moral, epistemological, and ideological potential, of the role of criticism (whether it should be merely interpretative or evaluative, whether it should intervene in larger ideological debates), and of the place of literature and art in the new consumerist and digitalized world order. Indeed, what has emerged in recent years is a greater clarity of the terms of debate: for all of the perceptions that we are living in a postmodern world, that the operations of power are diffuse, that identity is multilayered, language polysemic, that difference is more original than identity, the lines of political opposition are in some senses clearer: between those who wish to promote the values enumerated above and those who fundamentally oppose them (while paying lip service to them). As both Marxists in the twentieth century (the Frankfurt School through Williams, Eagleton, Žižek) and liberal scholars (Nussbaum, Scarry, Carey) have recognized, these vast debates do not rest on purely economic foundations: a great deal of work needs to be done in the cultural and political spheres, and the knowledge accumulated through centuries in the traditions of literary criticism, the liberal arts, and more recently the social sciences needs to be more visible in its application to, and shaping of, these spheres.

Index